War, Coups, and Terror

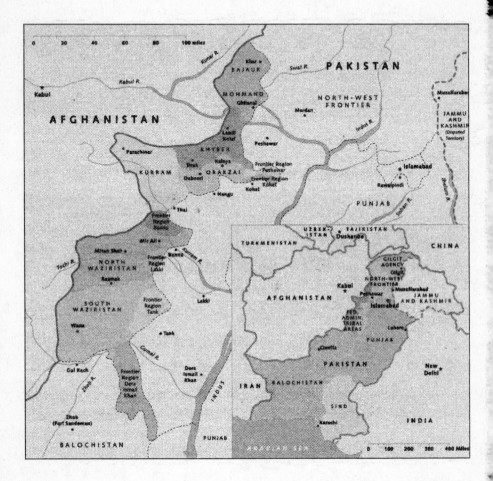

WAR, COUPS, AND TERROR

PAKISTAN'S ARMY IN YEARS OF TURMOIL

BRIAN CLOUGHLEY

SKYHORSE PUBLISHING

Skyhorse Publishing books may be purchased in bulk at special discounts for sales promotion, corporate gifts, fund-raising, or educational purposes. Special editions can also be created to specifications. For details, contact the Special Sales Department, Skyhorse Publishing, 307 West 36th Street, 11th Floor, New York, NY 10018 or info@skyhorsepublishing.com.

Skyhorse® and Skyhorse Publishing® are registered trademarks of Skyhorse Publishing, Inc.®, a Delaware corporation.

Visit our website at www.skyhorsepublishing.com.

10 9 8 7 6 5 4 3 2 1

Library of Congress Cataloging-in-Publication Data

Cloughley, Brian.
War, coups, and terror : Pakistan's army in years of turmoil / Brian Cloughley.
p. cm.
ISBN 978-1-60239-698-2 (alk. paper)
1. Pakistan. Army--History. 2. Pakistan. Army--Influence. 3. Pakistan--History, Military. 4. Coups d'itat--Pakistan--History. 5. Terrorism--Pakistan--History. 6. Pakistan--Politics and government. 7. Pakistan--Military policy. 8. Civil-military relations--Pakistan. 9. Pakistan--Strategic aspects. I. Title.
UA853.P3C63 2009
355.0095491--dc22
2009006154
Print ISBN: 978-1-62914-450-4

Printed in the United States of America

Contents

Introduction

Pakistan is a complicated country inhabited by a diverse people whose cultural divisions are acute. A tribesman from the North-West Frontier Province would feel as foreign in the house of a Punjabi as he would in that of a Portuguese or a Pole, even had they identical status in their respective social hierarchies. In language, habits and tradition they have nothing in common. Notwithstanding the practice of a common religion, there are wide differences in its interpretation, given the proclivity of some citizens, notably but far from exclusively the tribals, for the intricacies of sharia, religious law, which is often selectively interpreted by some spiritual leaders from motives of self-interest.

There are four entirely dissimilar provinces, plus the geographical anomalies of the federally controlled regions of Pakistan-administered Kashmir (still in dispute with India) and the Northern Territories, and the Federally Administered Tribal Areas (FATA) abutting Afghanistan, where since 2003 there has been grave instability, developing into insurrection.

Before 1971 Pakistan had an Eastern Wing, the land that is now Bangladesh. Political and economic mishandling of the East by the former West Pakistan caused deep dissatisfaction and growth of nationalist feeling among the almost entirely Bengali population, regarded as inferior by most of West Wing's Punjabis who were the majority of administrators. Matters came to a head following elections in 1970 in which East Pakistan's Awami League won a majority, entitling it to form a government. This was objected to by Zulfiqar Ali Bhutto, the West's most prominent politician and leader of the Pakistan People's Party, who refused to recognize the election results. Unrest in the East was suppressed in a brutal pogrom by the army, and there was open support by India for a growing insurrection.

The Indian invasion of the East Wing, to assist those regarded by West Pakistan as rebels, resulted in defeat of Pakistan's 80,000-strong army by an Indian force of over three times its size. The effects on the citizens of what remained of the country were immense.

1

Our story begins at this point, in December 1971, when the Army of Pakistan was shocked to the point of despair by defeat in battle.

The army gradually recovered from its humiliation. The country was ostensibly returned to democracy by Z.A. Bhutto, but there were disquieting facets to his exercise of power. Creation of the Federal Security Force, a body of 14,000 armed men that answered only to Bhutto, was hardly in accord with parliamentary democracy. Nor was his imposition of martial law in Karachi, Hyderabad and Lahore in 1977. In the last-named city three brigadiers showed great courage in refusing to have their troops put down riots, as this would almost certainly have involved killing civilians which they were not prepared to do. The army's chief, General Zia ul Haq, decided to take over the country and conducted a bloodless coup in July.

All Pakistan's army coups have been bloodless, successful and popular – but popular only for a while. The trouble is that military people are usually quite good at running large organizations, even civilian ones, but generally (if one may use that word) fail to understand politics and government, and the give-and-take so necessary in that esoteric world. It is said that following the first of the Duke of Wellington's cabinet meetings as Prime Minister, he complained about it having been 'An extraordinary affair. I gave them their orders and they wanted to stay and discuss them.' And even General Eisenhower, arguably the most successful world leader who exchanged uniform for plain clothes, distrusted, disliked and warned against what he called, at the end of his Presidency, the 'military-industrial complex' whose corrosive influence, with remarkable farsightedness, he saw as a threat to true democracy. But both Wellington and Eisenhower, for all their military background and irritation at those outside their control, were successful and highly regarded, elected, *civilian* leaders. They were subjected to checks and balances which, even in Wellington's time, were effective controls on those who had been accustomed to instant and unquestioning obedience. In Pakistan, however, none of the soldiers who have led the country has been a success. Had any of them placed the state on the path to democracy, no matter how forceful their methods, and then bowed out after a year or two, they would have been hailed as national saviours. None did. And all will be remembered for failure rather than for what they achieved, no matter their actual and in some cases substantial accomplishments.

Pakistan's third military ruler, General Zia, who deposed the charismatic and authoritarian Prime Minister Z.A. Bhutto, was a pious Islamic zealot who endorsed religious extremism. Following his mysterious death in a plane crash, and after a decade of chaotic democracy, General Pervez Musharraf deposed the corrupt and dictatorial Prime Minister Nawaz

Sharif in 1999, and encouraged benign Islam ('enlightened moderation') to the vexation and frustration of the clerics from the Dark Ages. Both began their period in power with vast popular support which diminished as the years went by, to the point of almost vanishing after they made major political errors: in the case of President Zia the dismissal of his government; in the case of President Musharraf the dismissal of his Chief Justice.

The army remained aloof from the controversies created by its professional heads. Its soldiers and officers, with only a few exceptions, as recounted later, cared as little for politics as they did for politicians, and did not relish being associated with suppressing the democratic wishes of their fellow citizens. Soldiering is difficult enough without having to help run a country, even if the politicians have made a mess of it. The story of the army's past four decades is essentially that of Pakistan itself, and in few countries can there have been such interrelation between army and state; but it is an unhealthy symbiosis and it is hoped that democracy will take root in Pakistan, even if it is initially flawed and frail.

Since 2003 the army has been involved in a low-level counter-insurgency in the Tribal Areas, with the attendant difficulties that face any army tasked to fight against its own citizens, no matter how intransigently brutal these may be. It has risen to the challenge, but has others to deal with, not least being that of difficulty in recruiting high-quality officers. As described in Chapter 6, the pay and pensions of Service personnel are tiny in comparison with what can be obtained by well-educated, intelligent people in civilian life. The consequences of this are examined, as are the well-publicized claims that serving and retired army officers form some sort of malevolent military industrial complex of the nature so deprecated by Eisenhower. The Army of Pakistan is not perfect, but it is far from being a den of corruption. It is led by honourable men and its members are in the main skilled and dedicated professionals. They are the guardians of the nation, but must never be its master.

The author is grateful to Oxford University Press, Karachi, for permission to use material from his book, A History of the Pakistan Army, *four chapters of which appear in amended and updated form.*

Chapter 1

Zulfikar Ali Bhutto

I have been summoned by the nation as the authentic voice of the people of
Pakistan ... by virtue of the verdict that you gave in the national elections
... I would not like to see Martial Law remain one day longer than
necessary ... We have to rebuild democratic institutions ... we have to
rebuild a situation in which the common man, the poor man in the street,
can tell me to go to hell.

Address to the nation by Zulfikar Ali Bhutto, 20 December 1971[1]

Bhutto pronounced these words four days after the end of Pakistan's war
with India over East Pakistan. The new nation of Bangladesh had arisen
from the wreckage of conflict, but the citizens of the remaining part of the
country that now called itself Pakistan were stunned at the defeat. They
were amazed and bewildered by the incompetence of their military
President, Yahya Khan, who had mislead them and caused the disaster.

Of course Yahya had to go. There was no alternative to that, other,
perhaps, than an army coup, and that way would lie disaster. The army
was unpopular and there would have been trouble if soldiers had been
deployed on the streets. And there was no alternative to Bhutto as Yahya's
successor. Bhutto was brilliant. Bhutto was the man for the time. But
Bhutto was deeply, irrevocably, disastrously flawed. There was no person
in Pakistan who could tell Zulfikar Ali Bhutto to go to hell and remain free
from vindictive retribution. But President Bhutto it had to be.

The days immediately after the ceasefire – the surrender – were confusing for all Pakistanis, not only those in uniform. Half the country had
vanished. Not that Bengalis and Biharis as such meant much to Punjabis or
Pushtuns, or almost anyone else in what had been called the West Wing;
but it was hard to come to terms with the fact that after twenty-four years
the country had ceased to exist in the shape and size in which it was
founded. Pakistanis had always considered themselves superior to
Indians, and most considered the outcome of the 1965 war to have been

bad luck. A defeat that was so open and dramatic ... and final ... was difficult to swallow.

The army felt betrayed by its Commander-in-Chief (C-in-C), to the extent that in at least one garrison, Gujranwala, there was near mutiny. Just why General Hamid, the C-in-C, chose to address the officers of GHQ in Rawalpindi on 19 December is inexplicable. Perhaps he thought it was 'the thing to do'.[2] The officers were silent at first; then restless; then vociferous and interruptive; finally, abusive. Hamid was shocked beyond speech. Gul Hassan Khan, still Chief of the General Staff (CGS), escorted him to the platform in the National Defence College auditorium but had little recollection of what went on other than 'The one incessant demand of the audience that I vaguely recall was that all officers' messes should be declared dry.' (As he also states in his *Memoirs*, it is difficult to see how this would solve anything either immediately or in the future, but some officers had seen Yahya the worse for drink and word had got round of his alcohol problem.[3] This, and a dash of overzealous religion, and the writing was on the wall for the old-style messes – although prohibition was imposed five years later by none other than the Scotch-quaffing Bhutto.) There was worse: the Quartermaster-General (QMG), Lieutenant General Mitha, was a close crony of Yahya's and decided to meddle in affairs by ordering a company of the Special Services Group (SSG) to be moved to Rawalpindi 'for the protection of the President, COS,* and GHQ'. The man he approached to carry out his wishes was the commander of the SSG, Brigadier Ghulam Mohammad Malik, 'GM',[4] who declined the order and at once reported to Gul Hassan. There was no good reason for a company of SSG to be used for close protection, and anyway the QMG had no business issuing orders of this type. Gul Hassan assured GM that he had acted properly. The exact nature of the conspiracy is not known (and conspiracy there undoubtedly was) but it is likely, according to several retired officers, that the COS and his QMG had ideas of ensuring that Yahya (who may or may not have known of the SSG affair) should remain in power. There was no hope whatever of this and the attempt showed that the two officers were as inept at reading the mood of the nation – and plotting – as they were at running an army. At the time, Bhutto was on his way home from the US, having first taken the wise precaution of telephoning Mustafa Khar, his close friend (then) and an astute politician, to ascertain whether it was safe for him to return in the PIA aircraft sent by the Chief of the Air Staff (and Gul Hassan) to fetch him from Rome. He was assured he would come to no harm.

* The title 'Commander-in-Chief' had been changed to Chief of Staff (COS) and would later be Chief of Army Staff (COAS), as still obtains. The air force and navy chiefs were renamed CAS and CNS.

When meeting with Nixon in Florida on 17 December, Bhutto apparently was given assurance that Pakistan would receive 'military and monetary support' – a promise Nixon would find hard to honour, as his policy during the war had little Congressional or popular backing. The gesture was welcomed by Bhutto in spite of his preoccupation with his own immediate political future. What seemed to be important was that he, Bhutto, was on cordial terms with the President of the United States – who, he perhaps did not know, was just as devious, untrustworthy and amoral as Bhutto himself.

One of the first things Bhutto did as President was to dismiss Hamid as COS and appoint Gul Hassan to take over on 20 December. Swift work, but Bhutto made up his mind quickly. The circumstances of the appointment took a strange form, of which the best description is in Gul Hassan's *Memoirs*.[5]

Bhutto wanted to broadcast the appointment that night and sent for Gul Hassan to tell him of his proposed elevation. Hassan was hesitant, but after about forty minutes contemplation he told his President he would take the job – on four conditions:

- The COS should be in the rank of lieutenant general, not general, as there had been too much 'rank creep', a request to which Bhutto 'consented with alacrity'. (Gul would find out almost as quickly just why he was so enthusiastic.)
- There must be disengagement of troops along the border, an important consideration when they were so physically close and emotionally tense; and the prisoners of war should be returned as soon as possible. Bhutto said he was working on this.
- It was time to lift Martial Law. Bhutto said that once a Constitution was composed [by a committee of his own nomination] and passed 'by all the political parties' [presumably meaning the National Assembly] 'he would bury Martial Law forever'.
- Last, said Gul Hassan, showing his firmness and complete lack of understanding of his President's character, he wanted 'no interference from anyone, himself or any of his ministers included'. Bhutto 'smiled and assured me that was the reason why he had selected me for the job'. Accepting this at face value showed that Gul did not know Bhutto. There was no possibility that any subordinate of Bhutto's would be allowed to run his own show without interference. And not only interference: strict, down-the-line obedience to decision and personal whim was demanded, however illegal or base these might be. Those who would not conform would be dismissed – or worse.

But there it was: the conditions were composed after less than an hour's thought by an honourable man who, before meeting Bhutto that evening, did not even know he was the new President (although some allege that it was Gul Hassan who forced Yahya's resignation and ensured Bhutto's rise to power).

That night Bhutto made his broadcast to the people of Pakistan, about two hours later than had been notified, but nobody minded. The saviour of the nation was to appear and would reassure them about the future. The new President would 'pick up the pieces' and would make 'A Pakistan envisaged by the Quaid-e-Azam' (the Founder of the Nation, the much-lamented Mohammad Ali Jinnah), with the co-operation of the people. This was precisely what the citizens of the new Pakistan wanted to hear. There had been mismanagement, exploitation, suffocation, but he, Zulfikar Ali Bhutto, although 'no magician', would lead his country from the squalor of recent years to recreate its pristine origins, from where it would develop, under the calm and majestic guidance of its new leader, to be once again the Land of the Pure. And in his first communication to the nation – everyone was listening, some watching, too – he told a lie.

Gul Hassan had good reasons for asking to be left as a lieutenant general rather being promoted to four-star rank, but Bhutto declared:

> I have asked General Gul Hassan to be acting Commander-in-Chief. He is a professional soldier. I do not think he has dabbled in politics and I think he has the respect and support of the Armed Forces ... But he will retain the rank of lieutenant general. We are not going to make unnecessary promotions. We are a poor country. We are not going to unnecessarily fatten people.

'This,' wrote Gul Hassan in his *Memoirs*, 'was out-and-out cheek'. Perhaps it was; but it was certainly an out-and-out lie by Bhutto for the sake of creating an impression *that he didn't need to make*. Bhutto didn't need to enthuse anyone about the new army chief. If he had announced that Gul would be promoted field marshal or demoted to corporal because he, Bhutto, considered that the most appropriate rank for the post, the people of Pakistan would have shouted approval until they were hoarse. Bhutto was a populist – but he didn't really understand, deep down, the feelings of the people he so desperately wanted to have follow him. He desired dramaturgy for its own sake. They did, of course, follow him – until his arrogance became too much for them; and so did Gul Hassan, with the difference that the arrogance showed itself to him rather sooner than it did to those whom Bhutto wanted to 'tell him to go to hell'. 'Why,' asked Gul Hassan of Bhutto, 'had [he] deliberately told a lie about my rank?' To

Bhutto this was a strange question. He had made a statement; its content was therefore unassailable. His answer was that his new army chief did not understand politics, which was certainly true. But Gul Hassan then ensured his later eclipse and banishment by telling Bhutto that 'he should keep politics out of his dealings with me or he was at liberty to get someone [to be army chief] who was familiar with such language'. Bhutto did not reply (and probably could not even begin to conceptualize how politics could be kept out of any of his dealings with anyone), but, according to one prominent figure,[6] he began to think again about his new army chief and to consider with whom he might replace him. Tikka Khan, the General who carried out orders without question, might be an alternative, thought some of Bhutto's associates.

Bhutto had appointed a man of honour as head of the army, but, being Bhutto, he did not – could not – understand that anyone could serve him and not be plotting against him. The army's chief would be especially suspect. He was to be lucky, for a while. Gul Hassan was loyal, as was his successor. The problem for Bhutto came when a few years later he appointed a Chief of the Army Staff whom he considered pliable or even quiescent, but who was to prove a more devious player than the brilliant Bhutto.

Bhutto got rid of the old title of 'commander-in-chief', a hangover from British days. This was an ideal time to do so, with the armed forces at their nadir of popularity and Bhutto at his zenith, but he also wanted to be rid of Gul Hassan who, Bhutto belatedly realized, was not the pushover he wanted. The army, thought Bhutto, should be put in its place, which was firmly under control of the civilians. This is a proper thing in a democracy, but Bhutto was no democrat. He proposed that the army be sent in to Karachi to enforce discipline amongst the restive work force; Gul disagreed and said the police should be used. Bhutto wanted to release National Cadet Corps members (students – PPP supporters) who had deserted and been imprisoned after court martial; Gul refused. Bhutto wanted to go with Gul on his first visit around the army; Gul was firm: 'As of tomorrow,' he said, 'I begin my visits to units, and alone.' Gul's days were numbered. And Bhutto, quietly and unheralded, visited units and headquarters on his own account. There were many pinpricks, many other instances of attempted interference by Bhutto, but two in particular showed his mindset: according to Gul, he proposed that all army officers should be 'screened by the police or intelligence, and those with political leanings or connections would be kept under surveillance'. This, too, was rejected by Gul, who was satisfied with the normal vetting process and, in any event, did not countenance 'meddling in politics' – but Bhutto would not be deflected from his desire to impose a personal mark on the army. He wanted to attend a promotion and selection board due to sit on 5 February 1972.

After the war it was obvious some officers would have to be retired. In the army twenty-nine senior officers were relieved of duty: two generals, eleven lieutenant generals, ten major generals and six brigadiers. (The navy and air force each lost their chiefs and six others.) Once the Military Secretary had done all the paperwork involving marshalling confidential reports, career outlines, vacancies and the promotion plot, a meeting of the senior generals was called to consider promotions between the ranks of lieutenant colonel and major general. They, in turn, would place recommendations before government in the normal way. Gul would chair the meeting. Bhutto told him he wanted to attend it, and, when Gul demurred, reminded him that he had been asked to attend cabinet meetings – as if there were any similarity between the two. Annoyingly for Bhutto, Gul had refused his invitations to go to cabinet meetings, so was able to parry that one, but in any case Gul was adamant: the President could not, would not, attend meetings of promotion boards. And it was so.

A strike of police in Peshawar took place at the end of February and Bhutto, not unnaturally, wished to have it resolved. His approach was much the same as he intended concerning the Karachi workers: force. Force against the 'common man', the people who could tell Bhutto 'to go to hell'. Gul had refused to co-operate concerning Karachi, but he was not consulted about the intention to employ military force in Peshawar. The National Security Adviser ordered deployment of two field guns to Peshawar from the School of Artillery at Nowshera, about 25 miles away on the Grand Trunk Road. He also ordered the move of a number of recruits from the Punjab Regiment Centre at Mardan, north of Nowshera, to Peshawar. Gul's staff told him of the orders, which he promptly countermanded. He was then surprised to receive a visit from a figure (of cabinet rank) who was none other than former Major General Akbar Khan, he of the 1951 'Rawalpindi Conspiracy' that had failed to overthrow the government, for which he had served a token period in prison. Akbar tried to browbeat the Commander-in-Chief but was sent off with a flea in his ear to (presumably) report to the President whose confidence he had. Just what a bunch of recruits and two 25-pounder guns would have achieved in Peshawar is not clear (chaos, most likely), but the orders show that Akbar was probably as expert in putting down disturbances as he had been at planning them.

Had Gul been more of a political animal, had he been devious and out to save his professional skin, he could have thwarted Bhutto – even to the extent of toppling him. Reports came to him that the police strikes, spreading throughout Punjab, had been engineered by Bhutto's People's Party in order to get the army involved and 'furnish Bhutto with a pretext to defame it beyond redemption'. Perhaps; perhaps not. But whatever was going on, it was nasty.

Some young officers indicated that he had only to say the word and they would 'sort out' Bhutto, an offer which appalled Gul, who calmed them down and sent them on their way. Matters were coming to a head. Given Bhutto's network of informers, it is reasonable to believe that he got to know, if not about this particular incident, then about the feeling in some sections of the army concerning himself. Little did he know – he was incapable of realizing – that he had a loyal chief who would brook no interference with government by the army. Gul simply wasn't interested in what to Bhutto was lifeblood: the manipulation of people and events. Bhutto seemed to attribute to everyone he met the more sinister characteristics he himself possessed; it appeared he was unable to believe that anyone could be disinterested enough to serve their country without an eye to the main chance.

The end for Gul came after he refused to provide a briefing on contingency planning for all ministers, especially as it was to be conducted, on Bhutto's orders, at a police facility (nice touch) and not at GHQ, where such briefings normally took place. This, combined with his refusal to become involved in putting down the police strike, and his remonstrance when Bhutto proposed creating the Federal Security Force, a para-military organization intended for such creative activity as strike-breaking, sealed his downfall.

On 3 March, a national holiday declared by Bhutto to mark the introduction of land reforms two days before, Gul Hassan and the Air Chief, Rahim Khan, were sacked. The drama – the 'needless drama', Gul called it – is described in detail in his *Memoirs*, but Bhutto's radio address to the nation that evening, in English, deserves to be recounted. He said, in part:

> My dear friends, citizens, the interests of this country are supreme, and it is in the interests of the country and the interest of the armed forces of Pakistan that today we have taken the decision to replace the commander-in-chief of the Pakistan Army and the commander-in-chief of the Pakistan Air Force. Both of them have been replaced by officers who are familiar with the armed forces [sic] and who have kept working with them with devotion and with splendid records. Replacements have been made on merits and in the highest consideration of the country and the armed forces.
>
> By now you must have heard that Lieutenant General Gul Hassan, who resigned this afternoon, has been replaced by Lieutenant General

Tikka Khan and Air Marshal Rahim Khan ... by Air Marshal Zaffar Chaudhury. From today we will no longer have the anachronistic and obsolete posts of commander-in-chief ... so we have changed the colonial structure of the armed forces of Pakistan and injected a truly independent pattern into these vital services ... And you must remember, my friends and compatriots, that the people of Pakistan and the armed forces themselves are equally determined to wipe out Bonapartic influences from the armed forces. It is essential so that these tendencies never again pollute the political life of this country. Bonapartism is an expression which means that professional soldiers turn into professional politicians. So I do not use the word Bonapartism. I use the word Bonapartic because what had happened in Pakistan since 1954 and more openly since 1958 is that some professional generals turned to politics not as a profession but as a plunder and as such, the influences that crept into Pakistan's sociopolitical life destroyed its fabric as the influences of Bonapartism had affected Europe in the eighteenth and nineteenth centuries.[7]

This was a fascinating insight into the man Bhutto. Not only did he use historical references to a defunct European emperor to make his points – a ludicrous choice, as only the highly educated would know what on earth he was talking about – he was deliberately and without conscience slandering Gul Hassan whom he had forced to 'resign'. But it was all over. Tikka Khan, the hard and loyal man to whom a superior's order was the final word and never to be questioned, took over as Chief of Staff and would remain so for exactly four years, at that time the tenure for the heads of the three Services.

Over the next six years, until Bhutto's fall, several measures were taken to modify, and in some instances improve, the structure of the armed services. It appears, however, that at least some of these moves were made for the sake of consolidating Bhutto's control, rather than by reason of improving efficiency.

The move of naval headquarters to Islamabad from Karachi in 1974 made sense in that the chief and his staff would be more readily available to government and the other Services, and could contribute better to overall defence planning and preparedness. There are those who argue that the place for NHQ is Karachi where the fleet is based, especially as the navy's part in conflict as fought in the subcontinent would not involve a great deal of 'jointery' – intimate co-operation with the other Services – and would never be required to be extensive. In the particular strategic circumstances of Pakistan this is a compelling point of view, but on the principle that all Service HQs should be collocated, the decision was proper. There were many arguments about how far 'jointery' should be carried. The debate is usually fierce and sometimes emotional in all staff colleges, and at any gathering of professionals – but in Pakistan in 1972 it was flaccid and undirected.[8] Proponents of joint doctrine went largely unheard. The half-hearted outcome was the appointment of a uniformed Chairman of the Joint Chiefs of Staff Committee on 1 March 1976[9] (until which time the chairman was the defence minister, who was Bhutto), but General Mohammad Sharif and his successors were not given the opportunity to mould their headquarters into a true command HQ.

The army seemed to have focused inwards, which is understandable in the circumstances (and might have been no bad thing had it lasted only for a year or so), but it needed a leader who had broad, bold vision so that it could break free from introspection and parochialism. Tikka Khan was a solid soldier, a firm believer in Constitutional propriety, a stickler for procedures and the chain of command. An original military thinker he was not.

The composition of the 1973 Constitution was to reflect Bhutto's pre-occupation with the loyalty of the military, but before endorsement of that document by the National Assembly there was another conspiracy to be dealt with. In early 1973, fourteen air force and twenty-one army officers were arrested on charges of plotting to overthrow the government. and went before separate Service courts martial. One army officer was acquitted and the others received punishment ranging from life imprisonment to stoppage of promotion. The air chief acted harshly. The case against one officer had been dropped and nine of the others were found not guilty, but Air Chief Marshal Zafar Chaudhury ordered retirement of all fourteen. His order was overruled by government in the case of seven officers. He resigned. 'In fairness to him,' says *The Story of the Pakistan Air Force*, 'it must also be stated that his abrupt departure may have been precipitated by the anti-Qadiani[10] sentiment sweeping the country at the time.' Things are not always what they seem. The trial of the army officers was presided over by a Major General Zia ul Haq, who reported to Bhutto, frequently in person.

The conspiracy case showed that the Services were not inclined to support calls for revolt against the government. They had, after all, detected the plot themselves and brought the offenders to justice. It seemed they could be trusted to remain outside politics and act against any within their ranks who would seek to do otherwise. Bhutto may or may not have agreed that this was so, but in any event he made sure that the 1973 Constitution authorized the Parliament to pass laws for the punishment of those found guilty of treason, and included an oath to refrain from indulging in political activity. The old tradition that officers did not involve themselves in politics was not enough; the Constitution formalized it:

> I ... do solemnly swear that I will bear true faith and allegiance to Pakistan and uphold the Constitution of the Islamic Republic of Pakistan which embodies the will of the people, that I will not engage myself in any political activities whatsoever and that I will honestly and faithfully serve the Pakistan Army/Navy/Air Force as required by and under the law.

The trouble with an oath of this nature is that it can be used by an autocratic regime to destroy those whom it fears. 'Any political activities whatsoever' is a catchall phrase. With checks and balances, a strong and independent judiciary, a parliament monitored by a free Press, and a sense of honour and responsibility on the part of political leaders, a phrase like this may have meaning (it will also, probably, be redundant). It does not appear to be recorded if the oath was taken by General Zia.

Bhutto realized that he could not remain as unelected (indeed, self-appointed) President indefinitely. The Constitution would be of dubious legality were it not to be endorsed by an elected Assembly, and in any event the people wanted an end to autocracy. Memories of 1958 had faded. The 'social vermin' to whom Ayub had referred at that time had been replaced by Bhutto's military 'traitors' who had 'beaten the workers ... lashed the peasants'[11] and, in his eyes, deserved their relegation to the blacker pages of Pakistan's short history. But martial law suited Bhutto. He was able to enact legislation as Chief Martial Law Administrator that would have been impossible, or at best extremely difficult, to push through a democratically-elected assembly, even were the Pakistan People's Party to have a majority. He begged protesting students and striking workers to 'Give me some time' to introduce democracy, largely because the powers of martial law were required 'for the sole purpose of bringing ... basic reforms ... Once this first phase of reforms is over ... the ground would be laid for the full flowering of democracy.' Fair enough, one might think, after such a long period of rule by diktat: use the methods of the autocrats to nurture the long-dormant seeds of fairness, equity, civil law and freedom for the masses. But it didn't work out quite like that.

Pakistan's economy was placed under severe strain by the nationalization of hundreds of private enterprises. Its international standing (and credit rating), already low in spite of Bhutto's charisma, took a hard knock. The army, of course, was not involved in the nationalization process – but in later years it was to reap benefits by undertaking, through its charitable agency, the Fauji Foundation, many commercial enterprises which were exempt from imposts paid by businesses that had been re-privatized.[12]

13

(The exemptions lasted until 1993.) Nationalization was unpopular with industrialists and businessmen, many of whom sent much capital abroad. In some cases the entrepreneurs went, too; a grave loss for Pakistan and, perhaps strangely, a loss for the army, as most of them were middle class. The army's officers were being recruited in increasing numbers from the middle class rather than the landed gentry and the aristocracy, and enlistment of such officers was a good thing. Ayub and Yahya had encouraged the grandees to send their sons to serve for at least a few years – like the old British system. And Ayub and Yahya were, in fact, just a wee bit snobbish about it all. Neither was of the real aristocracy – but Bhutto was; and he cared about the middle class just as little as his predecessors had. In a society such as Pakistan's it was a real step forward to broaden the social base of the officer corps, but the flight of so many of the middle classes meant a reduction in the number of educated young men from whom officer selection could be made.

Martial law was unpopular with the army, which does not seem to have disturbed Bhutto greatly, but it was also unpopular with his political supporters, especially the young. That was serious. In April 1972 its retention was about to come under attack in the Supreme Court – not critical, but definitely annoying for Bhutto. So on 14 April he announced that Martial Law would be repealed a week later, which it was. But he did not give publicity to the fact that the Interim Constitution, proclaimed concurrently, omitted to guarantee Fundamental Rights. These were suspended under a Proclamation of Emergency. Bhutto was not yet prepared to be *entirely* democratic.

The army was occupied with internal reform. Tikka Khan could be relied upon to reorganize it without drama and without creating any political waves. There is no record of Bhutto again insisting on attendance at a promotion board meeting, but there would have been no need for that, anyway – Tikka would ensure that only those whom he considered politically reliable would be promoted or appointed to sensitive posts. But there was one thing that even the loyal Tikka could not equivocate about: the prisoners of war. Of the 90,000 prisoners held by India some 70,000 were military, the others being civil servants, military dependants and private individuals. Article 118 of the Third Geneva Convention (1949) states that 'Prisoners of War shall be released and repatriated without delay after the cessation of active hostilities,' but Mrs Gandhi ignored the Article, just as she ignored Security Council Resolution 307/71 of 21 December, which called for her forces to be withdrawn and for compliance with the Convention. Tikka Khan was not much of a one for humanitarian conventions, any more than was Bhutto, but he knew it would be difficult to concentrate the minds of the army on re-equipping and reorganizing while his officers and men fretted about their comrades in Indian prison camps. He wanted action and for different reasons Bhutto also wanted their return. His electoral support would depend on such things; therefore, the sooner the POW problem was resolved, the better. In the short term it was as easy as it was justified to blame India, but Bhutto knew that odium could soon begin to shift.

Bhutto released Mujib from confinement (he could hardly have done otherwise) and the erstwhile captive became the President of Bangladesh, with whom Bhutto wanted to have talks as well as with Mrs Gandhi. But Mujib wanted some POWs to be tried as alleged war criminals, which made it difficult for Bhutto to propose including him. Mujib, too, was under pressure at home: the Bengalis considered Bhutto just as much an oppressor as Tikka Khan and Yahya, so it would be politically unwise for Mujib to have talks with Pakistan. Mrs Gandhi, alone, it had to be.

They met at Simla on 28 June and signed an agreement on 2 July.[13] The woman whom Bhutto had described as being 'mediocre ... with mediocre intelligence ... she'll never succeed in impressing me' negotiated with the national leader she had described as 'not a very balanced man' who, 'when he talks, you never understand what he means'.[14] A lovely couple.

The accord was cobbled together without benefit of reasoned input by Bhutto, whose efforts were limited – naturally – by the fact that he was more a supplicant than an equal party to negotiations. He had to get *some* sort of agreement. Bangladesh was not discussed, and there was therefore no mention of the POW question because Mrs Gandhi refused to permit this unless Bangladesh was recognized by Pakistan – a diplomatic venture that Bhutto could not possibly make only seven months after East Pakistan had been lost. For want of something better, Bhutto accepted the Simla (now Shimla) Accord, which the Indians seized upon as justification to treat the Kashmir question as bilateral – nothing to do with Kashmiris and certainly no business of the UN, whose 'good offices' were forever eschewed. The Security Council Resolutions concerning the holding of a plebiscite (agreed by Nehru) were, to the Indian mind, 'overtaken' by this bilateral accord – as curious an interpretation of the Simla Agreement as it was of UN procedure. India's contention that the Accord invalidates UN involvement in the Kashmir issue is, apparently, based on paragraph (ii) (under the heading 'Harmonious Relationship'), in that:

> The two countries are resolved to settle their differences by peaceful means through bilateral negotiations or by any other peaceful means mutually agreed upon between them.

This does not expunge, cancel, amend, or deny the Security Council Resolution about a plebiscite, any more than it excludes the UN from involvement in the Kashmir dispute. India holds that 'mutually agreed' is in some fashion equivalent to 'bilateral'. The 'peaceful means' must be bilateral or ... well ... bilateral. 'Mutual agreement' will, of course, never obtain about 'any other peaceful means', but this does not make it irrelevant; nor does it render UN resolutions or involvement inapplicable. The fact that the UN Mission in Kashmir remains in existence is evidence that the UN Security Council, although unable or unwilling to enforce some of its own most important Resolutions, confers legitimacy upon its involvement in Kashmir, even if by omission rather than commission. India can hardly renege – formally at least – from the first paragraph of the Simla agreement: 'That the principles and purposes of the Charter of the United Nations shall govern the relations between the two countries,' but it is probable there will continue to be arguments between India and Pakistan about the Accord, the other terms of which are anodyne. But what is decidedly not anodyne is the

DELINEATION OF THE LINE OF CONTROL IN JAMMU AND KASHMIR RESULTING FROM THE CEASE FIRE OF 17 DECEMBER 1971 IN ACCORDANCE WITH THE SIMLA AGREEMENT OF 2 JULY 1972

This document, composed by twelve army officers (six from each country), is, so far as it goes, unambiguous. Its territorial precision is remarkable. It contains such descriptions as:

The Line of Control runs from NR 313861 to NR 316865, thence to NR 319867, thence EAST to NR 322868, thence NE to NR 331872, thence to a monument on ridge line at NR 336874 approximately five hundred yards SE of Point 10008 (NR 3387), thence to a point NR 338881 on the Nullah such that point NR 336874 and point NR 338881 are connected by a counter clockwise arc with a radius of five hundred yards, thence NE to junction ...

and so on. What was not precise, unfortunately, was where the termination of the Line should be in the east. To be sure, the description ended with a grid reference: NJ 980420 – but what then? There was a cairn erected in 1972 at 980420; it was still there in 1982; it may still be there now; but there was, and is, about a hundred miles of mountainous snow and ice between 980420 and the border with China – at the junction with Aksai Chin, a large area in dispute between India and China.[15]

What was to be done about allocation of this area? It was of no commercial advantage, and of interest only to the most dedicated mountaineer. Dark rock, jagged ice, deep snow, foul weather. There could be no attraction in the region. And as such it was described to the author by one of the signatories to the *Description of the Line of Control* (short title). Lieutenant Colonel B.M. Tewari was one of the Indian representatives who

16

held meetings (nine altogether) with their Pakistani counterparts from 10 August to 11 December 1972. Ten years later, a brigadier, he was garrison commander in Srinagar (in Indian-administered Kashmir) and, like most Indian officers, genial, comradely and good company when sure that the intelligence services were not looking over his shoulder. Tewari said that delineation of the Line of Control was effected in the most gentlemanly manner and the reason the description of the Line stopped at grid reference NJ 980420 was that nobody in their right mind (or words to that effect) could possibly want any of the land between there and the Great Wall of China, and that they (the Indian officers and their Pakistani colleagues) agreed that anyone who wanted to lay claim to ice, snow and rocks was welcome to them.

Nobody, at that time, imagined that there might be military confrontation in the area. It would be futile to attempt to wage war at such heights, at the end of long lines of communication, with no strategic or even tactical aim, in an area in which mere existence (and no one lived there) would involve great hazard in moving tiny distances. Who would send troops to occupy a terrifying wasteland where there was no threat of invasion or even territorial infringement?

Sensible but incomplete delineation of the Line of Control sowed the seeds of the Siachen Glacier confrontation of 1984, but in the 1970s there were other external and internal factors that affected reorganization of the army and the attitude of its leaders.

Bhutto took Pakistan out of the Commonwealth on 30 January 1972 (because Commonwealth nations had recognized independent Bangladesh), which had the effect of denying the army and the other services co-operation at the very time when this would have been most welcome. His decision to withdraw from SEATO (7 November) was less sensitive and was based on his wish to begin to play a part in the non-aligned movement, which would be difficult for the leader of a country aligned with the West and not sympathetic to the Soviet Union; but in any event SEATO was dying and was wound up three years later. Withdrawal resulted in the cutting of links with other SEATO nations (who were disinclined to continue them on a purely bilateral basis with Pakistan), but so far as practical planning for war was concerned, SEATO had never mattered greatly to Pakistan. Bhutto also wanted to withdraw from CENTO and sent word of his intention far and wide, but never got round to it. (That grouping was also moribund and finally collapsed in March 1979.) 'Clearly,' say S.M. Burke and Lawrence Ziring in *Pakistan's Foreign Policy: An Analysis* (University of Minnesota Press, 1990), 'Pakistan's continuing presence in CENTO was an expression of friendship towards Iran and Turkey rather than a commitment to the American anti-Soviet policy,' which Bhutto considered irrelevant to Pakistan. The army's leaders had not been enthusiastic about either organization since it had become apparent that they would be of no consequence in conflict with India.

It was necessary to rebuild the army to be capable of planning and fighting a conventional war. Mrs Gandhi said she had no further territorial designs on Pakistan, but the Kashmir problem had not gone away – if anything it had been exacerbated by the terms of the Simla Accord – and Pakistan was right to be wary of what might happen next. In fact, there was little need to be concerned about India's rearmament programme in the early 1970s. The view of the authority Chris Smith is that 'It seems that through the 1970s India's defence procurement policy was low key, especially with regard to the army' and that, although the only reliable and comparatively inexpensive supplier of weaponry was the Soviet Union, availability of equipment was limited.[16] This, combined with the fact that India's army had not appeared overwhelmingly efficient during the war (although some units and formations conducted operations with distinction), might have been enough to convince Bhutto that there was no threat from across the border. He had other ideas, and in June 1972, just before going to Simla, produced an intriguing document on military strategy based on having 'read quite a bit on military matters and warfare'. He wrote that India had about 975,000 troops, 1,050 combat aircraft and 1,650 tanks (all of which figures were exaggerated),[17] and, dangerously, that India would depend 'largely on material superiority and not the human factor, upon technique and not the force of an ideal. In this can lie their weakness and our strength.'[18] This rubbish was followed by the contention that there should be plans for an offensive against Delhi, a thrust in the south to cut off Bombay, and a 'massive wave of raiders', similar, presumably, to those who conducted unsuccessful forays into Kashmir in 1965 during Operation Gibraltar. In this one might detect the advice of failed coup leader Akbar (now defence adviser to the President), as he had been involved in (badly) training the unfortunate 1965 raiders who went bravely but fruitlessly to death or capture. This was to be 'people's war' – but with what aim was not made clear. Was Pakistan to defeat India militarily? Occupy it? What was to be gained by waging all-out war? GHQ was making plans anyway – that was its job – but the idea of Bhutto becoming involved in the higher direction of war was alarming. Bhutto had been a hawk in 1965 and 1971; it seemed that he had not learned from his country's defeat. But (perhaps fortunately) he and Tikka Khan were to be more concerned about alarms within the country.

In Balochistan in December 1972 the Marri tribe attacked settlers in the area of a disputed canal. At about the same time, the Bugti tribe tried to force the resignation of Ahmad Nawaz Bugti, a minister in the Provincial government. There was general unrest. Troops were deployed but not committed, but in February next year an insurrection began, caused mainly by Bhutto's dismissal of the Provincial government. (He also 'swept aside' that of the North West Frontier Province, both having a majority of the National Awami Party, opposed to the PPP.)[19] The army was used vigorously by Tikka Khan (who became known as 'the Butcher of Balochistan') until the revolt was put down and operations ceased, officially, at least, on 15 May 1974. It was a (relatively) short and a bloody campaign, and thoroughly alienated much of the Baloch population which, fortunately for Pakistan, was tiny, numbering only 2.4 million.[20] According to a retired senior officer, about twenty battalions were deployed in the Province (although it is not clear whether they were all there concurrently) at a time when the army should have been concentrating on training for conventional operations. One benefit, as in all counter-insurgency campaigns, was improvement in junior leadership; but it would have been better had there been improvement in senior leadership.

Bhutto became prime minister on 14 August 1973 (and a new President, Chaudhry Fazal Elahi, was elected by the National Assembly and the Senate), but there appeared to be no change in his methods of governance. He retained the defence portfolio and appointed a Minister of State for Foreign Affairs and Defence, Aziz Ahmad, to undertake business not appropriate for a prime minister, and it was Ali who went to Delhi to negotiate the POW repatriation which finally took place in April 1974. An exchange of prisoners taken on the western front had been effected on 1 December 1972, and Bangladesh (which Bhutto recognized in February 1974, immediately before chairing an Islamic summit conference in Lahore) agreed to drop charges against the 195 alleged war criminals; 72,795 POWs and 17,186 civilians came home. Some had come home earlier: six officers and soldiers escaped and walked back over the Himalayas – a remarkable feat. One of the officers was Tariq Pervaiz Khan, later a lieutenant general and Commander XII Corps, whose dismissal from the army by General Musharraf in 1999 is described in Chapter 5.

Absorbing the returnees was not easy. Some, of course, did not wish to continue to serve and were pensioned off. Others were unsuitable, mentally or physically, to undertake military duties, and still others bore resentment against the government which, they thought, had not done enough to secure their release. Problems abounded, but Tikka Khan and his staff rose to the occasion and, by a combination of sympathetic treatment, allocation of money for resettlement, and the embrace of the regimental system, managed the transition well. Army strength was maintained at about 300,000, including 25,000 Azad ('Free') Kashmir (AK) troops recruited in their eponymous area and to all intents and purposes regular soldiers. (AK battalions and brigades have fewer heavy weapons than other units.) The loss of the East Wing had little effect on recruiting, as there had been few Bengalis in the army, but it did have considerable effect on the Gross National Product of the new Pakistan (and on the new Bangladesh, too).

Defence expenditure rose in the 1970s, as might have been expected, but authorities differ as to the increase in percentage of GNP, with one claiming that it went up to 9.2 in 1972 from 3.7 the previous year. Figures below are those of Omar Noman and are considered accurate.

The defence budget was modest. There was no alternative. The country had grave economic problems, but it seemed that Bhutto thought he could achieve growth by nationalization alone, which would result, he was convinced, in greatly expanded production and export of manufactured goods. Subventions by such luminaries as Colonel Gaddafi of Libya were forthcoming, but it must have been apparent that the economic management of the country could not depend on irregular subsidies. The fiscal base was tiny and skewed, and financial management was badly affected by Bhutto's virtual disbanding of the Civil Service of Pakistan and his appointment to responsible positions of PPP loyalists with few or no qualifications in administration.

Another destabilizing factor was the Federal Security Force (FSF), creation of which had been opposed by General Gul Hassan. It appeared that its role was to enable Bhutto to deal with politically motivated violence, or the threat of it, without having to resort to the army. It was 'responsible only to the Prime Minister and its actions were not subject to scrutiny or debate by Parliament, nor, as matters worked out in practice, was it inhibited by too nice a regard for the law'.[21] Had he remained army chief, it is likely Gul Hassan would not have permitted the FSF to exist, but Tikka Khan had no such qualms. What Bhutto ordered, Bhutto got. The FSF was raised without parliamentary endorsement in October 1972, and came into being officially by an Act of Parliament in June the following year. Equipped with automatic weapons and rocket launchers as well as rifles,[22] its strength in 1974 was almost 14,000: 8,000 in Punjab, 4,000 in NWFP, 1,100 in Sindh, 300 in Azad Kashmir, 200 in the Tribal Areas, and a mere 23 in Balochistan. (Bhutto did not need to cow Balochistan any more than it had been by the army's brutal suppression.) 'The ranks of the FSF,' says Lawrence Ziring, 'were filled by generally repulsive former members of the police and military communities',[23] however its significance lies not only in its creation as an unsavoury parallel institution to the armed forces and its entirely unconstitutional use as a private army (ironically, such elements had been explicitly banned by Bhutto), but because its Director-General, Masood Mahmud, a former policeman, eventually testified that Mr Bhutto had ordered the Force to murder one of his political opponents. The perceptive Hasan Askari Rizvi wrote in 1974 (and courageously republished in 1976, at the height of Bhutto's revengeful viciousness) the observation that, 'Once the political leadership [of Pakistan] is sure of the military's support, they assert their authority in society and deal with [political] opposition effectively,' which was precisely what Bhutto did.

So Bhutto intended and largely succeeded in having the army divorced from enforcing civil law, or the version of it applying at the time, and military re-equipment and training programmes went ahead, although not without some interruption. Floods and earthquakes in 1973–5 required support to the stricken populations of Punjab, Sindh and NWFP, the earthquake in Swat and Hazara of December 1974 being the worst calamity, with over 5,000 dead. The army provided aid and also undertook road, well and dam building. Gradually the army regained the trust of the people.

Military hardware is not difficult to obtain on the world market, providing the purchaser has hard currency with which to buy it. There are some problems with Western suppliers, such as reluctance of governments to permit exports to regimes of which they do not approve (or if they consider that selling arms to these countries would cost them votes), and a proclivity to deny spares or replacements at the time they are most needed. But Pakistan could not afford to pick its suppliers. China had given assistance, but it was European and US systems the services wanted – although some had been obtained via Iran, some directly from France. President Nixon wanted to help, but was involved with Vietnam and Watergate and had to choose his moment carefully. On 14 March 1973 he partially lifted the embargo in effect since 1971, and military sales were resumed on a case-by-case basis to an initial value of $14 million, which would, in 1973, purchase a lot of equipment, especially if prices were kept low by benevolent suppliers. Holdings of some main equipments in 1972 and 1976 were:

Equipment	1972/3	1976/7
M-47/M-48 tanks	200	250
T-55/T-59 tanks	250	750
M-113 APCs	250	400
Naval patrol boats	1	17
Mirage aircraft	30 (approx.)	60 (approx.)
MiG-19 aircraft	50 (approx.)	80 (approx.)

Source: *Military Balance*, International Institute for Strategic Studies.

The table does not show changes in artillery inventories. Chinese and US 105, 122, and 155 mm guns were acquired in lieu of older pieces such as 25-pounders, which were phased out of front-line service. The difference in quantity was small – 900 in 1972 and 1,000 in 1976 – but quality was much superior. Army strength increased from 278,000 to about 400,000 in the same period, and military expenditure surged immediately after the war, but levelled out later:

Year	Amount (US$ millions)	As percentage of GNP	As percentage of Budget
1969	350	5.0	55.52
1970	372	4.8	53.91
1971	436	5.6	56.17
1972	522	6.7	59.10
1973	522	6.6	58.10
1974	572	5.7	53.22
1975	569	6.3	53.41

Reproduced from Noman, O., *Pakistan – a Political and Economic History since 1947*, Kegan Paul International, 1990.

The armed forces were gradually regaining self-confidence and seemed less perturbed about India's nuclear test on 18 May 1974 than was the Prime Minister. India protested to the US about the resumption of defence co-operation with Pakistan, especially as it involved training as well as supply of equipment, but its complaints seemed less convincing when the 'peaceful' 12 kiloton device exploded in the Rajasthan desert. It was, said the chairman of India's Atomic Energy Commission, 'a part of the research in peaceful uses of nuclear explosives'. A later, independent comment was that 'Besides claiming that their bomb was a strictly peaceful one, which was as hypocritical as it was brazen, New Delhi also boasted that, "Not a single thing in it was foreign".'[24] But Pakistan could not ignore the bang: the existence of a nuclear weapon over the border meant a rethink of defence policy. The cost of defence against nuclear attack would be impossible to meet, and it seemed that the only counter to a hostile nuclear state was possession of a similar weapon. India was instrumental in causing the nuclear arms race in the subcontinent on which both countries have spent billions of dollars at the expense of human development. Bhutto was vehement about India's perceived intentions. Two weeks before the test he had indulged in a barbed comment at a banquet in Beijing (after the Indian ambassador left in diplomatic dudgeon because a reference to Kashmir had been made by Deng Xiaoping) by asking, 'Does India want conflict and confrontation instead of co-operation and friendly relations? If India wants that, then I can tell you Pakistan is prepared for it.' Which it wasn't, of course, any more than it was prepared for a new Ice Age – but after the explosion Bhutto became even more defiant and 'conscious of the dire necessity of our having a coherent nuclear programme'.[25] Pakistan was already engaged in nuclear research, with a focus on electricity generation centred on the Canadian-supplied 'Candu' reactor in Karachi which began operating in 1972, and was subject to IAEA inspections. The weapons programme began in earnest in 1974–5 and gathered pace in following decades.[26]

Some officers were concerned about the way India was being run. Mrs Gandhi had made belligerent statements about Pakistan and Kashmir, and it was feared that, in order to restore her waning popularity, she might manufacture an incident from which conflict could erupt. Neither the army nor the other services were in good enough shape to fight another war. The army's senior officers were being selected increasingly for their docility and perceived allegiance to the 'Qaid-e-Awam' (or 'Leader of the People', as Bhutto had taken to calling himself) rather than for ability to command troops in battle. But it was apparent that the army was beginning to resent the selection process. Even the iron man Tikka Khan had been given a rough time when addressing groups of officers in 1975.

On 12 June 1975, Mrs Gandhi was found guilty of electoral corruption. On the 26th she declared a State of Emergency, arrested 676 of a later total of several thousand political opponents, imposed censorship and damaged (but only temporarily) her credibility as a democrat. GHQ warned units along the Line of Control and the border to be vigilant, and the PAF increased combat air patrols and surveillance (using its newly delivered French Mirage IIIRPs) to monitor Indian movements. But Mrs Gandhi had more than enough problems to deal with in New Delhi and elsewhere to give her attention to Pakistan.

Bhutto had a good year, diplomatically, in 1975. He obtained assurance from President Ford that Pakistan was important to the US, which resulted in the complete lifting of the arms embargo of 1971 that had been partially lifted in 1973; pushed along an agreement with France for the supply of Crotale missiles, more Mirage aircraft, and more helicopters; discussed regional security with the Shah of Iran, including Bhutto's proposal for a conference of Indian Ocean littoral states on the subject; and tabled a resolution in the UN General Assembly about safeguarding the integrity of non-nuclear states which was adopted unanimously. Pakistan was making its mark in the world, and when the meeting of Islamic countries' foreign ministers agreed at Jeddah in July to support Pakistan's candidature for a vacant seat on the Security Council, Bhutto's cup was made full. But at home, Bhutto was not doing so well. Bombings, assassinations, plots and political mayhem were rife. The former Bhutto loyalist Mustafa Khar (whom Bhutto had telephoned from Rome in December 1971 to find out if it was safe for him to return to depose Yahya Khan) tried to play Bhutto at his own game of unscrupulously manipulating political affairs, as he had tried to do in 1973, and again lost. The political scene resembled that at the court of a particularly paranoid and malevolent Kabuli chieftain.[27]

General Tikka Khan retired on 28 February 1976 from the position of army chief, to become Special Assistant to the Prime Minister on Defence and National Security, and was succeeded by General Zia ul Haq. (Bhutto had wanted the COAS to remain for another year but it had become apparent that an extension of Tikka Khan's tenure would not be well received in the army, which was conscious that it was being politicized.) Zia was not Tikka's choice by any means, but Bhutto wanted him.[28]

It seems Zia was thought to be a reasonable fellow who, while deeply religious, was apparently not a zealot, and Bhutto considered he would not question his authority. At the time, he was commanding II Corps, the armour-heavy 'strike force' based in and around Multan. An officer who had been on his staff at that time told the author in the early 1980s that Zia was a good corps commander who let his staff get on with what they should be doing while 'doing the right thing' by getting around visiting units and assessing their capabilities. Zia's exercises were perforce small-scale, but seem to have been realistic enough, and his corps was as effective as it could be in the circumstances. He seemed the ideal man to be Chief of the Army Staff, as the seven officers senior to him either had political question marks against them or were disliked by Bhutto (same thing, in the end), who had dossiers on them all.[29] He was fifty-two, a good age for an army chief, not yet being in the bracket that could be called old and out of touch, yet not so young as to attract the 'wet-behind-the-ears' calumny. (But he had one remarkable deficiency for an army officer: he was hopeless at adhering to a timetable or keeping appointments, and sometimes exasperated his staff by forgetting engagements arranged days in advance. This trait became even more marked – and exasperating – in later years.)

Zia made no waves on arrival in GHQ at Rawalpindi. He seemed 'a bit withdrawn at first', according to one of his staff officers, but soon settled in to run a fairly humdrum headquarters whose officers had not been encouraged to indulge in original thinking, or question conventional wisdom as to what the army was all about and where it was going. And he did 'run' it: he wanted to know who was doing what and why – although he seemed to have an unfortunate proclivity for 'sitting on' files. Initially he did not wish to delegate to subordinates too much of what he saw as important. In later years he changed completely, and, in spite of being an autocrat, delegated a great deal to his Chief of Staff, General K.M. Arif, whose *Working with Zia* is a valuable account of his association with his master.

In GHQ there was no 'Mission Statement' (not that the phrase existed then), and training directives produced by the Military Training Directorate were decidedly low key, even banal. Operations Branch had a lot to occupy it, what with Balochistan, Sindh and the Afghan border, but planning was poor. Nobody quite knew what would happen if the Indians

24

were to commit their armour in Punjab, or try a 'vertical envelopment' (the OK phrase of the day, meaning a parachute drop) to cut the road to Karachi, or simply engage in a war of nerves along the border. (There was already a war of nerves along the Line of Control in Kashmir, but the orders to troops there consisted, basically, of: 'If you are fired at, fire back, but make sure the UN Observers are informed as soon as possible.' Which was one reason why the UN Mission in Kashmir was so unpopular in India. An examination of its independent reports on ceasefire violations makes interesting reading.) The War Book, as such, had given way to contingency plans, but these were pedestrian, imprecise and seemed in many ways impractical to some who had to examine them. Unfortunately, Zia was not the man to inject imagination into the minds of the planners. They carried on churning out what they considered to be staff college solutions to problems they had not examined in a spirit of challenge. But Zia did no harm to the army in his first fifteen months as COAS. He did not take over a happy team, but that was not his fault, and he tried to place it back on the rails in the best way he knew: with calmness, professional integrity, a genuine religiosity that struck a favourable chord with many of the younger officers and most of the soldiers, and a middle-class pragmatism that was beyond the comprehension of Zulfikar Ali Bhutto.

Bhutto was a bully whose aristocratic origins and upbringing contributed to an air of superiority that many thought irritating. One of his party tricks was to humiliate Zia, who he referred to in public as 'my monkey general', and there is no record of Zia ever sticking to an independent line after Bhutto disagreed with him. One instance was Zia's proposal in 1976 to have the captain to major promotion examination, usually confined to tactics and purely professional matters, include a test on the content of the Koran. Bhutto didn't like the idea and told Zia to think again, which he did, right away. Then he sent a minute to all units stating that 'We, in the army, are not Mullahs and we do not need anyone's certificate for being the followers of Islam.'[30] Zia was dissembling, and although he appeared to agree with Bhutto's contention that concentration on religious matters in the army would be 'highly injurious', he simply slid away and prepared to slither back later.

One of Bhutto's concerns was the approach of general elections, and it is puzzling why he appeared to be so worried about what was bound to be a victory for the PPP. At the end of 1976, the *Far Eastern Economic Review* commented: 'Even his staunchest rivals conceded privately that he did not face any serious challenge. Considering the plight of the Opposition, brought about partly by Bhutto and partly by its own ... political ineptitude, its despondent mood seemed fully justified.' But it seemed that Bhutto wanted overwhelming endorsement by the people. This he was determined to achieve.[31] It is difficult to disagree with Lawrence Ziring that 'He not only wanted to defeat his adversaries, he was determined to destroy them forever.'

During 1976, an agreement with the US was signed for the supply of arms worth $38.6 million, and Congress was asked by the Administration to approve a further $79.5 million. The equipment took some time to work its way through the pipeline, but it played a part in convincing the Services that they were not being neglected. Of considerable importance to the armed forces, Bhutto decided to provide plots of land at giveaway prices to junior commissioned officers because they were 'not financially well-off and their continued service to the country should not go unrecognized' (see Chapter 6) – and nor should the thoughtfulness (in the months before elections) of Zulfikar Ali Bhutto, who hoped that Zia would 'let [the grants] be known to all ranks of the Pakistan Army'.[32]

Bhutto's despairing comment in mid-1977 that 'There has been complete polarization – both horizontal and vertical – and it has left hardly any walk of life unaffected,' was quite true, but he would not admit to responsibility for this polarization any more than he could admit that the resurgence in political opposition owed much to his own confrontational stance. He had treated the opposition parties with contempt and was surprised when they established an alliance, the United Democratic Front, to fight the elections of 7 March. In spite of this development, the PPP would probably have won the elections even had they been conducted fairly.[33] It seems that in much of Sindh and the North-West Frontier Province the ballots were as fair as possible in the circumstances, but nobody believed that the results in Punjab were anything but well and truly rigged. General Gul Hassan, ambassador in Athens, and his friend Air Marshal Rahim Khan in Madrid, resigned as publicly as possible, but there were no major outbreaks of discontent in the country until the middle of April. Then the real trouble began.

The country was riven and shaken by demonstrations. In May, Bhutto tried 'to buy another parcel of time by offering Pakistan a referendum on whether he should stay in office. On Monday the national Assembly, consisting only of members of his own People's Party, amended the constitution for the seventh time in four years to authorise such a referendum before the end of September.'[34]

By mid-June, more than 11,000 people were in prison. Leaders of the opposition Pakistan National Alliance (PNA), the coalition of nine opposition parties (the 'gang of nine' as Bhutto referred to them) were as unprincipled as the Prime Minister in encouraging violence throughout the country. Once it became apparent that violent agitation was working in their favour, they refused to negotiate with Bhutto, who at first prevaricated about discussing the rigged election, then arrested many of the

PNA's leaders. Bhutto banned demonstrations and, in a desperate throw for popularity with the Islamic parties, declared the prohibition of alcohol and gambling.[35] Mosques became centres of agitation. Congregations were whipped to fury at Friday prayers and then held demonstrations which were suppressed by the police and, later, by the army. In an attempt to influence the population, the Chairman of the Joint Chiefs of Staff Committee and the Service Chiefs issued a statement towards the end of April declaring that Bhutto's government had the loyalty of the armed forces. It was ignored. Immediately after this, Bhutto declared martial law in Hyderabad, Karachi and Lahore (and later Multan), and the army imposed a curfew on these cities. Three brigadiers, all in the 10th Division in Lahore, refused to involve themselves or their troops in putting down riots, as this would almost certainly have involved killing civilians.

The country was becoming ungovernable and the economy had suffered greatly from the unrest, but it seemed that Bhutto did not realize that time was running out. The PNA wanted his resignation, the formation of an interim government and fresh elections. After much behind-the-scenes negotiation (including mediation by some Arab countries), the PNA dropped the resignation demand, agreeing that the Constitution required a PM to be in office until election of a successor (as pointed out by the wily Bhutto), and even compromised on their insistence on an interim government. They could not have gone much further and Bhutto was forced to consent to hold elections on 8 October. But the two sides could not continue to agree on anything for any length of time and kept altering their positions. The country was seething with dissatisfaction. A crisis was approaching. The President, Chaudhry Fazal Elahi, was unable to resolve matters because the Constitution forbade any action on his part except on the advice of the Prime Minister. As the Prime Minister was the major part of the problem, the President was powerless.

On the evening of 4 July 1977, the Chief of the Army Staff called a meeting of senior GHQ officers, having already discussed the nation's predicament with his corps commanders. Both sides in the political struggle, said Zia, had weapons. There was danger of a full-scale civil war. Operation Fair Play had begun. The army was going to take over.

Notes

1. Bhutto, Z.A., *Address to the Nation, Speeches and Statements*, vol. 1, 20 December 1971–31 March 1972, Government of Pakistan, 1972.
2. As suggested to the author by an officer present at the time.
3. The Hamoodur Rehman 'Commission of Inquiry into the 1971 War' (released in 2001) goes into this in some detail, as it does about Yahya's womanizing. Chapter 26 of the Report, 'The Moral Aspect', makes sad reading, as it deals with widespread moral decay in the army, as well as making observations about Yahya himself. The statement that he

'was extremely friendly with a number of ladies of indifferent repute' is substantiated by the visitors' log of the President's House, Karachi. It was all sordid stuff.

4. 'GM' was Director Military Operations (a brigadier's appointment) in the early 1980s when the author first made his acquaintance. Amongst later appointments he was Commandant of the Military Academy and commander X Corps in a very sensitive period. He had been awarded the Queen's Medal at Sandhurst and never looked back. A man of deep religious conviction and complete integrity.

5. *Memoirs of Lieutenant General Gul Hassan Khan*, OUP, Karachi, 1993. Gul Hassan was commissioned in 1942 and died in 1999.

6. Who retired in the 2000s but still does not want to be identified.

7. Rizvi, Hasan-Askari (ed.), *The Military and Politics in Pakistan 1947–1976*, Progressive Publishers, Lahore, 1976.

8. Discussions with senior officers of Joint Staff HQ, 1990–94.

9. As recommended by the Hamoodur Rahman Commission.

10. Qadianis are members of a movement formed by Mirza Ghulam Ahmad Qadiyani (1835–1908) and often referred to as Ahmadiyas or Ahmadis. (A split into Qadianis and Lahorites took place after Mirza Ghulam's death.) One tenet is the belief that Jesus Christ escaped death on the Cross and died and was buried in Srinagar in the Kashmir Valley. The sect is regarded with suspicion and often intolerance by many Muslims.

11. Speech in Karachi, 3 January 1972, in *Speeches and Statements*.

12. The US magazine *Business Week* of 12 November 2001 carried a major piece on the Fauji Foundation. It began 'It's early morning in Islamabad, and a middle-class child sits down for breakfast. He pours sugar refined from Fauji Sugar Mills into a bowl of Fauji oatmeal, which his mother cooked using gas bottled by Fauji LPG. In the next room his father logs onto his computer running on electricity produced by the Fauji Kabirwala power plant and clicks onto a program that uses Fauji software. The house they all live in was, of course, built with Fauji cement. The Fauji group is as pervasive a commercial presence in Pakistan as General Electric is in the US. And the Fauji companies, all part of the Fauji Foundation, are closely linked to an even more ubiquitous institution – the Pakistani military, itself a formidable force in the economy. See http://www.businessweek.com/magazine/content/01_46/b3757138.htm and Chapter 6. The Foundation is excoriated in a book by Dr Ayesha Siddiqa, *Military Inc*, Pluto Press, 2007, in which the most up-to-date statistics given are those of 2001 and 2002.

13. One of Mrs Ghandi's advisers, Parmeshwar Narain Haksar, told her that the object was not to humiliate Pakistan but to create confidence and trust. 'You must not forget the Versailles Treaty [that humiliated Germany in 1919 and led to the Second World War],' he said. 'You don't trample a man who is down and out.' See Frank, Katherine, *Indira*, HarperCollins, 2001, an elegant and most readable account of Mrs Gandhi's life.

14. Fallaci, Oriana (trans. John Shepley), *Interview with History*, New York, Houghton Mifflin, 1976.

15. Which, if it ever went to international arbitration, would probably be awarded to India. But India has spoiled its chances of international arbitration over Aksai Chin (and other areas in dispute with the PRC) by refusing such on Kashmir. Hoist by its own petard, India can attempt only bilateral negotiations – and China will not mention Aksai Chin.

16. Smith, Christopher, *India's Ad Hoc Arsenal*, OUP, New York, 1994.

17. The IISS *Military Balance* for 1972–3 gives the figures as 960,000 troops, 650 combat aircraft and 1,490 tanks.

18. Wolpert, Stanley, *Zulfi Bhutto of Pakistan*, OUP, New York, 1993. Wolpert records that the content of Tikka Khan's reply to the memo is not known.

19. Wirsing, R.G. *Pakistan's Security under Zia, 1977–1998*, Macmillan, London, 1991.

20. The army was assisted in its operations by Iranian helicopter gunships (supplied by the US) provided at the orders of the Shah who did not wish tribal troubles to spread to the Iranian provinces of Balochistan and Sistan. In 2004–5, as serious tribal and religious violence began again in Balochistan, its self-appointed leaders of dissident groups lost no opportunity to recall the events of the 1970s.

21. James, Sir Morrice (Lord Saint Brides), *Pakistan Chronicle*, OUP, Karachi, 1993.

22. Arif, General K.M., *Working with Zia*, OUP, Karachi, 1995.

23. Ziring, Lawrence, *Pakistan in the Twentieth Century*, OUP, Karachi, 1997.

24. Burrows, William E. and Windrem, Robert, *Critical Mass*, London, Simon and Schuster, 1994. See also the masterly George Perkovitch' *India's Nuclear Bomb*, California, 1999.

25. Wolpert, *ibid*.

26. In 1976 Dr Henry Kissinger, on behalf of the Ford administration, offered Pakistan 'a substantial conventional arms package' if Bhutto agreed to forgo the reprocessing plant. See Kux, Dennis, *The United States and Pakistan 1947–2000*, Johns Hopkins University Press, 2001.

27. Dennis Kux (for example) states in *The United States and Pakistan 1947–2000* that Bhutto 'was acting more like a feudal autocrat than a democratic political leader'. This is a superbly written book and most informative.

28. There is an account of the selection process, perhaps not altogether unbiased, in Chishti, F.A., *Betrayals of Another Kind: Islam, Democracy and the Army*, Jang Publishers, Lahore, 1996.

29. Arif recounts that Bhutto made 'unsavoury' comments about all seven.

30. Copy in the Bhutto Archives in Larkana, quoted by Wolpert.

31. He had also learned about propaganda, and the PPP produced thousands of little red booklets on the lines of Mao's *Thoughts*, entitled *Bhutto Says: a Pocket-Book of Thoughtful Quotations and Writings of Chairman Zulfiqar Ali Bhutto*. In 1980, while hill-walking, the author met a PPP loyalist (who had prudently decided to move out of Rawalpindi to his house on a Kashmir hillside) and asked him if the title was really intentional, or had someone been ironical and the joke got out of hand? No, no, said the former politician, the whole thing was genuine enough – but, anyway, those who could read were already convinced that Bhutto would win.

32. Wolpert, *ibid*. The allocation of plots of land to the military has been assailed by some writers and politicians, for reasons of their own, but they tend to ignore that Bhutto endorsed it.

33. In *Years of Upheaval*, Weidenfeld & Nicolson and Michael Joseph, 1982, Kissinger observed that 'Bhutto destroyed himself by seeking a popular mandate too rapidly and then manipulating the electoral result.'

34. *The Economist*, 21–7 May 1977. It is interesting but perhaps not surprising that recollections of this era by many later commentators excludes description of the viciousness of Bhutto's regime.

35. A close associate of Bhutto, Colonel Ismail Khan, described the institution of Prohibition to me on several occasions over many years. He and Bhutto 'cracked a bottle of Scotch' to celebrate.

Chapter 2

The Years of Zia

The experience of Pakistan, however, suggests that it might be easy for a disciplined army to take over the reins of government in a developing country ... but the military cannot solve all the problems facing a new nation. It may check instability, introduce certain social and economic reforms and accelerate the rate of economic growth but it cannot tackle the real problem which leads to a coup d'état – creation of a viable framework of political action which can function smoothly without the backing of the military commanders.

Hasan-Askari Rizvi, 1976

Rizvi forecast correctly on all counts: the army's takeover in 1977 was easy (and without violence – *The Economist*'s headline was 'A small coup, nobody killed'); instability was checked; social and economic reforms were introduced; and the rate of economic growth was accelerated. But there was no development of an alternative system, the 'viable framework' of civil government that would serve the country without the threat of bayonets in the background. Of most importance was approval and encouragement of religious intolerance. Zia's immediate introduction of punishments supposedly consistent with Muslim (sharia) law was greeted with dismay by secularly inclined Pakistanis and horror by Western liberals, but no one at the time had any notion of how disastrous his religiosity was to be for Pakistan and the rest of the world.

Zia was not prepared in any way to run a country. He had no concept of the intricacies of government; no agenda for social reform (other than imposition of crude religiously based diktats); and no training in economics (which he found boring). But for many years under his rule the country was prosperous and comparatively stable. Certainly he told a lie when he first promised to hold elections. Was it a lie at the time he told it? Or did it become a lie when, after a few weeks, he realized that elections would free the vicious and unforgiving Bhutto to stomp the country with his private army, making rabble-rousing speeches which would be equalled in ferocity by his political opponents?

Zia's regime began benevolently enough but became progressively more autocratic and eventually dismally directionless. There were improvements to the lot of the common man, there were undemocratic fiats that restricted personal freedoms, and judicially awarded punishments that appalled the liberal West. Emergence of religiosity of a weird and wonderful brand was undoubtedly at Zia's behest, and the seeds of future discord and violence were well and truly sown by his encouragement of Islamic bigots. But in the villages, towns and cities the people could relax for the moment, at least – provided they did not indulge in political machinations – and begin to enjoy life free from surveillance by Bhutto's FSF and the PPP petty functionaries, who had delighted in their power over the man in the street; those who, only six years earlier, Bhutto had said he wanted 'to be able to tell him to go to hell'.

The Zia regime lasted from 5 July 1977 to 17 August 1988. In these eleven years the army grew from 400,000 to 450,000 and its inventory of equipment increased in quantity and quality. The outlook of the army altered. Its members were encouraged by the example of the COAS to pay more attention to religion, which some did as lip service, some as genuine devotees. Some, of course, ignored the call and were quietly shunted sideways or out. Some ignored the call and were too valuable to dismiss. There was a gradual growth of national pride within the officer corps. They came to consider that although America had influence over their country, they could take as much US advice as they wished and discard the rest. China was an ally, although at times it appeared reluctant to offer more than token approval for Pakistan's policies – perhaps because America was so much to the fore – but the Chinese did not have much effect on military doctrine or training. The days of hankering after a 'people's army' were over. However, the army was weakened, especially at the beginning of Zia's regime and in the early 1980s, by the requirement for officers to be involved in martial law. A constant complaint was that many good officers who should have been gaining command experience were forced to have their postings cut short or disrupted by 'double-hatting' – carrying out administration of martial law in addition to normal military duties. It is impossible to quantify this, but it is obvious it existed.

The President, Chaudhury Fazal Elahi, remained in office, to the satisfaction of Zia, who gave him the respect he almost invariably afforded older and wiser men. The position, however, was a hollow one, just as Bhutto intended it to be, and Elahi was a tired man. He had borne with equanimity the insults of Bhutto and his henchmen ('no ministry . . . should in future deal directly with the President's Secretariat')[1] and wanted to leave at the end of his tenure in September 1978 in spite of Zia's sincere request that he remain. Under the Constitution, his successor should have been elected by both Houses of Parliament, but martial law overrode this, and on 16 September Zia was sworn in as Pakistan's fourth military President.

He charted the way ahead in his first speech to the nation on 5 July (written by the talented Siddiq Salik),[2] of which one theme was the lack of political ambition on his own part: 'My sole aim is to organise free and fair elections which [will] be held in October this year. Soon after the polls power will be transferred to the elected representatives of the people. I give a solemn assurance that I will not deviate from this schedule.' They weren't; it wasn't; and he did.

Zia formed a military council of the Chairman of the Joint Chiefs of Staff Committee (who was senior to Zia) and the three Service Chiefs of Staff, of whom he was but one – but it was obvious who was calling the shots because he announced that the Chief Martial Law Administrator was to be Chief Executive of the Nation and that Martial Law Orders and Regulations were not to be challenged in any court of law. By proclamation he suspended the Constitution, dissolved the federal and provincial assemblies, sacked the Prime Minister and all ministers (federal and provincial), dismissed the provincial governors and brought the entire country under martial law. All within forty-eight hours of taking power. Interesting stuff, especially as replacements were needed at once for a large number of experienced officials. Which makes one imagine that Operation Fair Play might have been thought out in detail over a considerable period. Some sources state that Zia was in the hands of junior officers – majors and colonels – who forced him to go ahead with the coup. Perhaps, but interestingly, Zia had been keeping track of young officers' career profiles for many years. When he was the senior administrative staff officer on the HQ of 6th Armoured Division, it was noted by a fellow officer who had known him for many years that he 'paid a lot of attention to the confidential reports' of officers in the formation, which was not what administrators normally do.[3] His dislike of files did not seem to extend to detailed examination of personal records. And later he was very careful in selection of officers when it was within his gift to do so. One wonders whether Zia might have been planning ahead in some way.

The stage was set for a restoration of stability and then progression to what one might call the Third Republic. But Zia discovered two things: that Zulfikar Ali Bhutto had been even less principled than had been supposed – to the point that he was strongly suspected of ordering a murder; and that he, Zia, thought he was rather good at governing the country, which he wasn't. The legal rights or wrongs of Bhutto's trial and execution are neither here nor there so far as this narrative is concerned, except to state that the army itself acted with propriety and dignity. There were many wild allegations made concerning the circumstances in which Mr Bhutto died, but the facts are horrible enough. The execution was carried out in a manner that caused the utmost misery and grief to his wife and family, especially his daughter Benazir, probably his favourite person, who understandably distrusted and hated the army from that moment onwards.

The system of martial law throughout the country was consistent with the military chain of command. Initially the corps commanders were appointed governors in each province (except Balochistan, which at that time did not have a Corps HQ in the capital, Quetta). This resulted in protocol problems and was also unwieldy. Dignity (and its close kin, pomposity) was at stake, of course, when a governor who was a lieutenant general considered that he should be treated as senior to a full general when the latter was a visitor in the former's province. The somewhat bombastic (but, to the author, at least, most likeable) Lieutenant General Fazle Haq[4] of the North-West Frontier Province objected when the Deputy Chief of the Army Staff, General Muhammad Iqbal, was to be given precedence over him at a passing-out parade at the Pakistan Military Academy. Fazle Haq refused to attend the parade, but Zia took no notice and continued to place confidence in him. It became necessary to appoint full-time governors from the army, which was done in NWFP (Fazle stayed), Punjab and Sindh. Balochistan continued to be governed by Lieutenant General Rahimuddin Khan, Zia's son-in-law. The insurrection in Balochistan was ended, simply, by ceasing military operations, granting amnesties and turning 'confrontation into reconciliation'.[5]

The federal cabinet, at first styled the Council of Advisers, did not originally include many military officers, and in its final composition had none at all. Many members were able enough but had ideas above their station and became embarrassing, and some outstanding ones left because they considered they were wasting their time. The retired Lieutenant General Habibullah Khan, an industrialist of energy, honesty and wealth, became weary of having his advice ignored and went home to Peshawar. The Minister for Finance and Planning, the sagacious Mr Ghulam Ishaq Khan, became President of Pakistan in later years, and some others continued to exercise their talents in the interests of their country, but it cannot be said that the cabinet was a happy organization (perhaps few cabinets are). The army, too, began to lose direction. It became unsure of itself, and the chain of command became imprecise and unclear. Perhaps it became unsure of itself because the chain of command was unclear. It had a chief who was also President, which resembled a rerun of the Yahya period, when it seemed the President was never quite sure about which hat he was wearing at any given time. Zia had to concentrate on running the country, which was his own choice and nobody else's, but surely, thought the army,[6] he should pay attention to reorganization, re-equipment and getting rid of 'Bhutto boys'.

In fact, Zia had got rid of several 'Bhutto boys'. Some were included in the first bunch of thirty or so that he ordered sidelined or sacked when he sent for the Military Secretary to talk about the career plot the day after he took over, and some others went later. 'Bhuttoism' did remain in the army (and more so in the air force), but was of little consequence. (The navy ignored all this vulgar stuff.) In spite of this, Zia was never quite sure about some senior officers who remained in command positions and made it clear they were on probation. Those who seemed to be in the pattern of the old Ayub and Yahya style were suspect – although Fazle Haq and some others were undoubtedly in this mould.

Of the many Zia loyalists, few were more dependable than Lieutenant General Muhammad Sawar Khan, who was appointed Governor of Punjab in 1978. He performed the difficult task of managing the province for two years and was then made Vice Chief of Army Staff – a new appointment redesignated from Deputy Chief – which carried the rank of full general. The duty statement of the Vice Chief was: 'To exercise and perform all the powers and functions vested in the Chief of Army Staff under the law, rules, regulations, orders and instructions for the time being in force'. Further, the Vice Chief was allowed all facilities 'as authorised to the Chief of Army Staff for so long as the COAS holds the office of the President'.[7] He was head of the army – but not altogether, because he could not take independent action in matters that Zia considered his sole province, such as senior promotions and appointments. Zia had three hats: COAS, CMLA and President. The anomaly that, although senior to the Chairman of the Joint Chiefs of Staff Committee by virtue of being President, he was his junior in military appointment and length of service, was overcome by tinkering with the Constitution. He based his right to do so on the dubious Supreme Court decision that imposition of martial law was validated 'as it was found to be dictated by considerations of state necessity and public welfare' – although the nine judges rejected the argument that legitimacy of the coup (or any coup) was conferred by success.[8] The judgment resulted in modifications to the Constitution that were designed to legitimize and prolong Zia's Presidency. They included amendment of Articles governing senior military appointments, which suited Zia's purposes but were untranslatable when the country reverted to parliamentary rule, and almost caused a constitutional upset when Benazir Bhutto, as Prime Minister, attempted to exercise what she considered her powers to appoint a Chairman of the Joint Chiefs of Staff Committee in 1989. In any event, the amendment to the Constitution that was relevant to Zia's Presidency and the armed forces was that: 'Without prejudice to the generality of the foregoing provision [that the Federal Government shall have control and command of the Armed Forces], the Supreme Command of the Armed Forces shall vest in the President.'[9] So Zia was senior to the Chairman, after all.

It has been claimed that Zia was a hypocrite as regards religion, but it is difficult to find a convincing argument for this contention. Allegations are usually based on the fact that the regime was harsh and that many PPP adherents suffered because of their connections to Bhutto. The regime was indeed harsh on those who sought to undermine it and PPP loyalists were treated appallingly in squalid jails.[10] (Although there is no possible excuse for their treatment it should be remembered that many of them had behaved outrageously, illegally and brutally during the time in power of their protector.) All this might not have been unIslamic *per se*, although that is cold comfort to those who suffered. Zia was a genuinely religious man and tried his best to encourage the people of Pakistan to observe the Faith in the manner he wished. In the army this had mixed results. For the country (in hindsight) it was a disaster.

The problem is that there can be conflict between encouragement, suggestion, discipline and obedience. In a strictly structured military society there is little room for exhibition of originality. In modern military services eccentricity is distrusted and conformity approved. And there is a fine line between the highest level of conformity and the lowest of compliant obsequiousness. Once that line is crossed, the subject can move quickly to ever-greater levels of ingratiation, thereby compromising integrity in the desire to appear efficient. It can appear to junior officers that sycophancy is not only acceptable, but that without it the road to advancement is blocked. In an officer corps this can be a speedy way to disaster. It is not detectable at first, but once it becomes apparent it is usually too late to alter course without a wholesale cleansing, which usually means excision of some of the innocent along with the guilty, and also of some who could be saved by restoration of good practices.

This does not mean that the holding of religious beliefs and their practice are in any way undesirable in a defence force. It does mean that the flaunting of religious belief in the hope that this will meet with the approval of superior officers is unhealthy. But there are problems here, too. Common worship in Islam is desirable because it 'strengthen[s] the awareness of one Muslim for another in times of gain or of adversity. In many respects [acts of common worship] serve to cement communal bonds by stimulating the individual's sense of belonging.'[11] So where is the line between public worship because it is an essential part of religion, and public worship because it is a good thing to be seen by a senior officer performing one's devotions? The answer lies in the application of common sense by all concerned – but as this is unlikely to obtain at all times, it must be accepted that a military hierarchical system with theocratic overtones will be difficult to manage.

Many of Zia's new senior officers were by upbringing and education more inclined to religion than their worldly predecessors whose secular approach he had long distrusted. (Even as a divisional commander he had banned alcohol in officers' messes.) Omar Noman (*Pakistan, a Political and Economic History Since 1947*, Kegan Paul International, 1990) wrote:

> One of the first changes made by Zia, after his appointment as COAS, was to upgrade the status of the maulvis attached to each army unit. Hitherto they had been regarded as comic figures which the military elite tolerated as a gesture to religious obligation. Zia integrated [them] into the everyday ethos of the military and made it compulsory for them to go into battle with the troops. This initial gesture was a harbinger of things to come. Thus, when the military-bureaucratic apparatus regained power in 1977, it was the religiously inclined generals who were dominant.

Well, not altogether. There were several influential senior officers who, while perfectly good Muslims, had a more lenitive interpretation of what their leader required. It seemed, however, that the writing was on the wall for those who wanted wider and more secular horizons. But events moved in favour of wider horizons, at least. First, most religious parties objected to martial law (for reasons that would take too long to examine) and were unwilling to support Zia; and outside developments took place that perforce encouraged a less conditional approach to the Profession of Arms.

It was Zia who furthered polarization between Shia and Sunni Muslims. Little as this may have been his intent (and there are varying views), he exacerbated the problem (never far below the surface) by introducing zakat, an Islamic wealth-sharing arrangement which was objected to by Shias. He then reversed his decision (not for nothing was CMLA known as Cancel My Last Announcement), thereby alienating extremist Sunnis. The short-term result was the usual rioting, but the effects lasted and the Sunni-Shia divide continues to be a matter for serious concern in Pakistan.

Zia was helped in development of the country by instability across the western border. When the Soviet Union agreed to provide Afghanistan with 'urgent political, moral and economic aid, including military aid' in 1979, it was obvious that a Soviet military takeover was in progress. On 1 January 1980 the Kabul government admitted it had 'invited' Russian troops into the country a few days before 'in view of the present aggressive actions of the enemies of Afghanistan', without specifying who these might be and ignoring the fact that the need for Soviet intervention stemmed largely from the Afghans' own proclivity for internal strife. Events then moved quickly. Thousands of refugees (soon to be over three million) began to cross the border into Pakistan (and some hundreds of thousands to Iran). President Carter said the US would provide defence equipment;[12] Saudi Arabia and the Gulf States sent donations, the former giving $100 million in its first tranche; the EEC promised $20 million in refugee assistance; China said it backed Pakistan 'against foreign aggression and interference' and, in one of the more improbable developments of the era, later received indirect CIA funding for provision of weapons to the freedom fighters, the mujahideen; Japan signed a $50 million aid package and gave $1.5 million for the refugee programme; the world was beating paths to Zia's door. The economy of Pakistan, in reasonable shape but already skewed by such fiscal subsidies as the earnings of Pakistani workers in the Gulf, was put even further out of kilter by these donations, and by an outflow of capital caused by fear of the Russian presence. It is now known 'that the leaders of the Soviet Union never wanted to invade or occupy Afghanistan',[13] but the fact remains that they did occupy it. And so far as most of the rest of the world was concerned the situation was grave, for what other sovereign country might be invaded by a stronger power in the future?

The Services benefited greatly from the quantities of money and weapons that began arriving in the early 1980s. Pakistani officers were once again welcome in the US for briefings, training, and visits concerned with provision and use of weapons and intelligence. The threat of terrorism (as much from the Al Zulfiqar organization[14] as from across the border) brought a British team of 'mountaineers' to instruct the Special Services Group in some of the arcane skills employed by Britain's counter-terrorist experts.[15] Zia even went to the US to have talks with Mr Carter in October 1980, and a year later Mrs Thatcher visited Pakistan and recorded that 'Pakistan's was an unsung story of heroism, taking in hundreds of thousands of refugees and bordering the world's greatest military power ... if Pakistan was to stand as a bulwark against communism it would need still more help from the West.'[16] (Mrs Thatcher did not like Zia,[17] but her support for him was to bear fruit during the Falklands Campaign, when he refused to sell Exocet missiles to Argentina in spite of approaches by Italy which was supposedly an ally of the UK.) When President Reagan entered the White House in January 1981, there was a surge in support and especially in provision of military equipment, including F-16 aircraft, much to the vexation of India.[18] The CIA, according to Brigadier Mohammad Yousaf of the Afghan Cell in ISI, 'supported the Mujahideen by spending the American taxpayers' money, billions of dollars of it over the years, on buying arms, ammunition and equipment ... A high proportion of CIA aid was in the form of cash. For every dollar supplied by the US, another was added by the Saudi Arabian government.'[19] Pakistan was full of dollars, international goodwill, spooks of all nations, and amazement that the world suddenly seemed to care about what was going on in their country and to its west.

The Pakistan Army had produced plans, years before, to take account of a threat from the west (in addition to the unending one from the tribes). These involved positioning of artillery and armoured units in North West Frontier Province and Balochistan, and reinforcement from the Multan-based 'strike force' – even were there a concurrent threat from India – and creation of a corps HQ in Quetta, which was undertaken. If the Soviets crossed the border, the tactical plan was to hold the Khyber and Bolan passes and then strike into Afghanistan with special forces and ground-attack aircraft. (There had been a request for provision of Crusader aircraft on Pakistan's wish list for a long time but the US would not supply them. They had been part of the offer by President Ford as a quid pro quo for agreeing to cease nuclear weapons development, but Carter withdrew the carrot.)[20] The rest of the army would have time to deploy westwards and would be able to hold the advance. Enemy air attack in the passes would be suicidal at low level and ineffective from high altitude. Attempts at outflanking would be dealt with by ambush, just as they had been by the tribes in the days of the British. There was to be no reliance placed on foreign troops or aircraft. Pakistan would be on its own and could handle matters nicely, provided it had the equipment. This time, of course, it could be assured that the supply of spare parts would not be cut off.

The Americans had a plan, too. US forces were to be involved, but it is not known from where and how quickly they would come, the closest troops other than Marines being in Germany. The Soviets were to be permitted to advance through the passes and to 'fan out' on the plains, where they would then be defeated by overwhelming US military might. It is not known whether the Pakistanis were officially informed of this.[21] It is doubtful if the DMO in the early 1980s would have paid much attention to such a scenario, other than, with characteristic politeness, to thank the Americans for such original thought. Zia thanked the Americans for their largesse and laughed up his sleeve about their change of policy. The defence forces of Pakistan increased in size, capability and credibility. The mid-1980s saw a remarkable change in all three, but, all the same, one had reservations about the effectiveness of collective training and the quality of leadership. Statistics covering the decade show the difference in holdings:

Strength/Equipment/ Order of Battle	1979	1989
Army	400,000	450,000
Air Force	17,000	17,600
Navy	12,000	16,000

Army Corps HQ	3 plus 2 forming	7
Infantry Divisions	16	17 plus 1 equivalent (Northern Areas)
Armoured Divisions	2	2
Armoured Brigades	3	4
Infantry Brigades	3	8
Tanks	900	1,600
Artillery Pieces	1,000 (many obsolete)	1,200
Armoured Personnel Carriers	500	900
Advanced Combat Aircraft	–	39
Other Combat Aircraft	250	300
Surface-to-Air Missiles	1 battery	7 batteries

Sources: based on IISS, *The Military Balance*, amended by later information.

The Pakistan Military Academy increased its intake but had to lower its standards in quality of instructors and the educational standard of entrants. Expansion of the army meant much more than a mere increase in quantities of advanced weapons: it required more officers and soldiers, of course, but it demanded a commensurate improvement in technical skills, which depended on an education base Pakistan did not possess. The Education Corps was hard pressed to keep up with instruction in English, the language needed for understanding foreign manuals and for communication at higher levels. One of Zia's more disastrous priorities was the use of Urdu as the national language. English was to be downgraded. Regional languages were to be acknowledged, but Urdu was to be paramount. Remonstration was useless so far as Zia was concerned. He was as happy in Urdu as he was in English and failed to grasp, or perhaps didn't want to grasp, the implication of the comment by Dr A.Q. Khan, the now-disgraced nuclear expert, who is said to have observed that there were few textbooks about nuclear technology written in Urdu. (One of Zia's doctors told the author that he mentioned that there weren't many medical books in Urdu, either, but Zia just grunted.) Higher education in Pakistan was set back considerably by the introduction of 'Urdu-medium' schools that emphasized religious instruction. It became noticeable in the 1990s that many cadets entering the Service academies required coaching in English (just as they do, unfortunately, in some Western colleges and universities).

The army could not be directed properly with only a few corps headquarters. There was a limit to how many divisions could be commanded by a single HQ or be under effective direct command from GHQ. Both wars had shown that arrangements were inadequate. Expansion would exacerbate difficulties if more headquarters were not raised. In the late 1970s this was begun and the army gradually developed a more balanced structure. It was necessary to take account of the threat from the Soviets to the west, but planners realized that the defence of Karachi and the routes linking the industrial centres of Pakistan with its only port must be given greater priority than had hitherto obtained. The Indians had doubtless learned their lesson and, if there were another war, it could not be expected that the failure in 1971 of India's 11 and 12 Divisions in the western theatre to press their advantage would be repeated. In any event, India's Southern Command had been overhauled and was better organized to conduct offensive operations. It was not enough for Pakistan to have only an incomplete division to hold the southern sector. There had to be more troops and a higher HQ to command them and to act independently of GHQ if necessary. Tanks from the US and the workhorse Type 59s from China permitted the formation of more armoured regiments, and Pakistan complemented foreign weapons by giving emphasis to indigenous production of small arms under licence (such as the German G3 rifle) and manufacture of ammunition.

The influx of weapons had many effects on Pakistan, which had never been a country where the carrying of arms was unusual, especially in the Tribal Areas and North West Frontier Province in general. Large stocks of small arms and other weapons were built up, with suitable quantities of ammunition, by many tribes and groups. The Afghan factions increased their armouries, with some weapons being used against the Soviets and the Kabul regime, but many being stockpiled for use against each other when the day came that the Soviets left Afghanistan and the real fight for control of the country would begin. The Al Zulfiqar organization obtained weapons, too, including an SA-7 shoulder-fired anti-aircraft missile which was used on 7 February 1982 against a Falcon aircraft just after take-off from Islamabad/Rawalpindi.[22] It was carrying Zia, who was unperturbed about the attempt on his life but disconcerted that a missile could be launched so close to the airport. Some wild rumours flew round at the time as Zia was loath to have the incident publicized, yet ordered improvements in security which were implemented without explanation. More SA-7s were discovered later, including two in a private house in Lahore. Pakistan was becoming an ever more dangerous place, courtesy of Western, Chinese and Saudi support for the war against the Soviets in Afghanistan.

On 16 January 1983, the first three F-16s arrived, a symbol of US commitment to Pakistan, irrespective of the nature of the government in place. This support was a matter of concern not only to India but to the opposition political parties which had formed an alliance named the Movement for the Restoration of Democracy (MRD). They had hoped that the Zia regime would not receive so much backing, but reckoned without realpolitik. Zia was intent on retaining power for some years to come, but was also trying to come to terms with transforming martial law into a regime more akin to civilian rule. This was impossible, as Bhutto had discovered. It had to be one thing or the other. For Pakistan there was no middle way;

no possibility of melding the civil infrastructure and the military ethos on the lines of Indonesia, to which Zia was drawn, but realized was impracticable in Pakistan (and eventually proved unsuccessful in Indonesia). So he tinkered with alternatives and announced a three-phase programme of elections: municipal in 1983; provincial the next year; and federal in March 1985. The problem was that the MRD was excluded from taking part as it had been declared an illegal organization. Disturbances began in August, and anti-government rallies were held throughout the country resulting in several hundred deaths (official figure sixty-one) and the imprisonment of thousands of demonstrators and political activists, mainly of the PPP, whose leader, Benazir Bhutto, called on the army to overthrow the President. This caused Zia, in a display of severity (and showing a lack of understanding of the country at large), to ban political activity by the PPP for a further ten years. But in spite of the violence encouraged by the PPP, there was considerable domestic satisfaction with the Zia regime. Very many Pakistanis were enjoying prosperity such as they had never known before, much of it engendered by the spin-off from the Afghan war and the benefits accrued from Saudi approval of Zia's theocratic approach to government. Not only were there substantial subsidies with no strings attached, but Pakistani workers were employed in large numbers throughout the Kingdom, adding to an already increasing flow of cash from the extensive Pakistani diaspora. There was also a Pakistan military presence in Saudi Arabia which grew to over two divisions, some 40,000 men.

So far as the US was concerned, Zia was in a similar position to Nixon's Yahya Khan. Deference and dignity were the keywords. He was being treated as a world figure, an important personage in international relations. Secretary of State George Shultz recounts in his book *Turmoil and Triumph* that he met Zia in Delhi at the time of Indira Gandhi's funeral, then at Chernenko's in March 1985: 'The vice president and I visited President Zia' and at the funeral itself, 'I stood beside Zia and Yaqub Khan of Pakistan to show our unity in opposition to Soviet occupation of Afghanistan.' This would turn the head of most Third World rulers. It did not turn Zia's. He knew exactly the motivation of the US, and it certainly was not to support Pakistan because of sympathy for a developing nation. He had seen how American policy towards his country had changed over the years. He was grateful for the aid and actually liked the style of many Americans, but knew it could end the moment the US ceased to be concerned about Russia's activities in the region.

The navy and air force faced more problems with the introduction of new systems than did the army. There were advanced detection devices fitted in the navy's surveillance aircraft and in the F-16s, whose radar was the most up to date in the world (and to whose provision the USAF objected but was overruled). The French Mirage Vs were equipped with Exocet missiles, and Harpoons were provided by the US. There had to be expansion of technician training and many were trained overseas, but even with this assistance there was strain placed on facilities and training systems.

India was worried about all this new technology. The fact that Soviet aircraft were violating Pakistan's territory was neither here nor there so far as India was concerned: New Delhi considered that additions to or improvement in Pakistan's military hardware presented an increased threat to India. And that point of view was reasonable. Although there was belligerence on the part of India (especially during Rajiv Gandhi's election campaign in late 1984), and while it was becoming an ever more close associate of the USSR, which was still perceived as the aggressor rather than an unwilling participant in the Afghan mêlée, it was apparent that Pakistan's army improvements were greater than could be justified by Soviet adventurism – although in 1986 the Soviets had some 250 combat aircraft and 140 attack helicopters in Afghanistan.[23] There was an increase in army strength in Balochistan and some upgrading of capabilities in North West Frontier Province, but most improvements were taking place in Punjab and Sindh, on the border with India. Little wonder India was worried; but it compounded its fears by increasing its own military capabilities, which caused Pakistan and its Western backers to be even more suspicious about its intentions and those of its Soviet ally, for such the USSR was perceived to be.

In spite of Ms Bhutto's encouragement to rise up and depose Zia the army as a whole remained loyal to the President (who was also Chief of the Army Staff; shades of later years), although there were some problems. There had been arrests of several officers in January 1984 following a shooting incident in Lahore Cantonment, and the army was worried that her call to overthrow the regime might be heeded, especially by younger officers. In some cases it appeared that this was so. Several officers had heard they were to be arrested on 3 January and managed to leave the country, perhaps with the help of the Al Zulfiqar organization (which had contacts among the PIA staff[24] in Islamabad and Karachi airports), but others were detected and a few attempted to fight it out. All appear to have been junior officers, but they had received encouragement from some senior figures whose involvement could not be completely proved. Several were tried by court martial and served their sentences in Attock military prison. Others were encouraged to quit the service. Zia remained in power – threatened by PPP/MRD extremists; suspicious of some of his officers (especially in the air force); dubious as to how he should continue to govern the country; confused by the religious political parties' failing to give him the support he had expected; wary of permitting political activity lest it get out of hand; and worried about the enormous number of Afghan refugees within the country. He had not lost his sense of humour, however. On one occasion he had to fly to Saudi Arabia at short notice to argue that the Pakistan Army contingent's Shia Muslims should be permitted to serve in the Kingdom.[25] The diplomatic corps were present to bid him farewell, as were the most senior officers, one of whom, to his surprise and not to his delight, had been appointed to act as Chief Martial Law Administrator in Zia's absence. Brigadier M.A. Durrani,[26] Zia's senior aide, watched the aircraft take off and, as the wheels left the ground, turned to the acting CMLA, Admiral T.K. Khan,[27] saluted, and asked for orders. 'Ah,' said TK, 'I've only got one: Prohibition is repealed at once.' Zia heard the story, of course, but in spite of his anti-alcohol stance he laughed about it and never let it interfere with his dealings with his Navy Chief.

Zia had a lot on his plate in the mid-1980s, including the Indian occupation of Siachen, in what had been regarded as Pakistan-controlled territory. Most cartographers had drawn the Line of Control as extending to the Karakoram Pass leading to China, and mountaineers wishing to attempt peaks further north went through Islamabad rather than Delhi to obtain clearance. This appeared to vex Mrs Gandhi.

As foreshadowed, an Indian force advanced from Ladakh to the northern end of the Siachen Glacier in the spring of 1984, there having been a lodgement the previous year. New Delhi could have made a reasonable case in international law for a claim on the region, but chose to use force rather than negotiation. Its agreement at Simla – 'That the two countries are resolved to settle their differences by peaceful means' – was apparently annulled by contemporary considerations whose urgency and essentiality have never been satisfactorily explained. India's claim was based on the fact that the Line of Control ended, as agreed by representatives of India and Pakistan, at Grid Reference NJ 980420, there being no further delineation in any direction. India came to consider, eleven years after agreeing with Pakistan about the Line of Control, that because there was no formal accord governing the barren lands between the end of the Line and the Karakoram Pass, the area should belong to India. No attempt was made to enter the contiguous Aksai Chin area occupied by Chinese forces.

Of some consequence in the Indian position – had it been decided to follow diplomacy rather than take military action – would have been the fact that Pakistan and China concluded an agreement on 2 March 1963 concerning demarcation of territory between Xinjiang Province and Pakistan-controlled Kashmir, a sensible arrangement to which India took exception at the time.[28] It could be argued with some reason that Pakistan and China had no right to apportion territory to each other (1,350 square miles to Pakistan; 2,050 to China) while some of it was in dispute with a third party. A case could have been made for adjudication by the International Court of Justice, or even by an independent body of assessors, but India, since the decision of the tribunal concerning the Rann of Kutch in 1968, has resisted mediation or 'good offices' intended to defuse tension in the subcontinent. One Indian argument was that:

The strategic Tibet-Sinkiang road passes through territory captured by China east of Siachen. Northwards we have the new road from Pakistan going through the Khunjerab Pass. These form a noose round India's jugular. If they took Siachen they would be holding a dagger to our backs in the Nubra Valley.[29]

There is no point in examining this contention (by a general, alas), as anyone knowing anything about the region would ridicule it.

The Siachen dispute continued, with many casualties on both sides, most caused by respiratory ailments, frostbite, avalanches, crevasses and losing sense of direction in white-outs. 'We take Siachen as a test case,' said one supporter of India's thrust. 'We want to assert that the Indian strategic doctrine of the 80s goes way beyond the docility of the 50s and 60s, that it is no longer possible to gnaw at our far flung territories and then get away with no more than filibustry at the United Nations.'[30] The cost to both countries has been enormous in lives and money. Indian defence attachés around the world were tasked to buy sleeping bags, high-altitude tents, boots, clothing and snow vehicles. Pakistan was more fortunate: it had much cold-weather gear in store and received more from friendly nations. Instructors in mountain warfare came to Pakistan, and Pakistani officers and soldiers went to the UK, the US, Germany, France and Italy for such training. Many countries regarded India's foray into the wastes as ridiculous and, although there were few protests, made it clear that Pakistan would receive assistance if requested.

The Pakistan Army has a major advantage: its lines of communication to Siachen are much shorter than India's. It does not require the Sno-cats and other expensive equipment needed by India to supply its troops along the glacier. India's expenses in maintaining its presence in the north are immense. A foreign intelligence estimate in the early 1990s placed them at $100 million a year, as against one-tenth of that for Pakistan. Pakistan has one brigade of three battalions, an artillery regiment and a company of SSG in the area, while Indian strength is about twice that. The conditions in which the soldiers live (as witnessed by the author on the Pakistani side, and there is no reason to believe they differ on the Indian side) are the harshest in the world. There are no soldiers, anywhere else, who undergo the privations of the men at Siachen. At heights of over 20,000 feet the soldiers of both sides display great tenacity and courage – over a dispute which the politicians could settle in ten minutes.[31]

Zia was concerned about his soldiers in the north. The author was his guest in September 1985 and during discussions Zia expressed regret about the futility of operations in Siachen, but, he said, what else could be done other than to counter the Indian advance? What might come next? The move of the Indian Army towards Skardu? What, he was asked, if an offer were made to India to have the Line of Control declared the international border? Would not that solve the whole Kashmir problem? No, Zia said. He had a political problem anyway with the Kashmiris and didn't want an uprising, as would surely happen if they thought he was dealing with India behind their backs.

This is one of the main difficulties. India's insistence on bilateralism excludes Kashmiris from discussion about their own future. In December 1985 Zia went to Delhi to talk with the new Indian Prime Minister, Rajiv Gandhi. They agreed that there should be a peaceful solution to the Siachen Glacier confrontation, but later meetings of defence secretaries ended in the usual inconclusive manner.

In 1985 Zia ended Martial Law. He had received a 98 per cent approval vote in a referendum (of very low turnout) on 19 December 1984 asking if the electorate approved Islamization of the state. This he interpreted as endorsement of his rule. The poll was undoubtedly rigged, but he went ahead in March the following year with elections, permitting no political parties as such to participate. All candidates were 'independents', but political parties were allowed to resume their functions in 1986. The Prime Minister, Mr Mohammad Khan Junejo, assumed leadership of the Pakistan Muslim League (PML), and in the same period the PPP of Benazir Bhutto began to conduct itself again as a normal political party (although it excluded itself voluntarily from the National Assembly). There was a move towards polity by Zia, but the military scene was giving cause for some concern.

Relations between India and Pakistan were poor in the mid-1980s. There were allegations by New Delhi that Pakistan was involved in an assassination attempt on Mr Gandhi by Karamjeet Singh, a Sikh; there were more clashes in Siachen, and neither Gandhi nor Zia appeared willing to compromise over the dispute; India, having exploded a nuclear device in 1974, criticized Pakistan for having a nuclear programme; Zia brought up the subject of Kashmir at a non-aligned conference in Harare, immediately after which Gandhi criticized Pakistan's counter-terrorist assault on a hijacked aircraft at Karachi airport. Neither country was behaving well.

Outside influences contributed, too, to distrust: the US arranged a further aid package for Pakistan in March 1986, for $4.02 billion. Mr Gorbachev visited India in November and had the pleasure of hearing Mr Gandhi criticize the US for assisting Pakistan. This did not appear to cause Pakistan much concern but annoyed the US which, in turn, criticized the Soviet Union for not making genuine efforts to quit Afghanistan, which it was trying to do without losing face.[32] Altogether the subcontinent was in a mess and did not need another drama, especially one that might seem to be overplayed by some domestic and foreign observers.

In the second half of 1986 the Indian Army began a major exercise, Brass Tacks, which became the subject of intriguing comment concerning Indian intentions and Pakistani reaction. Curiously, *The Economist* did not cover the matter in spite of having both a 'Survey' of Pakistan and a cover-piece on India in January 1987. The *Far Eastern Economic Review* first mentioned the exercise on 12 February in the context of a meeting between foreign secretaries in Delhi earlier that month that was aimed – and successful – at easing tension. It appears that the whole affair was given rather more attention than was warranted, but it was and remains difficult to sort truth from unsubstantiated allegations.

Both sides overreacted; their media, including government-controlled radio, was often irresponsible;[33] and both sides told lies. Pakistan was not given official notification before the exercise began, although the *Pakistan Times* carried a report on 14 November that 'The major manoeuvres of the Indian armed forces will last four months, an unusually long time.' The Indian Defence Ministry would neither confirm nor deny, on 11 November, that an exercise was scheduled, as reported by AFP and other agencies. Next day New Delhi 'categorically denied reports that India has massed troops on its western borders for major manoeuvres',[34] which, as events showed, was patently untrue. According to *India Today*, a critic of Delhi's handling of Brass Tacks, Mr Gandhi forbade telephone contact between the two Directors-General of Military Operations which, if correct, was a lamentable way for him to behave.[35] When it became apparent that Indian troops were indeed massed for large-scale manoeuvres, the Pakistan government – Zia and his Prime Minister – at first reacted cautiously, but, in response to the unscheduled move of more troops in India's western sectors, later sent forces to the border area.[36] The affair is perhaps best summed up by the International Institute for Strategic Studies' Strategic Survey 1987–88, which noted briefly and pithily that the two countries 'demonstrated that their mutual antipathy could be contained when they backed away from a major build-up of forces on their border which was the result of poor communications and some posturing on both sides'. A storm in a teacup? Not quite. Although the antipathy was 'contained', there remained grave distrust. Zia was as placatory as he could be in February when he said that the agreement to end tension along the border was 'proof of the wisdom of the Prime Ministers of the two countries', which he may or may not have believed but was a generous public statement.[37]

Zia scored a propaganda success by visiting Jaipur in February for a Pakistan-India cricket match at which Gandhi had to meet him. Zia was no cricket fan, but used the opportunity to score runs which annoyed Gandhi but placed him in a position in which he might appear churlish if he objected to the approach. Zia was demonstrating that he was not concerned about India's military manoeuvres, but might not have been so sanguine had he known of India's plans. A week later, Gandhi's budget increased military spending by 43 per cent to about $10 bn a year. This, given friendship prices and other arrangements for Soviet equipment (the first Kilo Class submarine had just arrived), did not reflect true military expenditure. Pakistan's defence budget was artificial, too, because of aid and other subventions. It is impossible to calculate the real expenditure of either country during the cold war years; only since the early 1990s can reasonably accurate, unclassified estimates be made, and these, of course, do not take into account nuclear programmes.

The Indian government enjoyed irritating Pakistan (and the US) about the situation in Afghanistan. The External Affairs Minister, Mr N.D. Tiwari, visited Kabul in early May 1987 for the seventh session of the Indo-Afghan Joint Commission and held a press conference. Pakistan, he said, was obtaining weapons 'clearly designed for use against India' and not against the Soviet Union or 'any hypothetical threat from Afghanistan'. There have been many outrageous statements made by representatives of both governments over the years, but this minister deliberately tried to undermine what consensus had been obtained during discussions about troop withdrawal from Afghanistan by stating that 'Pakistan has not shown the degree of flexibility that was expected of it at the proximity talks,' on which record the signatures were barely dry. This was bumbling stuff, and it is hardly surprising that the US Administration was exasperated with such meddling but continued assistance to Pakistan in spite of knowing full well about its nuclear programme. US concerns rose in June, when India sent fighter aircraft to escort its An-32 transports that violated Sri Lankan airspace to drop supplies to rebel Tamils in Jaffna – and threatened to shoot down opposing aircraft. The *Guardian*'s Derek Brown, who travelled in one of the transports, wrote that he flew 'through Sri Lankan airspace where we have no right at all to be,' and that, 'the mission is a spectacular success. Not as a relief operation, for 22½ tonnes of supplies won't feed many people, but rather as a message to Colombo that it can no longer defy the regional superpower.'

Pakistan, too, got the message, as did other regional countries and some further afield: India's fast-growing military capabilities seemed to be intended for power projection. India was 'invited' by the government in Colombo to send troops to Sri Lanka to intervene in the campaign against

Tamil terrorists. But the Indian Peace-Keeping Force (IPKF) was disorganized, poorly trained and unprepared to fight the guerrilla war in which it became involved. In spite of much bravery by individuals, the IPKF, the cream of the Indian Army, eventually over 50,000 of them, suffered terrible casualties, including some 1,500 killed. They withdrew in 1990.

GHQ Rawalpindi was aware of Indian problems of poor leadership, bad planning, almost no training in counter-revolutionary warfare, and a 'very peculiar, off-beat command and control structure', as they were of Indian tactics being 'predetermined, strait-jacketed, predictable and reactive'.[38] But that was in Sri Lanka. Would the Indians display similar incompetence on the plains of Punjab and Sindh where their tanks, outnumbering Pakistan's in 1988 by about 2:1, with massive close air support, might swamp Pakistan's defences? It was time to construct better plans for the defence of Pakistan. But who would put forward such plans? The new Vice-Chief in 1987, a small, rather unsmiling (enigmatic, some considered),[39] and energetic man called Aslam Beg might be the fellow to do this, thought the bright young officers.[40]

Prime Minister Junejo was trying to interfere in the army's internal affairs, which its chief, the President, would not permit. Amongst other things, Junejo insisted on the removal of General Akhtar Abdul Rehman as Director-General of Inter Services Intelligence and questioned the promotion of two officers to be corps commanders (Pir Dad Khan and Shamim Alam Khan, both admirable officers). Zia considered that Mr Junejo, nice fellow as he was, was becoming too big for his boots and dismissed him, with his cabinet, on 29 May 1988, on the grounds that:

Whereas the objects and the purposes for which the National Assembly was elected have not been fulfilled

And whereas the law and order in the country have broken down to an alarming extent resulting in tragic loss of innumberable [sic] valuable lives as well as loss of property

And whereas the life property honour and security of the citizens of Pakistan have been rendered totally unsafe and the integrity and ideology of Pakistan have been seriously endangered

And whereas public morality has deteriorated to a serious level

And whereas in my opinion a situation has arisen in which the Government of the federation cannot be carried on in accordance with the provision [sic] of the Constitution and an appeal to the electorate is necessary

Now therefore I, General Mohammad Zia-ul-Haq, President of Pakistan in exercise of the powers conferred on me by Clause (2)(b) of Article 58 of the Constitution of the Islamic Republic of Pakistan hereby dissolve the National Assembly with immediate effect and in consequence thereof the Cabinet also stands dissolved forthwith.[41]

Zia's speech to the nation in Urdu on 30 May was poor.[42] 'Life,' he said, 'continues normally. There is no ban on political parties or political activities. The press is free, as usual ... The only difference is that the National Assembly and all four Provincial Assemblies and Federal and Provincial cabinets have been dissolved.' He reminded listeners that in 1977 his 'sole purpose was to hold free and fair elections' – without mentioning the ninety-day caveat – and went on to emphasize that an Islamic form of governance was paramount, and that the Junejo government's 'greatest crime was that the enforcement of Islam was put aside'. He was floundering. His speech was full of inconsistencies.

Benazir Bhutto tried to bring her supporters into the streets to show popular condemnation of the government. Only a few thousand people demonstrated against Zia, but there was a groundswell of opinion against the President, even if it was not necessarily in support of the PPP. He was becoming unpopular and the army was restive. His death on 17 August 1988 caused little mourning.[43]

Notes

1. Letter from the Cabinet Secretary, Waqar Ahmad, of 19 December 1974, quoted in Wolpert, Stanley, *Zulfi Bhutto of Pakistan*, OUP, New York, 1993.
2. General Arif had been told to write the speech but found it difficult to find 'populist phrases', and was in any case writing in English, so Salik was brought in to write it in Urdu, which he did very well.
3. Discussion with a colleague of Zia, April 1988.
4. Alas it became clear in later years that Fazle became involved in skimming off money from drug smugglers and in other unsavoury activities.
5. Khan, Roedad, *Pakistan, a Dream Gone Sour*, OUP, Karachi, 1998.
6. Discussions with many officers serving at the time.
7. Arif, General K.M., *Working with Zia*, OUP, Karachi, 1995.
8. ' Introduction' by Makhdoom Ali Khan (also ed.) to *The Constitution of the Islamic Republic of Pakistan 1973*, Pakistan Law House, Karachi, 1986 (1990 edition).
9. Amended 1973 Constitution, Part XII, Chapter 2, Article 243 (1) and (1A).
10. In January 1999 I attended a dinner party hosted by Prime Minister Bhutto and sat next to a woman who described how rats had been deliberately placed in her cell and even on her body.
11. Farah, Caesar E., *Islam*, Barron, New York, 1970.
12. On 4 January. The amount – $400 million – was deemed 'peanuts' by Zia and was increased to over $3 billion in 1981.
13. Walker, Martin, *The Cold War*, Fourth Estate, London, 1993.
14. 'Al Zulfiqar' was an amateur terrorist organization formed by Bhutto's sons. See Anwar, Raja, *The Terrorist Prince*, Verso, London, 1997, for a description of this extraordinary organization.
15. The final exercise in 1982, the storming of a PIA aircraft parked on the PAF side of Islamabad airport, went well. The SAS officer and the British Defence Adviser then went

to Army House to be congratulated by Zia. On their return to the British DA's house I remarked on the handsome rug the SAS officer had been given. 'Best carpet shop in town,' said the DA.

16. Thatcher, Margaret, *The Downing Street Years*, HarperCollins, London, 1993.

17. Information from Sir Oliver Forster, former Ambassador and High Commissioner to Pakistan, February 1988.

18. It is often claimed that India's acquisition of Mirage 2000 aircraft from France was caused by the provision of F-16s to Pakistan. In a way this is correct: the F-16 agreement was signed in December 1981, but the Mirage negotiations had been under way for over a year before this – although the final signature was not applied until January 1982.

19. Yousaf, Brigadier Mohammad and Adkin, Mark, *The Bear Trap*, Jang Publishers, Lahore, 1992.

20. Kux, Dennis, *The United States and Pakistan 1947–2000*, Johns Hopkins University Press, 2001.

21. The author learned of this when visiting the US Army War College in 1993.

22. There had been an attempt in the previous month. Both tries failed because the firers were poorly trained. See Anwar, R., *The Terrorist Prince: The Life and Death of Murtaza Bhutto*, Vanguard Books, Lahore, 1998.

23. *Strategic Studies*, Islamabad, winter 1986. The Institute had excellent sources.

24. One of whom, in spite of there being no firm evidence of any wrongdoing, was sacked and not reinstated until after Zia's death. He still refuses to give details of the affair, which is understandable.

25. He lost, and withdrew almost the entire force – a principled action.

26. Appointed Ambassador to the US, 2006.

27. A close friend of the author.

28. *Sino-Pakistan 'Agreement' March 2, 1963, Some Facts*, Ministry of External Affairs, Government of India, 16 March 1963.

29. *India Today*, New Delhi, 31 July 1985.

30. *Ibid.*

31. I am grateful to Usman Shabbir for drawing my attention to *Fangs of Ice* by Lieutenant Colonel Ishfaq Ali, which gives details of engagements in Siachen. Published by American Commercial Private Ltd, Rawalpindi, 1991.

32. See Cordovez, Diego and Harrison, Selig, *Out of Afghanistan*, OUP, 1995. Myra Macdonald of Reuters has written *Heights of Madness*, Rupa & Co., New Delhi, 2007, a definitive book on Siachen which covers all aspects of this tragic and senseless adventure.

33. The *Washington Post* was not blameless in the period. It carried an absurd story on 3 November, quoting an alleged intelligence report, that Pakistan had 'tested the bomb' between 18 and 21 September.

34. BBC *Summary of World Broadcasts*, 12 November 1986 (henceforth *SWB*).

35. *India Today*, 15 and 29 February 1987. The edition of 15 February is remarkable for its estimate that 'The Cost of a Day's Fighting', excluding deaths and injuries, would be 'around Rs 4,700 crore [about $3.4 billion at the then rate of exchange], a horrendous expense that neither side can realistically afford'. It also noted that there 'are now no outstanding international issues over which the two countries could be propelled into a war'. *India Today* was a sensible magazine and robust about Indian policies as well as being forthright concerning Pakistan. Unfortunately it has now become more of a 'Bollywood Gazette'.

36. Seymour Hersh had an interesting piece in *The New Yorker* on 29 March 1993 in which he stated that 'studies showed that the main intelligence services for both sides – India's Research and Analysis Wing and Pakistan's Inter-Services Intelligence Directorate – had exaggerated their reports to their senior leadership. It was clear that, in a crisis, both RAW

and ISI were eager to provide incendiary intelligence without being sure of its reliability. Such eagerness could become deadly.'

37. Karachi Home Service, 7 February 1987; BBC *Summary of World Broadcasts.*
38. Sardeshpande, Lieutenant General S.C., *Assignment Jaffna*, Lancer, New Delhi, 1992. A summation of Indian Army capabilities by an honourable and most capable officer.
39. According to Seymour Hersh: 'I [Robert Gates] looked straight at Beg [at a meeting in Islamabad in 1990] and said, "General, our military has war-gamed every conceivable scenario between you and the Indians, and there isn't a single way you win."' It was a tough message for a proud and bellicose Army Chief of Staff. Beg said nothing and Gates detected no visible response. 'He was very cool,' Gates said. 'That was the high point' (*The New Yorker*, 29 March 1993). Another source has Gates saying that he would never play poker with Beg because of his impassive countenance.
40. Based on conversations with many of them in following years.
41. *Pakistan Times*, 20 May 1988.
42. BBC *Summary of World Broadcasts*, 2 June 1988.
43. In former writings I ended with the words 'but he left his country in better shape than he had found it eleven years before.' The distinguished academic Dr Ian Talbot told me I was talking rubbish. He was quite right, so I have omitted this claim and altered many observations on Zia in the text.

Chapter 3

Democracy Again

In 1988 the US was trying to sell M-1 Abrams tanks to Pakistan. Production tanks were provided for trials and evaluation, which did not go well. Zia wanted to attend a demonstration of the Abrams at the Bahawalpur field-firing range and flew there on the morning of 17 August in a PAF C-130 transport, callsign Pak One. The US Ambassador, Arnold Raphel, and his senior military sales officer, Brigadier General Herbert Wassom, were present, as were some twenty Pakistan Army officers who were to fly back to Rawalpindi in Pak One with Zia.[1] The aircraft left Bahawalpur runway at 1546, carrying, in a late and unpredictable arrangement, as invited by Zia, Raphel and Wassom. The aircraft crashed, killing all on board. The US/Pakistan Inquiry determined that there had been sabotage. There is no point in attempting to theorize about what occurred.[2] The Vice Chief of Army Staff, General Aslam Beg, in another aircraft which had taken off at about the same time, flew on to Rawalpindi and, after consultation and deliberation, announced that the days of military dominance were over. This was an historic decision and a wise one on his part. The Chairman of the Senate, Ghulam Ishaq Khan, was appointed President, as provided for by the Constitution. A caretaker National Emergency Council was formed and elections were scheduled for November.

The Pakistan People's Party, although well organized to conduct electioneering, did not win an outright majority in spite of the split in the Pakistan Muslim League (which must have had a death wish to indulge in internal quarrels at such a time). Benazir Bhutto became Prime Minister following the elections. There was hope throughout the land that, this time, there would be a new dawn for Pakistan. Not only had the armed forces left the scene of governance (and were happy to do so), but the politicians had surely learned their lesson, and would not behave irresponsibly and fall again to the temptations of deceit and corruption. It was thought that ministerial selection would be on merit, and that there would be no attempt to politicize the Civil Service. The atmosphere in Islamabad, amongst the educated classes at least, was euphoric. When a PTV female

52

announcer appeared on the screen to read the news without her headscarf there were telephone calls all round the capital. It seemed there might be relaxation of Islamic laws and practices, especially as the religious parties had not done well in the elections.[3]

Unfortunately the PPP did not meet the expectations of most people and President Ghulam Ishaq Khan dismissed it on 6 August 1990. There is little doubt that the leaders of the armed forces were involved concerning the President's action, which was lawful under the Constitution even if it was not in the spirit of the times. The government had had many problems, not the least of which was the Senate, which had been appointed during Zia's time and was opposed to the PPP. Ms Bhutto concentrated her energy on preserving her narrow majority in the National Assembly and the long-awaited reforms were not introduced. There was no legislation of any importance passed, and the country's economic and social problems worsened to an alarming extent.

One of the problems was the situation in Sindh Province. The *Guardian* (UK) reported on 16 July 1990 that some 3,000 people had been killed in communal violence in Sindh since 1985, mainly involving *Mohajirs* – settlers or descendants of settlers from India at the time of Partition – and Sindhis. The PPP ran the Province and was in direct confrontation with the Mohajir Qaumi Movement (MQM). On 10 February 1990 an incident occurred which perhaps encapsulates the bizarre situation.

Armed activists of the PPP and MQM had each kidnapped about a dozen of the other's supporters. In the office of the commander of V Corps in Karachi, the leaders of the parties arranged an exchange of twenty-seven hostages.[4] The significance is twofold. First, that leaders of political parties were involved in patently illegal affairs; second, that the army was being drawn into civil matters once again.

The army had enough to worry about concerning increasingly bellicose statements from New Delhi, which had become concerned about the insurrection in Indian-administered Kashmir that began in 1989. The Kashmiris, indignant about years of Congress (I) Party ballot-fixing, lack of political representation, and the arrogance with which they were governed, had finally had enough. India immediately accused Pakistan of involvement. The 'foreign hand' was once again blamed for India's ills (and did indeed, later, take advantage of the rebellion in Kashmir); but it was nonetheless serious, for all the Indian posturing. Tension was high along the Line of Control. Ceasefire violations increased and there were incidents of firing on 'Azad' Kashmiri demonstrators by Indian soldiers. Both countries sent reinforcements to the Line and the international border. Pakistan was not involved in the insurrection to begin with, but there is no doubt there was later, and very deep dabbling when the indigenous rebellion was hijacked by jihadi militants, whose motive was not so much freedom for Kashmiris as establishment of fundamental Islamic rule throughout all Kashmir, and elsewhere in the world. The army was also concerned about two figures close to the Prime Minister: her special assistant, former Major General Nasirullah Babar,[5] a close confidant of Zulfikar Ali Bhutto; and the adviser on defence, former Major General Imtiaz Ali, who had been Bhutto's military secretary, with neither of whom was there an easy relationship. (Babar considered Beg 'a coward'.) But it is interesting that two such influential people were former military men. Accusations were made that the army chain of command was being bypassed by them and other government-associated figures, and that decisions were being taken on defence procurement matters without consultation with GHQ. It was said that the Prime Minister's husband, Asif Zardari, was involved in such matters.[6]

The chain of command is sacrosanct in any armed force. If it is ignored, there is a danger that orders will not be carried out. If it is bypassed by what is perceived to be a legal authority, it places subordinates in a difficult position: whom are they to obey if they receive conflicting orders – their superior officers or the political associates of a government? Meddling with the military chain of command is a dangerous thing for politicians to do. It creates confusion and resentment. An intriguing development was that on 24 May Ms Bhutto dismissed the Director-General Inter Services Intelligence, Lieutenant General Hamid Gul,[7] and replaced him with Lieutenant General (retired) Shamsur Rehman Kallue.[8] Gul was appointed commander II Corps at Multan. He was a hawk concerning Afghanistan, and his support for the more fundamentalist political groups did not meet with the approval of some members of the PPP (or with many other people, for that matter); but the manner of his going – although completely lawful, as ISI was a discrete government body – did not give the army confidence that the government wished to refrain from interference in military affairs as much as the army wished to stay out of politics.

In mid-1990 the PPP government appeared to be rudderless. This was regrettable, although hardly cause for its dismissal, but the President gave detailed reasons including allegations of 'persistent and scandalous "horse-trading" for political gain', breakdown of law and order in Sindh, corruption and nepotism, and use of statutory corporations, authorities, and banks for political ends and personal gain. A state of emergency was declared and a caretaker administration under Mr Ghulam Mustafa Jatoi was appointed. It governed until elections were held in October, when the Islami Jamhoori Ittehad (IJI)[9] alliance of parties led by Nawaz Sharif obtained 105 seats, Benazir Bhutto's People's Democratic Alliance 45, and the MQM 15 (all in Sindh). The election was rigged.[10] It seemed that the new government, with a large majority, might be able to concentrate on domestic reforms and urgent foreign policy affairs that demanded its immediate attention.

Ms Bhutto blamed the army for her dismissal from power. At a press conference on 8 August 1990, she stated that 'military intelligence forced the President to make this decision' and that the army had 'from the first day [of her government]' planned a conspiracy against her. She asked why, if there was no military involvement, the army had seized records of the Intelligence Bureau (the civilian counter-intelligence organization) and why troops had been posted at radio and television stations.[11] 'Within two to three weeks they'll roll back and it will be proper martial law.'[12] These were grave allegations and deeply resented by many in the armed services who considered that strain had been placed on their loyalty by the activities of some people in or associated with government in the recent past. There had been disagreements between the Prime Minister and the President (in his capacity as Commander-in-Chief) and, in spite of efforts to stay outside politics, the army considered it should take a stand. Whether this was justified or not, is another matter.

In August 1989 Ms Bhutto had sought to appoint a new Chairman of the Joint Chiefs of Staff Committee in place of Admiral Iftikhar Sirohey, who had succeeded to the position in November 1988. It seemed clear from the usual interpretation of tenure that he would serve until November 1991, when he would retire after his three-year tour. In any case it was the prerogative of the President to appoint a new Chairman.[13] On 8 August Begum Nusrat Bhutto, mother of Benazir, told a reporter that the Admiral had 'completed his three years' and stated that her daughter was attending a meeting concerning 'the security of our country and democracy', a remark, according to one newspaper, 'which only added to the impression of a crisis being played out behind the scenes'.[14] The Prime Minister had chosen to interpret the three-year tour as being from the date of Sirohey's promotion on 14 August 1986, when he took over as Chief of Naval Staff. If implemented, such a procedure could be awkward, as an officer appointed to one of the senior positions might already have held four-star rank (general, admiral or air chief marshal) for some time before assuming his new position, and it was reasonable to expect him to carry out a full tour in the new job. But it seemed there might be another factor.

General Aslam Beg had been a four-star general since 1987 but COAS only since 1988. If the government was successful in restricting Sirohey's term, would it then insist that Beg retired in March 1990 instead of August 1991, citing curtailment of the Chairman's tour as a precedent? There were rumours that Ms Bhutto wished to sideline Beg to be Chairman (a non-executive post) and replace him by Lieutenant General Ahmed Kamal

Khan, the Deputy Chief, because of his perceived loyalty to the PPP. This was sensitive stuff.

In the end the Prime Minister had to back down. The President handled the affair gracefully (although, as the perceptive journalist Mushahid Hussain pointed out, he had been in favour of Junejo's position concerning military appointments in 1987 – which contretemps with Zia contributed to Junejo's dismissal) and the matter came to a close. It petered out rather than ending on a conclusive note of agreement by the President and the Prime Minister, but it was evident that the government had failed in its attempt to control military appointments, and the armed forces and the PPP were wary of each other from that time on. The President resented the attempt to encroach on his authority and prerogatives (as he saw them) and bided his time.

The armies of Pakistan and India still faced each other in Siachen. Casualties in the icy wastes mounted as the years went by. There was no possibility of a military solution. Neither side could advance beyond the areas they held. There was stalemate – until mid-1989, when a break-through took place. Or seemed to take place. An excited journalist (well, as excited as that phlegmatic race can be) contacted the author on 17 June and said he had just sent a piece to the effect that the Indian and Pakistani foreign secretaries (respectively Mr S.K. Singh and Mr Humayun Khan) had agreed that troops would be withdrawn to the positions occupied at the time of the Simla Accord. The journalist said it was a final agreement that was, obviously, authorized by the two governments and only needed the armies to implement it forthwith. A major occurrence in the sub-continent, he said; at last an indication that the countries seemed to be serious about rapprochement and working for peace; there might even be a new era of trust and co-operation. (He was quite enthusiastic, for a journalist.)

The BBC reported that the foreign secretaries:

> had been meeting for two days and their discussions set the seal on the earlier meetings ... between the defence secretaries. At a joint news conference Mr Khan announced that both sides have now decided to withdraw to the positions that they held at the time of the Simla Accord.

A corresponding report was broadcast in Urdu on government-controlled All India Radio.[15] It seemed, even to the most sceptical observers in Islamabad and New Delhi, that, at long last, senior representatives of the countries were not only sitting down and talking about matters of substance, they were also authorized to take decisions that would smooth the way for further confidence-building measures. Wrong.

A 'clarification' was issued by the Indian Ministry of External Affairs. The 'chronology of events', said a spokesman, had been 'muddled and confused'. He went on to state that 'The Indian foreign secretary had endorsed the Pakistani foreign secretary's observations on their talks, whereas the report has made out as if he had endorsed the Pakistan foreign secretary's remarks on the defence secretaries' talks.'[16] Which statement was, of course, not muddled or confusing. The Indian government denied 'that Pakistan and India had reached an agreement on this [Siachen] issue'. The foreign correspondents in Islamabad shrugged their collective shoulders. 'What,' asked one of them, rhetorically, 'can you expect of a bunch of people like that?'*

If there has been one occasion, a single identifiable point, a precise moment in the history of the subcontinent at which India and Pakistan might have been placed on the road to the establishment of reasonable relations, it was that day in June 1989. An agreement such as the one that was reached and then denied would have saved hundreds of soldiers' lives and cost nothing in national pride. The strategic positions of the countries would not have altered one jot. The accord would have proved to the world that bilateralism actually worked (a real winner for Indian objectives concerning Kashmir) and terminated an unjustifiable drain on national budgets (India's much more than Pakistan's). But it was not to be.

The Doctrine of the Riposte

If a war is thrust on us then the broad strategy we are going to follow is that, while defending all territories of Pakistan, including Kashmir, the Pakistan Army plans to launch a sizeable offensive, thus carrying the war into Indian territory.

General Aslam Beg, 13 September 1989[17]

The author attended Exercise Zarb-i-Momin (the Believer's Blow) from 17 to 20 December 1989. There were several foreign observers, some of whom saw more of the exercise than others, and the consensus was that the Pakistan Army could fight a conventional war against India for several weeks, and stood a reasonable chance of carrying war into Indian territory but for one thing: insufficient attention to the enemy air threat. There was not enough PAF participation at all levels.

Battle procedures were effective much of the time but on occasions were poor. This gave the observers some confidence in what they were witnessing, in that, of course, real exercises generally have almost as many snafus as real battles. An exercise that goes exactly to plan is not without its uses – but mistakes show what commanders and staffs at all levels are

---

*He did not say 'people'.

made of, when they have to sort things out quickly. There is nothing like pressure for revealing proneness to panic. In Zarb-i-Momin there were some nonsenses, one caused by elements of the 'enemy' armour becoming overenthusiastic and advancing to overcome positions that should have remained inviolate until the following day. The exercise was, after all, they thought, the first trial of Riposte – the quick and devastating thrust into enemy territory – why not press on? This was the greatest fun for the visiting generals, many of whom had been in similar circumstances, and resulted in later exchanges of confidences about how poorly written exercises were these days, and how they (the Pakistani commanders and observing generals) would have dealt with things had they (the planners) been better organized. A telling comment was made by one visitor after we had bumped around in four-wheel drive vehicles for three hours without seeing an 'incident' of note (other than a fire caused by an unfortunate cavalry subaltern who was, apparently, trying to dry out his bedding). 'This,' he said, 'demonstrates the emptiness of the battlefield.'[18] To see this emptiness was of considerable value to commanders and staffs – and to participants at more humble levels. It is not often an exercise can give the 'feel' of the battlefield and show that engagements are rarely fought concurrently all over the area of operations.

Planning for the exercise began soon after Beg took over as COAS, and care was taken to notify India several months before it started. Maps were provided that included directions of advance and withdrawal – north–south – lest there be any misconstruction placed on Pakistan's putting over 200,000 troops in the field. Zarb-i-Momin was a very large exercise. It was perhaps too big, too extensive in its objectives, to be valuable in all aspects of tactics, and many soldiers were bored for long periods. This was realistic, but the troops were out of barracks for too long. But it had value in many other ways. It showed that the Pakistan Army was now out of the business of martial law, once and for all, and could concentrate on training. It gave the message to India that enormous numbers of troops could be moved quickly and with 'notional' ammunition (represented by sand-filled ammunition boxes), rather than causing alarm by moving real ammunition (which would deteriorate, anyway, due to handling and exposure to climate, as the Indians experienced during Exercise Brass Tacks and again, and more seriously, during Operation Parakram, the confrontation with Pakistan in 2001–2). It was a good exercise whose main results, following analysis by GHQ and input from elsewhere, included improvement in armour tactics, better passage of intelligence, enhanced co-operation with the PAF, creation of Air Defence Command, and introduction of higher-level co-ordination of artillery.

Thus far in his term as Chief of Army Staff, General Aslam Beg had proved to the army and to outsiders that there was some original thought in GHQ, an organization that had been singularly lacking in vision for some years. But the COAS had some other ideas that did not sit quite so comfortably with the government or with some other countries. These included the concept of 'Strategic Defiance'.

General Beg spoke to the Press frequently and did not appear to realize that he was not always reported on accurately and that occasionally he went further than he should. Sometimes his statements irritated the government. Had some of them been made by his counterparts in the US or the UK (for example), they would have swiftly become his former counterparts.

On 2 December 1990, exactly four months after Iraq invaded Kuwait, Beg gave a talk at the Pakistan Ordnance Factories' annual seminar at Wah Cantonment near Islamabad. Those present prepared themselves for the usual comments about how efficient Pakistan defence industries had become, and other mandatory platitudes. They sat up when he began speaking about the Gulf, and even more interest was displayed when he mentioned Iraq in terms of approbation in relation to defiance of 'the mightiest of the mighty'. He also said words to the effect that the audience should not mention what he had said once they got outside the auditorium – fat chance of that, especially as there were reporters and defence attachés present. Later, the office of Inter Services Public Relations was swamped by telephone calls from reporters, diplomats, defence attachés (and even, it was said, staff officers from GHQ), asking for copies of the speech. There wasn't one, said the harassed voice at the other end of the telephone. Why? Well, because there isn't. And it seems there wasn't. The Chief of the Army Staff appeared to have been speaking off the cuff. A version of his speech was produced but nobody had a definitive copy.[19] Outside the hall, when asked by reporters why the US was discriminating against Pakistan concerning aid (which the Bush administration had cut off in October), he said, 'I think I have spoken enough,'[20] which indeed he had.

A leader in *The Muslim* on 4 December was encouraging about the General's speech:

> his extempore remarks at a seminar in Wah Cantonment on Sunday with reference to the current Gulf crisis represent a forceful and highly significant reminder of the premium the Chief of the Pakistan army continues to place on strengthening collective defences of regional Muslim countries.

Well, yes; he had gone on record almost two years before with the notion that regional Islamic nations should present a united front of some sort, and had named Iran and Turkey (and, optimistically, a peaceful Afghanistan) as possible partners in a security arrangement. Pakistan is narrow east to west, and Beg had some idea of using Iran as 'strategic depth', which was a woolly concept and unlikely to attract much support in Teheran. And he wooed Iran assiduously. 'Iran,' he said on 13 September 1989, 'has gone through a revolution and after great sacrifices has emerged stronger in spite of the fact that many countries of the world joined hands to destroy the revolution.' Iran was ambivalent about strategic consensus, in spite of being willing to accept whatever assistance Pakistan could offer in provision of defence equipment and training (and wishing to exercise influence concerning the rights and treatment of Pakistan's Shia minority). Beg may have believed that some senior Iranians approved of his enthusiastic proposals. The Chairman of the Joint Chiefs, Brigadier General Shahbazi, said that Iran 'would appreciate such co-operation amongst the Muslim countries', and the Revolutionary Guards' minister, Ali Shamkhani, said that Iran and Pakistan 'will form an important part of the Islamic defence line in the region', neither of which statements meant anything definitive to anyone versed in international relations, which Beg was not. Neither was Turkey enthusiastic. As a secular nation drawing closer (it hoped) to Europe than to poor Eastern countries that had little to offer it, it distanced itself from Beg's proposal. This was no CENTO, with US approval and all the backing that went with that dubious accolade. Beg's ideas had little support within Pakistan, either, although some half-baked ideologists seized on his apparent fervour for Islamic solidarity to push their own theocratic barrow. No; 'Strategic Defiance' was not born out of 'strategic consensus', as it was known in some circles. It was a new concept and, given the manner in which it was presented, apparently not well thought through.

The Muslim newspaper sounded a note of caution – although that was not what the writer of its editorial intended in the penultimate sentence: 'It is striking that, though apparently in agreement with this [Beg's] approach, the political government of the day has not so far come out with such a clear statement of national policy.' Goodness me – the *political* government. Was there another one? Three days later *Dawn* commented: 'That the Chief of Army Staff chose to announce the policy, which in a civilian democratic set-up should normally have been the prerogative of the prime minister, is ... understandable. After all, Mian Nawaz Sharif does not mind keeping a low profile.' This was becoming dangerous. There was no one in authority in Pakistan who appeared to disapprove of this alteration in the nation's defence policy, or, if there was, they were not able or willing to speak out against it. Further, and of greater importance, it is not 'understandable' that policy should be notified by a general, no matter how eminent. It is the responsibility of a democratically elected government and *no one else* to do so. Beg was quite wrong to make the announcement. Even had the policy been agreed with government and the President (still

60

the supreme commander of the armed forces), it was not for the COAS or anyone in uniform to announce it to the world at a technical seminar, however prestigious.

But what did the concept, possibly the new defence policy of Pakistan, actually mean? It had a challenging ring about it, certainly. Strategic Defiance: 'Come the three corners of the world in arms, and we shall shock them.'[21] Stirring; nationalistic; even xenophobic. Was it self-reliance? If so, this was dreamtime. There was no possibility that Pakistan could become self-reliant in all or even most aspects of defence production. Well, then, was it based on refusal to accept assistance from larger powers, specifically the US, which had in any case curtailed its aid on the grounds that it believed Pakistan to be a nuclear weapons state, like Israel and India? Not much point in that: it was only from more sophisticated industrial economies that advanced weapons systems could be obtained, and the armed forces badly needed such equipment. It was difficult to pin down, this doctrine, unless it was – but surely not? – a catchphrase looking for a policy?

Beg said, 'We do not say no to friendly offers of assistance but that does not mean we can be dictated terms which I believe are not in the best interests of the country.' Referring to the 1965 and 1971 wars, he pointed out that US military aid had been suspended and 'we were left high and dry but we managed to live and the aid cut-off did not affect us.' This is simply not correct. The cut-off had a severe effect on the country's war-fighting capabilities and would have been critical had ceasefire arrangements not come into force. What was Beg trying to illustrate by this assertion?

The Nation was in reflective mood by 4 December:

> While one should stand by everything that is being said about not allowing the nation's sovereignty to be compromised, the question is whether the acceptance of aid, or loans to be exact, really compromises our sovereignty? It has not, so far. Again, since a US aid negotiations team is expected to be here soon, wouldn't it be better to wait and see if any demand against our national interests is made?

The editorial went on to question the right of the COAS to pronounce on foreign policy, and indicated that his 'view on the Gulf conflict could be at variance with our declared position on Iraq. It would have been better if all organs of the state were to be seen to speak with one voice, if all of them have to speak on national issues.' The responsible press of Pakistan had engaged gear. But it made no difference. 'Strategic defiance' was the jargon of the moment, whatever it meant, and the country's policy was not to become engaged in the Gulf War, for which the build-up in the Arabian Peninsula had almost ended.

It should have been worrying for Pakistan that in December the US Assistant Secretary of Defence for International Security, Henry Rowan, and a large delegation visited New Delhi to discuss ways of improving defence co-operation, but it seemed that neither Beg nor the government was perturbed about this development, or about others of considerable international significance.

The cold war had ended. On the day that Beg delivered his speech at Wah, Presidents Bush and Gorbachev, meeting in the port of Marsaxlokk, declared its demise. Pakistan's value to the US as a counter to what had been perceived as Soviet expansion in Afghanistan had disappeared, and the end of the cold war meant that Pakistan had no further strategic value for the US. India could no longer count on receiving weapons from the Russian Federation at the bargain rates of former years – but if the US were to distance itself from Pakistan and move closer to India, as seemed to be happening, then Pakistan could find itself in a difficult situation economically, and could have an even worse problem so far as defence was concerned. This did not escape the professionals in Pakistan's Foreign Office but, unfortunately, neither the government nor the army seemed to be paying attention to what was happening, at amazing speed, in the outside world.

Pakistan and the Gulf War

Pakistan did not join the coalition that provided troops to fight against Iraq in 1991. In a particularly maladroit manner, it compromised by sending, initially, 12 Independent Armoured Brigade Group to Saudi Arabia to 'guard the Holy Places'. The US was unpopular in Pakistan, for obvious reasons, and Iraq, under the unbeliever Saddam Hussain, was considered by many semi-educated people (and some educated ones, too) to be the aggrieved party.[22] They thought Saddam should be congratulated on his defiance of the mighty US-led coalition which, in any case, was only going to help the arrogant Kuwaitis who treated the rest of the Arab and Muslim world with contempt. It would have been difficult (but not impossible) for the government to justify committing troops under command of a power that had dumped Pakistan as an ally.

A hiatus in foreign policy decision-making was probably inevitable in this period that saw so many important international developments. The PPP government had been dismissed just at the time of the Iraqi invasion; the interim government had not been in a position to take decisions that in any case would not have been binding on their successor; and the new government of Nawaz Sharif was finding its feet, and lacked expertise in foreign relations. Into the vacuum where Pakistan's foreign policy should have been there came Aslam Beg, and it would have been better for the country had he refrained from trying to fill it.

Not only was the dispatch of the brigade to Saudi Arabia politically inept, it was an operational and administrative disaster. Had Pakistan acted under the aegis of the Gulf Coalition, it would have been welcomed with equipment and generous support. It would have been doubly welcome: its very presence would have demonstrated Pakistan's solidarity with important nations; and its expertise and professionalism would have contributed to the coalition's war-fighting capability. An armoured brigade is a potent force, and commanders, no matter how many troops they have, can always find tasks for more. The brigade would have fitted well alongside any of the coalition's forces and would doubtless have distinguished itself. But it was treated coolly by Saudi Arabia (although Saudi aircraft transported Pakistani soldiers) and, barely credibly, was almost ignored by GHQ. Immediately before the attack began, Beg went to Coalition HQ for a briefing which, according to US military officers, 'shook him'. (He was not given details of timings for the advance.) He had no idea what to expect and was amazed at the size of the build-up in spite of having been briefed on its progress by US officers in preceding weeks. He avoided discussion of Pakistan's reluctance to become involved in the coalition and appeared 'sort of apologetic, but he didn't say that'.[23] Beg had visited his troops, which by now included 330 Independent Infantry Brigade Group as part of the GCC element, but was seemingly not disturbed that morale was low, or that his soldiers were poorly equipped and lacked proper clothing.[24] Their mission was unclear (Saddam would have been insane to have attacked the holy places, even if his army could have crossed the Saudi border) and their rules of engagement non-existent. They were moved hither and thither throughout the country and were unpopular with almost everyone. There was not much evidence of 'Strategic Defiance' in this. Pakistan had distanced itself from the coalition that it was prevented from joining by a combination of reluctance on the part of Beg, and Iraqi propaganda. A government in Islamabad that was settled in power and had foreign affairs experience might have overcome the problems associated with propaganda, which was extremely effective. It could have employed all the publicity means at its disposal to counter pro-Iraqi agitators (many of whom were simply troublemakers, but no less effective for that) who chose to ignore the fact that Saddam was no more a Muslim than he was a soldier – although he was portrayed as a defender of the Faith and a mighty warrior in all the material circulating in Pakistan.

The Gulf War was a sad chapter for Pakistan. India, too, had problems with Desert Shield/Desert Storm, but somehow they were overcome. The minority government of Prime Minister Chandra Shekar had allowed US aircraft to refuel in India en route to the Gulf but rescinded permission when there was (quite cynical) objection from, amongst others, Rajiv

Gandhi. This did not affect the burgeoning of US-Indian relations because Washington wished to believe the best of 'the world's largest democracy' and was happy to ignore the decades of support by and for the Soviet Union. (Not much happened, in the end, on the defence scene. India's paranoia about secrecy exasperated American delegations, who reported to the State Department and the Pentagon that co-operation on the scale proposed by the Administration would present more difficulties than it would reap benefits. Some members of the US defence staffs in New Delhi had warned that this would be the outcome.)

Rumours of War

In 1990 tension rose between New Delhi and Islamabad. The main cause was the uprising in Indian-administered Kashmir. There were Indian allegations of Pakistani support for Kashmiri armed separatists. Representatives of the two countries indulged in unhelpful public comments, as in the cases of Indian Prime Minister V.P. Singh and Pakistani Chief of Army Staff General Aslam Beg. Mr V.P. Singh was asked in April if he could 'at this stage rule out an armed conflict with Pakistan'. 'You see,' said V.P. Singh,

> it is all one-sided. All action you see is the asymmetry of the action. It [Pakistan] is sending weapons of the highest calibre across the border: machine guns, anti-tank mines, rockets [sic] launchers, and even surface-to-surface missiles according to our intelligence sources. It is also sending armed and trained infiltrators in a well planned move to instigate insurgency [in Kashmir] while we are doing nothing like this on their side.[25]

It is charitable to imagine that Mr V.P. Singh may have been tired at the time of this comment, but only a few days before he made it, he said in the Lok Sabha that 'We have the capability to inflict a very heavy cost on Pakistan for its territorial goals against India,' when he was in possession of a prepared statement. On the same day, 11 April, General Beg said that deployment of the Indian Strike Corps between Suratgarh and Bikaner was 'most threatening' and the Pakistan Army had to take measures to counter it. The army did no such thing, as was made clear a week later by Lieutenant General Alam Jan Mahsud, the commander of IV Corps in Lahore, when he said that the army remained in peacetime locations. One might ignore the hyperbolic statements of the Indian Prime Minister – for he, after all, had a domestic constituency to address, placate and enthuse. But what constituency was Aslam Beg speaking to? Further, what message was being given to India by conflicting statements about Pakistan's preparedness to meet the move of an Indian division and a brigade close to the

64

border? [26] Who spoke for Pakistan? Was it the government in Islamabad (still, in early 1990, that of Benazir Bhutto), or was it the generals in Rawalpindi? Who was calling the shots in Pakistan?

Tension continued to increase. It appeared there was a harder line being taken in India because the uprising in Kashmir was gaining momentum and there was indubitably official support by Islamabad. Pakistan was being increasingly blamed for the insurrection, as the foreign minister Mr I.K. Gujral alleged on 8 May. Pakistan, he said, 'is aware it cannot take Kashmir by force. Its real design is to foment communal tension and to create a situation of 1947.'[27] (Mr Gujral's opinion of Pakistan did not undergo much modification during the 1990s. He became Prime Minister in 1997 – albeit for only seven months – and on 31 July, the day after India announced it was reactivating its intermediate-range ballistic missile programme, he said that Pakistan was spreading hostile propaganda, taking provocative actions and stockpiling arms: 'The government is aware that Pakistan maintains a military arsenal far in excess of its legitimate defence requirements.')[28]

Eventually, Pakistan moved some units close to the border. There was not much secrecy about the deployments. In fact, it appeared that Pakistan wished it to be known – or did not care if it were known – that reinforcements were on the move. The author witnessed the entrainment of an artillery regiment in Karachi which took place with all the stealth of a National Day Parade. Diplomats and defence attachés in Islamabad were aware of what was taking place and received information from many sources, in addition to raw and processed intelligence. They concluded that tension was high but that the situation was not dangerous. It appears that some other people considered it to be dangerous to the point that a nuclear weapons exchange could take place.

On 16 February 1994, a meeting of eighteen experts on the subcontinent took place at Washington's Henry L. Stimson Center, whose President is the highly respected Michael Krepon. The aim was to 'set the record straight' as to whether there was a 'near-nuclear war between India and Pakistan in 1990'. Participants included former ambassadors Oakley and Clark, who had been US heads of mission in Islamabad and New Delhi at the time, their then defence advisers, Colonels Jones and Sandrock, and General Sundarji, former Indian Army chief. The key findings included that:

> By all accounts the Gates Mission was extremely helpful in defusing the crisis (see below), and
> The participants knew of no credible evidence that Pakistan had deployed nuclear weapons during the crisis.[29]

Pronouncements by both sides appear to have relied on national intelligence assessments which, given the means at their disposal, could not present a full picture of each other's intentions. Commercial satellite photography was available but was neither high quality nor timely. There was confusion as to whether troop movements were exercises or operational deployments. Human intelligence sources were unreliable, and, even if credible, far from timely in the passage of information. Communications intercept was fragmented. Intelligence analysts were confused because movement was carried out using identical security measures whether it was operational or for exercise purposes. It may be that if the countries had had better intelligence systems, then mutual confidence would have been more readily established.

Apparently it was fear of a nuclear exchange that prompted the visit to Pakistan and India of a delegation led by Mr Robert Gates, deputy national security adviser to President Bush (and in 2007 appointed Defence Secretary to his son), from 19 to 21 May, an activity that intrigued several journalists.[30] India greeted the visit cautiously, stating that 'We have friendly relations with both the US and the Soviet Union, but there is no question of mediation by the US,' and Pakistan, which had been expecting yet another visit by the egregious Stephen Solarz, was grateful to be spared the latter,[31] but did not know what to make of the former.

From 15 to 24 May, Ms Bhutto visited Iran, Turkey, Syria, Jordan, Yemen, Egypt, Libya and Tunisia seeking support for Pakistan's stance on Kashmir. It was strange that the Prime Minister was out of the country when the emissary of President Bush came calling to stop a nuclear war, but Mr Gates met the President and COAS and, from what we are told,[32] convinced them that Pakistan should not proceed with plans for employment of nuclear weapons. It is said he achieved his objective in India as well. And, to be sure, there was no recourse to the atom; no nuclear Armageddon. But there are doubts as to whether there *were* any plans to employ nuclear weapons, or even intention to do anything, very much, in the conventional field.

Pakistan moved troops in Punjab and Sindh but was careful to avoid closing right up to the border itself. India was cautious, too. The Punjab canals are a double-edged obstacle: good for defence when your forces are on the home side; good for attack if your forces cross to the far bank within your territory to give them an advantage before the balloon goes up. Indian troops did not cross to their own far bank. Such an operation would have been practicable without interference; Indian troops could do what they liked in their own country. It would have signalled to the Pakistanis that war might be imminent, and who knows what might have happened then – but nothing happened. The armies moved closer to their borders, but refrained from provocation. There were no incidents of cross-border firing (there were many of firing over the Line of Control, but this was normal), and it was apparent to observers that, although the mood was one of disquietude, there was none of the expectant exhilaration that might be the prelude to operations. Satellite imagery and communications intercept provided an important part of the picture but could not tell the attitude of human beings. Washington knew the locations of tank squadrons and all sorts of other units – and it should have known the opinion of experienced observers on the ground concerning the behaviour of the army's leaders; but if it did, it paid more attention to the former than the latter. A photograph can indicate the position of a tank, and much else besides, but it cannot (yet) see if there is the light of battle in the eyes of its commander.

During the period of heightened tension there had been little evidence of leadership on the part of the government. A ten-day, eight-country tour by the Prime Minister to encourage support for Pakistan's stance on Kashmir was hardly a substitute for firm direction on the home front. General Beg had made pronouncements of national sensitivity that seemed to be at variance with the facts as reported elsewhere. His opposite number in India also made comments, but *they* reflected his government's position. In Pakistan, it seemed, important pronouncements were left to the military. Oddly – well, perhaps not so oddly – many people felt comfortable with that.

US intercession probably provided a fig leaf for both sides to calm down and withdraw troops without suffering loss of pride. The confrontation with India fizzled out – just in time for a row between the government and the army about the future of a corps commander and over the legal powers of the army in connection with the terrible violence in Sindh Province.

Army Appointments

On 10 July the author paid a call on the commander of IV Corps in Lahore, the genial and extremely competent Lieutenant General Alam Jan Mahsud, whose tour was about to end. His successor had been named and Alam Jan was preparing to retire. But there were rumours that he might be retained. What, he was asked, was the future? It all depended, he said, 'on the lady'. It appeared he had been told by someone – not in GHQ – that the Prime Minister wished him to become Deputy Chief of the Army Staff (as distinct from Vice Chief), a post that had not been filled since the retirement of the previous incumbent, Lieutenant General Ahmad Kamal Khan, some seven months before. It was Ahmad Kamal, so rumour had it during the Sirohey débâcle, who was Ms Bhutto's choice for Chief of Army Staff had Beg moved to become Chairman of the Joint Chiefs of Staff Committee, had Sirohey been retired as Ms Bhutto wished. All very complicated and smelling nastily of political meddling. Alam Jan would have made a good deputy chief (although one doubts if his heart would have been in it, as administration was not his scene; he was a soldier's soldier) and would not on any account have dabbled in politics – but what was going on was quite improper. He knew it, and was embarrassed; and the COAS knew it and was determined that no officer should be extended beyond retirement age, and especially that no officer should be appointed to *any* post because a politician wanted it. It was no fault of Alam Jan's that he had been placed in this position and he retired the next week, after General Beg prevailed, but it left a nasty taste in the mouths of many people. What was going on between the government and the army? Especially, what was going on between them concerning the situation in Sindh?

A Province in Chaos
The armed struggle between the political parties in Sindh, and especially in Karachi, had developed almost into civil war. Dreadful things were happening and it seemed the central government was powerless to control events. At the end of May 1990, when, allegedly, Pakistan was sharpening its nuclear talons, the respected Senator Mohsin Siddiqi was shot dead by a sniper in Karachi when returning from a visit to the scene of disturbances in which over forty people had been killed. On 4 June (about the time when he was supposed by some people to be considering nuclear war), General Beg toured the worst areas with the Corps Commander Karachi, Lieutenant General Asif Nawaz. It was obvious that firm action was needed if there was not to be anarchy. The trouble was that the PPP government felt itself unable to act decisively because of political complications. Earlier in May there had been some plain speaking at a meeting of the Defence Committee at the Prime Minister's Secretariat. The army was involved in Sindh – it had to be, simply because it was the only element that could combat organized terrorism (the police were politicized and ineffectual, and the para-military Rangers lacked authority) – but the army wanted power to arrest and detain malefactors. The government wanted malefactors to be arrested and dealt with, provided they were MQM malefactors.[33]

During a call on the commander of V Corps on 17 July the author was told the nature of some of the problems in Karachi and Islamabad, and specifically about relations with the government.

At a further meeting of the Defence Committee, ten days before, General Asif had been handed a list of persons against whom there were prima facie cases to answer concerning plans to disrupt affairs in Sindh. Certainly it seemed that all on the list belonged to the ungodly. Their detention would assuredly assist in restoring order in Karachi. There was only one problem, said the general to one of the ministers, in front of his Prime Minister and his chief (neither of whom took part in the subsequent exchange of views): all the names on the list appeared to be MQM adherents. Were there not any persons of evil intent who had other political allegiance? Like, for example, those on this list he happened to have with him, that contained not only many of those on the list of the minister, but the names of some who were of other political persuasion? There was strong disagreement. And Lieutenant General Asif Nawaz said it would not be proper for the civilian authorities to arrest only some of the alleged criminals, and, in any case, the army could not arrest *anyone* under present legislation. Where did they stand? If the government wanted the army to act, as it seemed it did, why did not the government permit the army to have the legal authority to take action? (The answer, of course, was that the army, if Asif Nawaz had anything to do with matters, would act against PPP thugs as well as MQM thugs.) The meeting ended in complete understanding and mutual antagonism. Two days later, a PPP spokesman in Karachi issued a statement urging the COAS 'not to indulge in politics'. Now, the COAS had undoubtedly been indulging in politics for many months. He had said what he should not have said on some occasions; he had explored the fascinating world of foreign affairs and enjoyed the heady brew of headlines; he had spoken without reference to government on matters that were the province and prerogative of government alone; he had taken unto himself the might and majesty of a national leader rather than a servant of the civil power who by virtue of his appointment should enjoy a proper dignity and respect – and no more. But the PPP had gone too far, in the eyes of the President and his Chief of the Army Staff.

The government was incompetent. The deliberations of the cabinet, solemnly issued to the Press, included matters so petty and inconsequential as to be embarrassing. There had not in eighteen months been a major piece of legislation that might have improved the lot of the common man or, especially, woman. Citizens in Sindh went in fear of their lives. Corruption was rampant, as the old Z.A. Bhutto loyalists claimed their rewards and the new adherents to 'BB' climbed on the gravy train. The country was becoming – had become – tacky, squalid, sordid, venal and dangerous to live in. *But*, the PPP government had been elected by the people and had a mandate that had not expired. What had expired was the patience of the President and of the Chief of the Army Staff, neither of whom was prepared to have their powers reduced or even questioned. The army, in spite of wishing to stay out of matters affecting the governance of the nation, was being drawn back into power politics by its chief – and it did not like it.

Change of Government

After Ms Bhutto and the PPP government were dismissed in August 1990, Mr Nawaz Sharif and his coalition were elected in October with rather more than a two-thirds majority in the National Assembly. Mr Sharif had been a protégé of General Zia (and was still young, at forty), but had little political baggage to encumber him. He was a populist, naturally, but had, perhaps, something more to offer the country. He had, after all, actually *run* something. He was an industrialist, albeit scion of a business family, but he had also run the province of Punjab, a major undertaking, and had done it well. In fact, considering the confrontationist stance of the central government and the machinations of his enemies, he had performed very well indeed, as he had always to keep an eye over his shoulder to watch for the next political dagger thrust.

On 10 November, the day that Mr Sharif and his cabinet were sworn in by the President, a compromise Prime Minister was selected in India. Unlike Mr Sharif, Mr Chandra Shekar had no popular mandate, nor a guaranteed majority in parliament, but within two weeks they met at a SAARC gathering in the Maldives and arranged for a meeting of foreign secretaries in December to 'discuss confidence-building measures'. There was no headway on Kashmir as, in spite of the Indian Prime Minister finding his counterpart 'very co-operative,' they both stuck to their briefs, which meant, in Pakistan's case, the raising of Kashmir as a problem to be discussed in the context of UN Security Council resolutions, and, on the Indian side, restatement of the stand that there must be 'no interference in India's internal matters'. Still, it was better to talk peace than shout about war. But at this juncture General Beg began to speak of 'strategic defiance', which left the Indians guessing just as much as everyone else. The foreign secretaries' talks included arrangements for weekly telephone links between the Directors-General Military Operations in Delhi and Rawalpindi, which was a step forward, and there was agreement to exchange the *Instruments of Ratification of the Agreement on Prohibition of Attack against Nuclear Installations* of 31 December 1988, which was largely symbolic, but nonetheless welcome evidence that agreement could be reached about *something*. It was unfortunate for the foreign policy of Pakistan that there had been a government upset in a crucial period, just as it was unfortunate for India that there had been eleven ministers and ministers of state for external affairs in the period January 1986 to January 1991. Construction and continuity of measured, farsighted, prudent policy was difficult for both countries in these circumstances. There appeared to be little gravitas in their exchanges. There were self-righteousness and mutual castigation in abundance; there were misunderstandings, wilful and otherwise and to spare; there may even have been a subliminal desire to seek resolution of their differences. But without governments on both sides that, concurrently, had massive popular support and an unassailable majority in both houses of their parliaments, there could be little progress.

After Aslam Beg (1991–3)

In mid-1991, the Islamabad rumour mill was working hard. General Beg, it was said, did not wish to retire in August. He wanted to stay as army chief, to take over as executive Chairman of the Joint Chiefs, to reintroduce martial law, to take over the country. Wild interpretations were placed on the fact that the US Ambassador said he was remaining in Pakistan until August rather than returning to Washington on the date his tenure ended. In Delhi, government-controlled All India Radio claimed that Beg wanted to invade and capture Kashmir before he retired. Nothing, it seemed, was too far-fetched to be retailed and, by some, at least, believed. Then it all stopped. It was announced on 12 June that Lieutenant General Asif Nawaz was to be appointed COAS on 17 August. General Beg would retire on time – but not before he made some startling pronouncements.

In July he stated that the situation in Kashmir could make it 'quite likely that in sheer desperation India could lead to venture [sic] against Pakistan', which statement was 'clarified' by a foreign office spokesman who explained that the army chief was not speaking about the immediate situation but was 'referring to problems being faced by India which could lead to a certain course of action in the long term'. Undeterred by clarification, the General returned to his theme of regional bonding. On 3 August he said, 'The tripartite accord reached by Pakistan, Iran, and the Afghan mujahideen to reach a peaceful solution of the Afghan issue [although abrogated almost immediately by the Afghans] was a prelude to achieving strategic consensus and regional security linkage between the three countries' – which was a strange statement to follow that by the Iranian ambassador on 20 June when, at a news conference, he said, 'Any sort of defence agreement is out of the question' because his country's Constitution excluded any such arrangement. Game to the last, a few days later the General said that 'the enemy' had 'launched a calculated campaign of disinformation to sabotage the political stability of Pakistan', which prompted *The News* of 10 August to note in an editorial that 'All too often we have chosen to externalise problems of our own making ... the danger lies in beginning to believe our own propaganda,' which was sagacious, perceptive, unbiased and probably completely ignored by all but a few, and they the wrong people.

It was small wonder that there was a sigh of relief from the bureaucracy and not a few politicians when Beg handed over. The new chief, Asif Nawaz, was different. Where Beg was taciturn, even enigmatic, when meeting with those whom he did not know well (and especially those whom he distrusted, like Mr Gates), Asif was straightforward and prepared to exchange views. Beg enjoyed publicity and the sense that he was at the centre of events. Asif eschewed the media and cared little for influence for its own sake. He was interested in foreign policy and relations, of course, but had no intention of making the first or interfering with the second. He liked senior members of the Ministry of Foreign Affairs, respected their expertise and recognized that there should be closer consultation. Beg had given approval for a strategy review to have input by the ministry and Asif was happy to endorse this. There was a changed atmosphere in the capital and in GHQ. No theatre; no thrilling statements – and no 'strategic consensus' or 'strategic defiance'. These inventions were quietly laid to rest.

This is not to denigrate the achievements of Aslam Beg, which were many. He placed the country back on the road to democracy when he could have continued in the shoes of Zia. It was not his fault that democracy was limping along, stricken by the perennial diseases of corruption, petty infighting and shallow thinking. He had interfered in politics, of course: his agreement with the President concerning the dismissal of the PPP government was improper – but what else could he have done? The President had been adamant that the government must go. The Eighth Amendment to the Constitution placed the loyalty of the COAS firmly at the office of the President, the supreme commander, who could 'act in his discretion in respect of any matter in respect of which he is empowered by the Constitution to do so'. The empowerment included dissolution of the National Assembly. But, although Beg interfered with the governance of the country, he was apolitical in the strictest sense. Never did he give the impression that he favoured one political party over another. He disliked and distrusted some members of both governments during his tenure, but did not let this affect the manner in which he carried out his duties. In fact, some said he should have been more resolute when the MQM's activities in Sindh began to resemble insurrection, but he was reluctant to commit the army wholesale to taking over from the civil power. Amongst other things, he introduced improvements in administration and operational planning. Promotion and selection procedures were speeded up, the role of administrative areas was examined and aligned with operational requirements, surface-to-surface artillery was included in tactical planning, armour tactics were re-examined, command and control of artillery was enhanced by introduction of the artillery division HQ, and air defence was given a much-needed boost in priority and inter-service liaison by the establishment of Air Defence Command. Not bad for three years in which he had a multitude of other matters to attend to. If only he hadn't talked so much and got himself more deeply involved in politics than was necessary.

General Asif was a tough man. The political parties were aware of his stance: he was uncompromising about aid to the civil power in that, if it was deemed necessary by the supreme commander, then it should be introduced by the parliament and implemented vigorously by the army. There could be no half measures. Asif preferred to keep out of things in Sindh, but, if there were no other means of controlling the vicious killers in the Province, then the army it would have to be – but without its hands tied. And he would make sure there were no favourites. There would be no question, either, of criminals coming to arrangements of mutual benefit with politicians, the police, or anyone else.

Unfortunately the Prime Minister dithered, probably because the MQM was an asset in the Assembly, and the lawlessness continued. The Chief Minister of Sindh, Jam Sadiq Ali, was a political ally (and a former PPP man), but when the Province was faced with even more violence after he died (of natural causes) in March 1992, Nawaz continued to dither. Along with growth in politically-motivated violence, there was a surge in 'ordinary' criminal activity. Dacoits – bandits – took advantage of the situation to indulge in rape, robbery, kidnap, extortion, drug-smuggling across the border with India, and general disorder. It was unsafe to travel by road and even by train, for gangs boarded coaches and stole what they could from the passengers – usually, of course, the poor. The rich travelled by air, or by road with well-armed bodyguards. The main sufferers were the villagers and their plight did not matter. There were not, after all, elections in the offing.

By the end of May the President had had enough. On the 28th he ordered Operation Clean-Up to begin, following a 'request' from the Sindh government. Article 147 of the Constitution was invoked,[34] and GHQ issued orders to the commander of V Corps (Lieutenant General Nasir Akhtar – just the man for the job) accordingly. The army began with operations against dacoits in an area along the Hyderabad–Lahore road, and along the railway (a favourite tactic being to leap onto trains as they slowed down). Asif Nawaz insisted that all operations be conducted 'in consultation with the civil administration', and whenever possible this was done; but sometimes it was difficult to distinguish between some members of the civil administration and those who were flouting its authority. Paramilitary Rangers were employed in conjunction with regular troops; curfews were imposed; the army was in control – but still without legal cover, which Asif continued to insist was necessary. The President finally agreed and issued a retrospective ordinance on 19 July to the effect that when troops were involved in police work such as search and arrest, they would be immune from legal procedures.[35] The President and the army had got what they wanted, but the Prime Minister was faced with problems of changing political alliances in the light of the crackdown. He had to perform a balancing act which took much time that should have been devoted to legislation, administration, and national leadership.

Disagreement between some members of the government and the army arose in September, when the country was hit by floods. *The News* of 25 September reported that the Prime Minister, although pleased with the way the emergency was dealt with by the army, was under pressure from some political colleagues to remove troops from relief work. Several million people lost their homes; livestock deaths and flooded farmland caused grave destitution; and the army worked wonders in cleaning up, restoring bridges, repaving roads, and administering distribution of relief moneys and supplies. But in one incident, local politicians informed the garrison commander in Multan that troops were no longer needed and that they should be withdrawn.[36] The order was rescinded, but there was unease locally and in the rest of the country about the motives behind such action. The sensitive aspects of this crisis, alas, were nothing to do with alleviating the distress of poor people rendered destitute, or with methods of restoring drowned land to productivity. Neither did they concern the best means of reconnecting canals, wells, sewage, tracks, roads, power supplies and telephone lines. They were to do with how relief aid could best be distributed in order to make it appear that a beneficent government was the sole agency involved in succouring the common man.

The army tried to ignore this sort of nonsense. It had a job to do and was getting on with it efficiently. If a politician wanted to strut into one of his villages and claim that what was being achieved was entirely his doing, then by all means let him. It was nothing to do with the army, provided he did not interfere. But if relief money and material was being diverted by local functionaries to their own benefit, the army was going to have none of it. The petty official concerned would get short shrift and might even be clapped inside for a while to show that, although he might be a big man to the peasants, he was not going to be allowed to get away with dishonesty. The army did not understand politics. It was vital to a local politician that he be seen to be helping the voters. It was traditional, and for him essential, that largesse be seen as coming directly from him or from the people appointed through his influence. The army might be a bit feudal in its approach to discipline and its place in society, but it did not subscribe to feudalism if the poor were going to be even further disadvantaged by the actions of pompous little men who were lining their own pockets.[37] Ms Bhutto, leader of the Opposition, wanted to visit the afflicted areas but was denied a helicopter by the government. This did not make much difference to her popularity – may even have enhanced it or at least not reduced it – because the Prime Minister had been hissed and booed when he arrived from the skies in one stricken village, and the Chief Minister of Punjab had been stoned in another. Political mileage should not be gained by Ms Bhutto if the government had anything to do with it – but if their own people were to be put in the shade by the army, things were getting dangerous.

In November 1992 the author attended a divisional exercise in Balochistan. The commander of XII Corps, Lieutenant General Abdul Waheed, was his usual jovial self but had a sense of humour failure when watching a television broadcast on the 18th which showed preparations for a 'Long March' by the PPP on the capital. The government made much of the threat to law and order and prevailed upon the COAS to have troops stand by in case of emergency. General Waheed, in what he expected to be the final posting of his career, was critical of both government and opposition. They were putting the country in an impossible position, he said. Let them have disagreements, of course, but don't let one side force the other to take action that set Pakistani against Pakistani. This was an interesting comment that showed the way Waheed – and the COAS and probably most of the army – felt about politics. It was an unsettling period for the government, which seemed to be unaware that the army took law and order very seriously indeed.

On 31 October 1992, Major Arshad Jamil was sentenced to death by a court martial in Sindh. Thirteen of his soldiers received life imprisonment. In June they had killed nine people in the village of Tando Bahawal, about 10 miles from Hyderabad, on the pretext of their being dacoits, while the real reason was a land dispute to which the major was privy. It was appalling that the slaughter had taken place, but the fact that it was reported, investigated and dealt with gave a message to the nation that the army was resolute about administration of the law. If the army could mete out punishment to an officer and his men, then, so notice was given, it could deal similarly with any who might fall within its jurisdiction. Curiously, this manifestation of respect for the law did not strike a resonant chord with either government or opposition.

The year 1992 was a poor one for internal stability and it was cyclic externally. The army remained alert in Kashmir but refused to be drawn into internal security affairs when the Jammu and Kashmir Liberation Front stage-managed a march intended to cross the Line of Control. One interesting aspect of the Kashmir dispute that year was the apparent but unintended volte-face by India regarding bilateralism. New Delhi slipped up in its conduct of relations with Pakistan by holding individual discussions with the permanent members of the Security Council in an attempt to persuade them of the justice of India's cause concerning Kashmir. Demonstrators crossing the Line of Control would be fired on, said its representatives. Pakistan's foreign ministry chuckled and went for the jugular. How principled, how proper, that New Delhi should enlist the support of the Security Council concerning Kashmir, they said. There was a still-extant Security Council Resolution about a plebiscite, was there not?

If India was so concerned about the disputed territory of Kashmir as to lobby the Great Five, then perhaps it might give similar attention to other matters, such as that?[38] The government did not seize this public relations advantage and Pakistan lost the opportunity to make a telling point, although it would have only been a PR victory, and nobody would have paid attention to it, so perhaps it didn't matter, anyway.

There had been many casualties in Siachen, but discussions in November were a waste of time. Neither government appeared anxious to reach a solution. Both had problems at home, and it seemed that political survival had priority over any initiatives that would save lives but endanger majorities.

Relations between the government and the army were looking shaky. While General Asif was on an overseas visit the government replaced the Director-General Inter Services Intelligence, Lieutenant General Asad Durrani,[39] by Lieutenant General Javed Nasir, a bearded Tablighi engineer officer with no intelligence background.[40] It was the government's prerogative to appoint the DG ISI, but it was not tactful to do so while the Army Chief was out of the country. It looked ... contrived. It also made nonsense of the claim that the army called the shots about who was to be DG ISI, because Javed Nasir was a figure of fun to many officers, mainly because his intellect was far from being as outstanding as his beard. Then there was the story that a senior figure allegedly close to government had approached two (perhaps three) lieutenant generals to ask them whom they would recommend to be Chief of the Army Staff if General Asif Nawaz was in some unspecified way to vacate the appointment in the near future. Would it, they were asked by the emissary, be regarded as a serious upset were General Asif to be replaced? When the army chief was informed of the approach he chose to ignore it, although his language was ripe and his suspicions were confirmed. He was, in any event, becoming disenchanted about some government activities, especially the attempt to prosecute The News newspaper for sedition. The government backed down eventually, after pressure, but Asif was worried that the Prime Minister might have been hijacked by some of his more aggressive colleagues, and convinced that there was a Press and army plot against him.

In the land of the conspiracy, nothing is impossible to the paranoid mind, but a plot by Asif Nawaz was inconceivable. The idea that the Chief Editor and Editor of The News could be plotting against the government was also ludicrous, but a charge had been laid and the process of prosecution was taken a long way before it was dropped. The public was becoming restive about allegations of corruption and mismanagement. The Muslim commented on 9 October that over a million dollars had been spent on sending politicians and bureaucrats overseas for medical treatment. 'Try as one might,' ran the editorial, 'it is impossible to unearth a single [medical] facility in this country which is not being misused ... What is happening in the corridors of power is downright dishonest.' *The News* reported two weeks later that the seats in the executive jet purchased for the Prime Minister had been replaced at a cost of two million dollars. A week later came the revelation that a ski resort had been sold to an entrepreneur of most dubious antecedents for a fraction of its value. The man in the street was becoming irritated about the extent of corrupt activities and one heard it suggested, more and more, that it might not be a bad thing if the army took over again.

General Asif Nawaz died of a heart attack on 8 January 1993 and was succeeded by General Abdul Waheed Kakar, the commander of XII Corps in Quetta. Much was made of the fact that six officers were senior to him, and there was in fact a considerable difference of opinion between President and Prime Minister concerning who should be the next Chief. The President had selected the CGS, General Farrukh Khan, but when he informed Nawaz Sharif of his choice the Prime Minister was violently opposed. Farrukh, alleged Sharif, 'had been responsible for all his problems with the late General Asif Nawaz'.[41] This was true, to the extent that Farrukh had been totally loyal to Asif. The President compromised and, after discussion with Roedad Khan, a close friend of many years, decided on General Waheed.

Whatever anyone expected of General Waheed, they should have known he would be his own man. Unfortunately for the ambitions of both President and Prime Minister – and most fortunately for the country – General Waheed brought hard common sense to the post of COAS. He was neither ideologue nor demagogue nor theocrat; no wild and dramatic ideas came from GHQ during his tenure. He was completely apolitical and determined that he and the army should remain so. He wanted the best for his country, and if he was forced to intervene he would become involved only in strict accordance with the Constitution. Some observers commented that his outlook was narrow. Well, it may have been, although knowing him as I did I doubt it. Whatever it was, it was a blessing for his country.

The President dismissed the government of Nawaz Sharif on 18 April 1993 on the grounds that it was corrupt and had mismanaged the country. An interim government headed by a feudal landlord, Balakh Sher Mazari, took over at an undignified ceremony and set about creating a cabinet of fifty-eight members – a record number – whose usefulness was entirely dubious. On 26 May the Supreme Court ordered the reinstatement of Nawaz Sharif and his group. The situation was developing into chaos and Pakistan was becoming a laughing stock. General Waheed, by a combination of tact, forcefulness, honour and tenacity convinced the President and the Prime Minister they should stand down, which they did on 18 July. A caretaker administration led by Mr Moeen Qureshi, another luminary of the World Bank, took over and was, it has been argued, the best government Pakistan had experienced since the country was created. He was, sums up Lawrence Ziring, 'an effective, efficient, no-nonsense and dedicated administrator'. In three months (the time laid down in the Constitution for elections to be arranged) Qureshi introduced many proposals aimed at restoring probity to the conduct of the country's affairs. Unfortunately these were discarded by the next government – and the decision to cap the expensive nuclear programme was also rescinded.

In a post-dinner conversation with General Waheed in mid-1993 I asked about a recent trip he had made to Singapore and Malaysia. He had obviously had an enjoyable visit to both countries, but sighed and was silent for a moment. Then he looked at me and said words to the effect that 'After a few days in Malaysia I thought, "We could be like this" – but what on earth went wrong with us?' It was illuminating that he thought the way he did and indicative of his approach to national affairs, in that he obviously favoured democracy although he had serious doubts about the willingness of some of his fellow citizens to embrace it fully.

After three eventful years as Chief of the Army Staff, General Waheed handed over to General Jehangir Karamat, an equally forceful and forthright character, in January 1996. His tenure had been successful but not without grave problems. There had been, for example, the matter of the failed coup.

Major General Zaheerul Islam Abbasi always appeared to the author to be a competent officer of some charm. As Director of Infantry he was, in the early and mid-1990s, in a position that any infantry officer would welcome. The incumbent could have great influence on his Corps, and could introduce – or at least endorse and fine-tune – many improvements. In tactics, leadership, equipment acquisition and structure he could contribute much to development. Unfortunately Abbasi thought he could and should do more than was permitted an officer in influencing military affairs. He wanted to influence political affairs, too – and dramatically.

General Waheed had made it clear he would not countenance officers interfering in politics or becoming involved with contentious matters outside their profession. Let them argue about river crossings by all means, and give their opinions on deficiencies in training – but don't let them put their noses into affairs that might be considered even remotely connected with politicians. He dismissed from service the popular, intellectual and competent Lieutenant General Asad Durrani (see Note 39) for daring to involve himself in politics. Well intentioned as Durrani was, he had to go (and told the author two days after his dismissal that it was 'a fair cop').

But Abbasi was not trying to be an honest broker. He was involved in Islamic extremism and thought he might be able to overthrow what he saw as an unIslamic government. He and another thirty-five officers were arrested on 26 September 1995, having failed to carry through a plan to kill all those attending a Corps Commanders' Conference (chaired by the COAS) and then eradicate the cabinet. The government tried to play down the significance of the attempted coup, which was made public three weeks later, but there is no doubt it was serious. Equally, it had no chance of success. The government of Benazir Bhutto was not anti-Islamic, any more than it was pro-anything other than staying in power, but the army was not prepared to have dissidents in its midst. Punishment was swift. The three dozen were dealt with, and others suspected of having connections with extremism were moved sideways or out. The coup attempt had effects throughout the army but was far from being an all-embracing defect.

Islam was not a 'problem' in the army. It could hardly be that, because the army is, after all, one of the armed services of The Islamic Republic of Pakistan. But those who advocate *extreme* Islam are a problem, as are bigoted militants who espouse extreme Christianity or extreme Hinduism or extremes in other religious and political beliefs, because those who advocate immoderation and intolerance, and condemn others for failing to adhere to their own particular beliefs, have lost touch with human purpose and dignity. The army does not seem to have gone overboard about religion, but there are lingering doubts about the cumulative effects of the Zia years and the persistent efforts of the ultra-religious political parties to influence those whose primary duty it is to defend Pakistan.

In the early 1990s, during an exercise, I crawled 100 metres to a dug-in artillery observation post where a young officer showed me a laser range-finder with which I busied myself. After congratulating him on his device I was treated to an exposition on how, in fact, there is no need for advanced technology providing one believes in Allah. On another occasion I was informed gravely by a junior officer that the beard of one of his soldiers (the luxuriance and shade of which had attracted my admiration) had turned red of its own accord because of the piety displayed during his Haj. His commanding officer buried his head in his hands, but made no comment. In more recent years I have met middle-ranking officers and been told in some detail of more senior ones (only a few) whose approach to their military duties has been based entirely on their interpretation of Islam, to the point of subordinating the relevance and practicability of military doctrine. I do not say that these officers are typical; but I do say that their attitude is disconcerting. One interesting, and to my mind healthy instance of disapproval of extremist tendencies in 2006 was the case of the bearded commanding officer who was becoming more influentially Islamic than deemed appropriate by his newly appointed formation commander. The CO was called in and told calmly and firmly that 'it' (the beard) would go, or he (the CO) would go. The beard went. But who knows what continues to pulse under it?

The PPP under Ms Benazir Bhutto won eighty-six seats in the October 1993 elections, which were conducted fairly, under the eyes of the army and independent observers, of whom the author was one. The Pakistan Muslim League of Nawaz Sharif obtained seventy-two seats. Ms Bhutto managed to construct a coalition with 121 seats and achieved government on 19 October. On the election of her candidate for President, Farooq Leghari, a PPP loyalist, Ms Bhutto stated that it was a triumph for democracy. Mr Leghari, she said, would contribute to the country's stability.

He did. Mr Leghari dismissed the government of Ms Bhutto on the night of 4/5 November 1996. There was little condemnation. The country had become nigh on ungovernable. One senior politician told the author later in November in Lahore that 'all is not lost' but that it had been a near-run thing. Anarchy had loomed, he said, and, with that, intervention by the army, as 'there would have been no alternative'. Mr Nawaz Sharif's Muslim League was voted in to power on 17 February 1997 with 181 seats in the 217-seat lower house. He faced enormous problems, as the country was on the verge of bankruptcy, but given his huge majority it seemed that Pakistan might be on the way to stability, because he could take action and institute reforms that would be impossible for a weak government to consider. Pakistan, thanks to the army, had avoided civil war (although Karachi resembled a battlefield later in the year, and clashes between Sunni and Shia fanatics in Punjab were mindlessly savage), and appeared to be able to start – once again – the long haul to stable governance thanks to an electorate that had become sick of corruption and mismanagement, and had voted for change.

In August 1997 the former caretaker Prime Minister, the wise Moeen Qureshi, sounded a note of caution. 'This is,' he said, 'the last chance for the parliamentary form of government of the kind we have now in Pakistan. I have often said before, if this experiment does not succeed, then I think we must consider a presidential form of government.' He was saying that the future of Pakistan lay in the hands of Mr Nawaz Sharif's government. He was right, but those hands eventually donned the iron gloves of autocracy. And the army would once again take over.

Notes

1. One of whom was the then Lieutenant Colonel (later Lieutenant General and commander of I Corps 2003–5) Javed Alam Khan who gave the presentation to Zia and the Americans about the tank trials. In his talk Javed mentioned that the engine filters ceased to be

effective after about 90 days of operation. He was surprised to see the President and the Ambassador guffawing at his plain statement of fact and wondered what could be so amusing. Later he was told that their laughter was caused by reference to '90 days' – the period in which Zia stated he would hold elections after his coup. An interesting insight to US policy of the day. Javed had wanted to go to Islamabad on the President's aircraft but was prevented from doing so by Zia's invitation to the US contingent to accompany him. Lucky Javed.

2. An excellent account of the crash is contained in Coll, Steve, *On the Grand Trunk Road*, Times Books, 1994. But a more stringent examination of the affair, agreed to be pursued by Coll and the author, was terminated by the former in the late 1990s. I am still wondering why. See also Arif, *op. cit.*

3. In the past I had commented that 'They never do,' which, alas, was proved incorrect in the 2002 elections when the MMA grouping of six religious parties achieved enough votes to govern in NWFP, which has set development and social welfare in the Province back by about fifty years.

4. *Gulf News*, 7 March 1990.

5. The *Globe* (Pakistan) of May 2001 carried a remarkable interview with General Babar, which is well worth reading for an intriguing interpretation of events in this period. See http://www.paksearch.com/globe/2001/may/babar.html

6. 'In 1995, a leading French military contractor, Dassault Aviation, agreed to pay Zardari and a Pakistani partner a $200 million commission for a $4 billion jet fighter deal that fell apart only when the Bhutto government was dismissed' – John F. Burns, *New York Times*, 9 January 1989. I have a copy of that edition of the NYT, given me by Burns, the Pulitzer Prize-winning reporter. Its front page headline is 'BHUTTO CLAN LEAVES TRAIL OF CORRUPTION'. Inside there are two pages under the banner 'The Bhutto Millions: A Name That Stood For Democracy and Greed'. Two entire pages of the *New York Times* were given to such pieces as 'Powerful Clan in Pakistan Is Stained by a Vast Record of Corruption', and 'A Pakistani Fortune Amassed From Graft Left Its Tracks Round the World'. The paper's libel lawyers went through his copy most thoroughly before publication.

7. Gul gave me a comprehensive briefing on 28 March 1989, when he was Director General ISI.

8. My despatch at the time was headed 'Intelligence Change: Not a Kallue'. Neither my attempt at humour nor pages of analysis was welcomed by those to whom they were directed.

9. The Islamic Democratic Alliance was not, in spite of its name, a religiously based grouping, although it included the fundamentalist Jamaat-i-Islami, which left the coalition in May 1992.

10. It was admitted by Beg in 1994 that the banker, Yunus Habib (jailed in 1995), had provided 1.4 million rupees to Beg in 1990 and that ISI spent part of that during the elections. See editorial in *Dawn* of 25 April 1994 and a more detailed description in *Islamic Pakistan: Illusions and Reality* by Abdus Sattar Ghazali, http://ghazali.net/book1/Chapter11a/page_4.html and published by the National Book Club (Pakistan).

11. I went to the radio and television studios that day. At the entrance to each establishment there was a solitary soldier, looking bored. On being asked his duties at the TV station, the soldier appeared unsure of what he was about other than to 'help the police'. There were eleven soldiers outside the Prime Minister's house, who left in the early evening.

12. Most newspapers, 9 August 1990. Steve Coll (*International Herald Tribune*, 8 August) was of the opinion that 'This was the Benazir Bhutto who ruled shakily over Pakistan for 20 months, who had difficulty sharing power, and who seemed increasingly to view the

world as composed of two groups: those who were with her and those who were against her.'

13. 'The President shall, subject to law, have power ... to appoint in his discretion the Chairman Joint Chiefs of Staff Committee, the Chief of the Army Staff.' *Constitution of the Islamic Republic of Pakistan*, Article 243 (2)(c).

14. *Dawn*, 11 August 1989; *The Nation*, 23 August; and Mushahid Hussain in *Gulf News*, 16 and 20 August.

15. Also carried by *Deutsche Welle*, Radio Australia and the Voice of America.

16. A recording was made of the press conference (in the VIP lounge at Islamabad airport) by, amongst others, the VOA correspondent, Gary Thomas, who alerted me to the run of events. Mr S.K. Singh said, 'I would like to thank Foreign Secretary Dr Humayun Khan, and endorse everything he said.' Mr Singh was an experienced diplomat who well knew how to choose his words. There is an excellent description of the affair in the *Indian Express* of 5 August 2004, by Jyoti Malhotra – available at http://www.indianexpress.com/print.php?content_id=52397.

17. Press briefing. Full statement in *Globe*, Karachi, November 1989.

18. Major General Murray Blake MC, Land Commander Australia.

19. *Defence Journal* [of Pakistan], vol. XVII, Nos. 6–7 of August 1991.

20. *Gulf News*, 3 December 1990. All Pakistani newspapers.

21. Shakespeare, *King John*, V.vii.112, if you really want to know.

22. The bazaars in Peshawar and other cities had many stalls with posters and badges portraying Saddam Hussein. Uniline Badges of Faislabad produced a particularly provocative 'Love For Saddam' badge which was worn by many schoolchildren.

23. US officer to author, January 1991.

24. I was given access to a report on the brigade's tour in Saudi Arabia.

25. The Indian reporter Anand Sagar recorded an exclusive interview with V.P. Singh, *Gulf News*, 30 April 1990.

26. Foreign country intelligence report.

27. *Gulf News*, 19 May 1990.

28. Reuters, 30 and 31 July 1997.

29. *Conflict Prevention and Confidence-Building Measures in South Asia: the 1990 Crisis*, The Henry L. Stimson Center Occasional Paper No. 17, April 1994, edited by Michael Krepon and Mishi Faruqee. I am grateful to Khurshid Khoja of Stimson for providing a copy.

30. USIS transcript of a press conference given by White House spokesman Marlin Fitzwater on 15 May 1990.

31. Only temporarily. He came on the 27th. Mr Solarz was disliked in Pakistan. As Chairman of the Asian subcommittee of the House Foreign Affairs Committee he appeared to have some influence on US policy, but his self-importance was hard to bear. There was much rejoicing when he failed to be re-elected. A proposal for his appointment as Ambassador to India fell through.

32. See Andrew, Christopher, *For the President's Eyes Only*, HarperCollins, 1995. I wrote to the author about the apparent discrepancy, mentioning that I was writing about it, but did not have the courtesy of a reply.

33. *Trial and Error*, Oxford, 2000 by Iqbal Akhund, Benazir Bhutto's National Security and Foreign Affairs Adviser places a rather different emphasis on the Sindh problem, and blames the army for failing to adhere to the law when troops were deployed after police had fired on a crowd in Hyderabad.

34. 'The Government of a Province may, with the consent of the Federal Government, entrust, either conditionally or unconditionally, to the Federal Government, or to its officers, functions in relation to any matter to which the executive authority of the province extends.'

35. The Criminal Procedure Code was extended to the military. Sections 46–9 dealt with powers of arrest; 53, 54, 55(a) and (c), 58 and 63–7 with seizure of illicit arms; and 100, 102 and 103 with powers of search.

36. *The News*, Lahore, 25 September 1993.

37. I drove down the Indus plain on 13–14 September and en route was given the views of some army officers concerning flood relief.

38. 'PTI said India asked the five permanent Council members to persuade Pakistan to "cease and desist" from escalating tension over Kashmir.' The request 'did not amount to an appeal for intervention by the Security Council members'. *Gulf News*, 7 February 1992.

39. There are two General Durranis relevant to this narrative, both outstanding officers: Lieutenant General Asad Durrani, the ISI head (later Ambassador to Germany and then to Saudi Arabia), is no relation to the Durrani who was Zia's PSO and later Chairman of Pakistan Ordnance Factories. The latter is author of, amongst other things, *India and Pakistan, the Cost of Conflict, the Benefits of Peace*, Johns Hopkins University, 2000, and was appointed Ambassador to the United States in 2006.

40. The Tablighi (sometimes Tableeghi) Jamaat is a Deobandi proselytizing religious movement. See Sikand, Yoginder, *The Origins and Development of the Tablighi Jama*, Orient Longman, New Delhi, 2002. An NBC news item of 18 January 2005 indicates the level of suspicion with which the Tablighi is regarded in the US (http://msnbc.msn.com/id/6839625/).

41. Khan, Roedad, *Pakistan: A Dream Gone Sour*, OUP, Karachi, 1998.

Chapter 4

Karamat, Kargil, Chaos

Change of Army Chiefs

General Jehangir Karamat took over from General Waheed in January 1996 and continued his predecessor's policies almost unchanged, but with the vigour and fresh personal approach that an energetic new appointee always brings to a demanding task. He saw his mission as being 'to put the army through a consolidation phase' because of the hiatus imposed by the coup attempt of Major General Abbasi, and severe financial constraints, and told the author his priorities were: 'Improving the institutional strength of the military system; and enhancing operational readiness and establishing a sound command and staff environment.'

The consolidation phase 'enabled us to make up shortfalls, improve manpower induction through a new short-term recruitment policy, and vastly improve our functional procedures'.[1]

There was much to do in the army, but it had to be done in a period of reduced activity. Major exercises, involving a division (which means more troops and staff officers are required from elsewhere to enable testing of the formation being exercised), were few and far between because there was not enough money to conduct them. One result of the nuclear tests in 1998 was to further reduce national defence capabilities, in addition to cancellation of defence co-operation by several countries. Nawaz Sharif was told by President Clinton by telephone that if Pakistan did not emulate India and explode nuclear devices, then the Administration would make every effort to have the F-16 ban lifted and would engage in a massive programme of military and other aid. The chiefs of the armed forces were in a difficult position, but 'internal dynamics made it inevitable that the nuclear programme would advance to conducting tests. Thus there was no room for dissent.'[2] In fact the overwhelming majority of Pakistanis approved of the tests. Even some highly intelligent people were enthusiastic, and at the side of main roads entering many cities there were constructed celebratory artificial slag heaps purporting to be replicas of the test site at Chagai. The national mood was decidedly in favour of

84

advancing to nuclear holocaust capability and I observed in print and in a BBC interview that this was because most people had no idea of what nuclear fallout effects might be, and imagined nuclear bombs simply made a bigger bang.

A major concern for the chiefs was that a new strategy was required if the country's defence was perforce to involve a nuclear posture. It had been much simpler before the tests (just as it continues to be for Israel), because the rest of the world was kept guessing about intentions and could even turn a (fairly) blind eye to what was going on.[3] Now that everything was public there had to be hard thinking concerning nuclear theory that would lead to doctrine, but first there had to be decisions about who would forge this doctrine. It could not be left solely to politicians and scientists. There would have to be a body established to define it, but its membership would have to reflect the responsibility of the military in development and employment of weapons as well as overall civilian control. In this context it is well to remember that military doctrine is:

> The combination of principles, policies and concepts into an integrated system for the purpose of governing a military force in combat, and assuring consistent, coordinated employment of these components. The origin of doctrine can be experience, or theory, or both. Doctrine represents the available thought on the employment of forces that has been adopted by an armed force. Doctrine is methodology, and if it is to work, all military elements must know, understand, and respect it. Doctrine is implemented by tactics.[4] [Doctrine can also take outside advice into account; but there was no possibility of that being offered by anyone.]

General Karamat's view was that the Defence Committee of the Cabinet, chaired by the Prime Minister, should be the 'apex body' (his words), with the Defence Council of the Ministry of Defence as the next tier. The Chairman of the Joint Chiefs of Staff and his headquarters would be the inter-service co-ordinator, but there would be input by the military at the level of a National Security Council.

The former Army Chief stated that 'My views were well known and I had discussed them with the PM often,'[5] but the problem that resulted in his resignation was more complex than reasoned debate concerning one of the most important issues facing the country. It concerned his frustration with the country's governance as such, which was a fundamental matter – and one that the Prime Minister could not regard, in any circumstances, as being open to question.

Pakistan had enormous problems in 1998. In the words of one reporter, it was suffering 'the worst financial crisis the country has faced, sanctions imposed for nuclear tests in May, and allegations and counter-allegations by the government and opposition of massive, systematic corruption'.[6] To this one might add *The Economist*'s comments on 17 October that:

> Almost anywhere but Pakistan the plug would surely be yanked out. With days to go before an IMF mission was due to put the finishing touches to a rescue package, the prime minister, Nawaz Sharif, announced a 30% increase in electricity charges. This is lunacy of a high order: Pakistan's utilities are already losing enough money to sink the foundering economy ... But Pakistan is no ordinary deadbeat debtor. It is a nuclear power engaged in a low-level war with another nuclear power, India, over the disputed province of Kashmir ... Every newspaper carries a litany of murder prompted by greed or group hatred. An economic implosion would make things worse ... the Sharif brothers seem to think that Pakistan can have sharia and constitutional democracy, holy wars and a peaceful society, economic populism and an IMF bail-out. The bet on the bail-out is a long shot. The other gambles are doomed.

This was blunt condemnation of the country's government, but seemed to be shrugged off by Mr Sharif (and his brother, in theory confined to Punjab's administration, but whose national role was growing). It was in this period that General Karamat gave an address to the Naval College. Amongst other sensible observations he said that Pakistan 'cannot afford the destabilizing effects of polarization, vendettas and insecurity-driven expedient policies', and while there must be 'a neutral, competent and secure bureaucracy', there was need for 'a national security council at the apex', backed by advisers to 'institutionalise decision-making'.[7] A senior figure of the establishment had spoken out. Having done so, he could not remain a member of the establishment – or, at least, not of Nawaz Sharif's establishment. He resigned.

There were many rumours following the resignation. Islamabad was rife with talk of an army takeover, pending constitution of a non-partisan government, and there were many who would have welcomed this. The Nawaz Sharif regime was all-powerful, politically, yet it was incapable of solving even the most basic economic problems, corruption scandals were of such magnitude the IMF wanted to walk away and wash its hands of the country, and in October said it was doing so, although it changed its mind. (US influence was brought to bear, on the grounds that total collapse would not solve anything and that it was better to bail out than to try to pick up the pieces afterwards.)[8] The independent press was under threat from Sharif's hoodlums (and later suffered grave assaults on its freedoms) and the bureaucracy was becoming increasingly politicized. Many distinguished civil servants were sidelined because preferment was being given to cronies of the brothers and their circle. But General Karamat is adamant that he was not forced out of his appointment:

> Dear Brian, [There was] no mystery or intrigue ... My comments were blown out of all proportion by the media and exploited by people in a politically unstable environment to target the government and create an army-government rift – the start point for all our problems. [The speech] was wrongly interpreted as a 'bid for power' by the military and a criticism of the government, which it was not – it was a review of the state of affairs and the [social and political] environment for which many governments and political factions were responsible – even past military rule.
>
> I left at my own request, to save my institution from controversial and uninformed public debate ... There was no conspiracy, no ambition and never did the PM ask me to leave. I acted in what I thought were the best interest of the army and the country at that time. Personal opinions should not plunge institutions into controversies in a politically divided atmosphere, because institutions suffer – individuals have to step aside.

This is an admirable explanation of what went on, by the man at the centre. Honour may be rare in politicians, but still exists in the military. And yet ... one wonders what Mr Sharif might have been thinking at the time. He has an unforgiving and vindictive nature, as was shown by his treatment of many loyal servants of government, not least being one unfortunate diplomat who was High Commissioner in London during Mr Sharif's first tenure as prime minister.[9] The Karamat episode was distasteful and served to accentuate the opinion within and outside Pakistan that the Prime Minister had become too powerful for the good of the country. One highly placed individual wrote to me to say that the 'great fear' was that checks and balances to prevent further lurches to erratic autocracy had been eroded to the extent that not only was the National Assembly becoming irrelevant, but the office of the President was seen as merely an extension of the ruling party's policy machine.

Consequential appointments came quickly. As General Karamat went into honourable retirement,[10] Lieutenant General Pervez Musharraf was appointed COAS, superseding Lieutenant Generals Khalid Nawaz (QMG) and Ali Kuli Khan Khattak who, as CGS, was considered the obvious choice to follow Karamat. Both Khalid Nawaz and Ali Kuli took the honourable course and resigned. They were regarded by foreign observers as well above average, although the betting was on the latter to succeed as COAS in the normal course of events. He, however, being of the opinion that he had the distinction of being detested by both Benazir Bhutto and Nawaz Sharif,[11] had no illusions as to his future under either, especially as the President was without influence in military appointments (or, indeed, anything of importance).

Musharraf had as many outstanding credentials as those whom he superseded. His career had been 'conventional-supersonic' according to a fellow officer,[12] and this is an accurate comment, given that he went up the command chain with excellent reports (two tours as CO of artillery regiments; command of divisional artillery and an infantry brigade; command of an infantry division and II Corps), as well as serving with the SSG and in all the 'right' Operational staff jobs in which he did well. His report from the Royal College of Defence Studies in London was glowing and it was obvious that he was a front-runner for the highest rank. His considerable charm might also have been a factor, although he is nobody's yes-man. He settled in quickly and brought in or moved some of his own team, promoting Muhammad Aziz Khan to three star rank as CGS (posted from ISI, where he headed the Afghan desk – a surprise) and appointing Lieutenant General Muhammad Akram as QMG. The chain was not controversial, although there were some disappointed faces around. As in all good armies, the shake-up did no harm, although the DG ISI, Lieutenant General Ziauddin, was a government appointee and there were some raised eyebrows – not because of any lack of competence on his part but because he had not been thought of as a 'Nawaz man', although he was one, most markedly, as was later shown. Now that the President was out of the loop, senior posts, except DG ISI, were the result of the recommendation of the COAS and the decision of the Prime Minister. (The ISI chief has always been a direct appointment as he answers to the PM and not, in theory at any rate, to a military superior, which is of interest when considering developments in October 1999.)

Less than two weeks after the upset it was announced by the then Minister for Power, Gauhar Ayub Khan, that military personnel would be seconded to electricity distribution regions because, according to the Prime Minister, 'WAPDA [the Water and Power Development Authority] itself could not contain line losses, pilferage and inefficiency.' The Minister said, 'We have to admit the fact that there is corruption in every cadre,'[13] which was a remarkable admission, given the much-publicized announcement of a campaign against corruption. The power sector was a shambles, but the army was not the long-term answer to appalling problems of institutionalized improbity. The solution lay in the hands of government, and it was the responsibility of the country's leaders to revitalize public utilities. The band-aid approach could work for a while, but unless there were culling and retraining at all levels in WAPDA (and in many other enterprises) the country would continue to be ripped off and would stagger along in the business-as-usual mode of extreme inefficiency which had come to be accepted by all but a few bold figures – and those were voices in the wilderness of venality that characterized Sharif's Pakistan. The views of General Musharraf are not known concerning the intervention to which he acceded, but other officers commented discreetly that it is not the business of the army to become involved in such tasks. They are right, for it is not in the best interests of the nation that the armed forces be associated with wider functions than national defence. Military involvement in detecting 'ghost teachers' (who were drawing pay for non-attendance, particularly in rural areas where they were most needed) was also regrettable, and was not notably effective.

However efficient the army might be in eradicating poor practices in civilian sectors, there is always a deferred price to pay, usually in reduced efficiency in the military element so employed. Units and formations have a 'training cycle' which, within a finite budget, is intended to improve standards. Not every type of skill can be practised within the training year, so there is emphasis, from cycle to cycle (and dependent on location and primary operational tasks), on different demands. To put it simply, it might be the Attack one year, then Defence the next. As every commander knows, the desirable number of months in a training year is thirteen plus, and any interruption of the cycle causes disruption. When units and individuals are required to serve with the UN, or natural disaster relief, or on internal security duties in aid of the civil power, they require much shaking down when they get back, because they have concentrated on acquiring and practising skills which are not their bread and butter. Some units, such as engineers, transport and signals, may have been demonstrating their particular expertise in bridge-laying, logistics, communications – but they have been doing this in a totally different environment and not within a structured fighting force. There is a world of difference for a signaller between reading and resetting an electricity meter that has been retarded on the orders of a Member of the National Assembly and manning the communications network for an armoured attack, although such skills can be transferred to civil life once a soldier retires.

The armed forces are efficient and are capable of managing almost any other institution, but that is not their job. If the government cannot run the country in the best interests of the people, and if the rule of law and provision of education, water reticulation, electricity and other services are so bad as to require the intervention of the armed forces, then it could be argued that one might as well have full martial law and have done with it; but this is not what democracy is all about.

One result of the government's deliberations about law and order was the Pakistan Armed Forces Ordinance, 1998, signed into law by President Mohammad Rafiq Tarar on 20 November. The Ordinance[14] was intended to legalize harsh counter-measures against terrorism and general mayhem in Sindh and especially Karachi (there is an excellent examination of armed forces' involvement by the ever-watchful Brigadier A.R. Siddiqi in *The Nation* of 13 January 1999), but the main features were disturbing. The old Article 245 of the Constitution,[15] one would have thought, would have met most requirements, in that:

1. The Armed Forces shall, under the directions of the Federal Government, defend Pakistan against external aggression or threat of war, and, subject to law, act in aid of [the] civil power when called upon to do so; and
2. The validity of any direction issued by the Federal Government under clause (1) shall not be called into question by any court.

This was deemed inadequate by the government and it tried to bring in a new set of laws, seemingly without seeking legal advice from those best qualified to give it. Tinkering with the Constitution was a hobby of General Zia ul Haq, who sought to maintain his autocratic power by equating legality with personal ambition, and to that end demanded that lawyers discover language whereby the convergence might be furthered. It seems that this inclination had not deserted Pakistan's leaders in 1998 (and it might be remembered that it was Zia who appointed Nawaz Sharif Chief Minister of Punjab in 1985), for the Ordinance gave authority for the convening of military courts 'to try offences trialable [sic] under this ordinance', and declared many activities as not only illegal but deserving of severe punishment. The terms of Section (3)(1) were Draconian enough to have been constructed by the Raj in some of its worst moments of retribution against malcontent natives:

6. *Creating Civil Commotion*: 'Civil Commotion' means creation of internal disturbances in violation of law or intended to violate law, commencement or continuation of illegal strikes, go-slows, lock-outs, vehicles snatching/lifting [sic], damage to or destruction of State or private property, random firing to create panic, charging *bhatha*, acts of criminal trespass (illegal *qabza*), distributing, publishing or pasting of a handbill or making graffiti or wall-chalking intended to create unrest or fear or create a threat to the security of law and order or to incite the commission of an offence punishable under Chapter VI of the Pakistan Penal Code (Act XLV of 1860 [sic]).

7. *Punishment for creating civil commotion*: Whoever commits an act of civil commotion shall be punished with rigorous imprisonment for a term which may extend to seven years, or with fine, or with both.

The ukase was as vicious as it was all-embracing. Legally appointed enforcers of the Ordinance could interpret a chalk mark on a wall as 'incitement' just as those zealous in enforcement of sharia could declare an

Pakistan Army tanks and armoured personnel carriers on a field-firing exercise. (*Courtesy of the Directorate of Inter-Service Public Relations*)

Part of a military cordon following a suicide bomb attack in which ten people were killed. (*Courtesy of the Directorate of Inter-Service Public Relations*)

Leaders of tomorrow. Passing out parade at the Pakistan Military Academy. (*Courtesy of the Directorate of Inter-Service Public Relations*)

Pakistan Military Academy parade. (*Courtesy of the Directorate of Inter-Service Public Relations*)

Dismounted infantry. Units sent to NWFP from the border area had to revise their battle skills to adapt to totally different terrain. (*Courtesy of the Directorate of Inter-Service Public Relations*)

Special Services Group (SSG) training. (*Courtesy of the Directorate of Inter-Service Public Relations*)

Weapons captured in South Waziristan. (*Courtesy of the Directorate of Inter-Service Public Relations*)

Militants' communications trenches in South Waziristan. (*Courtesy of the Directorate of Inter-Service Public Relations*)

Test firing of a Hatf VI
missile in April 2008.
(*Courtesy of the Directorate of
Inter-Service Public Relations*)

Artillery in close support in FATA, 2008. (*Courtesy of the Directorate of Inter-Service Public Relations*)

In the Eastern Desert. (*Courtesy of the Directorate of Inter-Service Public Relations*)

The President's bodyguard. (*Courtesy of the Directorate of Inter-Service Public Relations*)

Scene of terror: the aftermath of the suicide bombing in which the Surgeon General, Lieutenant General Mushtaq Ahmad Baig was killed in February 2008. (*Courtesy of the Directorate of Inter-Service Public Relations*)

Chief of Army Staff, General Ashtaq Kiyani. (*Courtesy of the Directorate of Inter-Service Public Relations*)

The author calls on President Zia in 1985 and, twenty years later, on President Musharraf.
(*Courtesy of the Directorate of Inter-Service Public Relations*)

innocent person a defiler of the Quran were he or she to offend against a landowner's greed-induced illegal land-grabbing, however contrary to the true precepts of the holy book and its interpretations their own actions might be. The Constitution was being violated, and the army was being drawn into endorsement of its violation; and the army did not relish its role as courts-martial provider to the nation.

In February 1999 the Supreme Court ruled against the use of military tribunals, and there was nothing – for once – that Mr Sharif could do about a body that went against his express desires. It was unfortunate that in the meantime tribunals had ordered the death penalty for two offenders and that the hangings had been carried out, but the Prime Minister's opinion that the military courts had 'shown good results' and that 'terrorists must take this idea out of their minds that they will be able to regain their foothold. Civility, truth and justice will be victorious in every circumstance. My mission is only peace and justice'[16] was interesting, given that two months before, Mr Sharif had said, 'Murderers and rapists roam around freely for years. Such people should be hanged publicly and their cases decided in twenty-four hours, three days or seven days.'[17] It seemed that justice in the eyes of Pakistan's government was to be weighed in favour of sharia law, objection to which Bill, according to Sharif, would indicate that the opponent was not a true Muslim. (It is presumed that Sharif did not mean that rapists should be hanged publicly *before* their cases were heard, but merely that hearings should be conducted rapidly.) It has to be said that the number of killings in Karachi and elsewhere in Sindh did decline markedly in the period of quasi-martial law, and did not again reach the appalling levels of 1998, when there was a total of over 800 murders, but the human rights' connotations of the Ordinance and the illegal actions taken as a result of its promulgation cannot be ignored. The army had been assured that its role was beneficial to the country, which it undoubtedly was, in the sense that malefactors were punished and removed from the society on which they preyed, but procedures were not satisfactory in law. As observed by the perceptive Brigadier Siddiqi, 'The question ... is whether the army is to be used for law and order enforcement and administration of summary justice, or to settle old political scores,' and it was this latter aspect with which the army was less than satisfied, according to one senior officer who wrote to the author at the time. Much of the slaughter was politically motivated, and was it right to place the army in the position of being associated with political matters, even if the overall benefits were tangible?

The army was to have other challenges in the coming months, not the least of which was the curious affair of incursions into Indian-administered Kashmir which gravely heightened tension in the subcontinent and led to even greater mistrust of Pakistan by India.

Kargil

The illegal incursion into Indian-administered Kashmir in early 1999, undetected by Indian forces until 6 May, was an aberration on the part of Pakistan. The aim of the operation has not been enunciated, and it is doubtful if it will be ever revealed – perhaps because the whole affair just seemed a good idea at the time, and got out of hand.

Analysis of the logistics of the incursion has drawn Western observers to the conclusion that planning and preliminary operations began during winter 1998/99, with movement of mujahideen from camps in Afghanistan for training by the Northern Light Infantry (NLI) around Skardu,[18] and considerable movement by the NLI and other Pakistan Army troops in the areas of Astore, Skardu, the Deosai Plains and forward to the Line of Control (LoC). In the event, mujahideen were not involved in organized combat.

I have walked and climbed in the precise areas in which movement across the LoC took place, in the course of a two-week visit to 3NLI, based at Gultari in the Shingo Valley. I visited the Battalion's picquets at heights up to 14,000 feet overlooking the LoC (some are 2,000 feet higher). The terrain is as beautiful and impressive as it is daunting and dangerous. Although the Line is not marked on the ground it is described fully in a document dated 11 December 1972,[19] and soldiers would find little difficulty in establishing where it runs vis-à-vis map and ground. It is incorrect to claim that the Line is indistinct. There can be no plausible claim made that the intrusion was in some manner justified because there is dubiety or confusion as to the Line's location.

Pakistan stated that no regular troops were involved in the incursions. Strictly speaking this might be so, at least initially, because the NLI is in theory subordinate to the Ministry of the Interior, but the Force Commander Northern Areas (HQ Gilgit) commands the NLI through the brigades in Astore and Skardu, and he, in turn, is subordinate to Commander X Corps in Rawalpindi. Almost the entire NLI was involved in one way or another with the incursion, together with other infantry units. Fire support was provided by regular army artillery units whose guns were moved along the Shingo Valley.[20] Stockpiles of ammunition were brought forward from Gilgit and from the south via the Skardu road along the Indus.

It appears that only a few militants were involved in the incursions, and that several hundred NLI and other regular soldiers occupied about 130 picquets on the Indian side of the Line from late March to early May. Indian troops had begun thinning out from the higher positions the previous September, as is usual, and completed their withdrawal at the end of October. The commander of 121 Brigade (HQ Kargil), Brigadier Surinder Singh,[21] is said to have written to his superiors concerning his threat perception in the area. This would be a normal action, as any commander in a sensitive sector would keep his higher HQ informed as to his appreciation of the situation (in the military term), but what is contentious is the substance of his communication. The war of words over the Brigadier's dismissal in early June and his claim to have informed his superiors of an unusual threat in his tactical area of operations will probably continue, but if he claimed (as has been leaked by official sources) that he was not permitted to send out reconnaissance or fighting patrols to check the area, then both he and his superiors are on dangerous ground. No commander requires permission to send out patrols unless this caveat has been included in formation Standing Orders or a specific directive to him. He would inform higher HQ and flanking formations of his patrol plan, but the converse is that if no patrolling had been done then the commander and staff at the higher HQ (3rd Division, Major General V.S. Budhwar) should have been uneasy that there was no information coming in about an important sector. It would be standard operating procedure to report on snow-melt, for example, if for no other reason than to give adequate notice to units about when they would be expected to reoccupy their summer positions. Commanders are (or ought to be) unhappy if there is no regular flow of information about terrain and movement conditions, for they never know when they might be required to commit troops to battle. The Line of Control has never been a holiday resort, and patrols from both sides have tended to stretch the envelope and even trail their coats by what General Pervez Musharraf called 'aggressive patrolling' – in other words, moving across the Line.

No matter the outcome of Indian official inquiries into the matter,[22] the fact is that there was failure of intelligence. Quite why some elements in India have tried to place the blame for this upon the intelligence services themselves is unclear, because it is the duty of soldiers on the ground to report on what is occurring – or not occurring – in their area. Intelligence agencies can employ many means of surveillance, but nobody expects a RAW (Research and Analysis Wing) or IB (Intelligence Bureau) man to be leaping from peak to peak at 16,000 feet while soldiers are snug in base camps below. If the US, with its enormously sophisticated technical intelligence methods, did not detect the build-up and incursions, it is hardly fair to blame IB and RAW.

No outside observer appears to have been aware of the movement to the Line of Control. While this is a sad commentary on the effectiveness of the Central Intelligence Agency (which at one time would have had at least a man in Skardu, where there was much activity before the incursions began, but mistakenly de-emphasized 'Humint' sources during the disastrous tenure of Admiral Stansfield Turner in the Carter presidency), it is also an interesting facet of the operations of the United Nations Military Observer

Group in India and Pakistan (UNMOGIP) which maintains observers in Astore and Skardu during the summer months. (It used to have a field station in Kargil, but Indian pressure and UN weakness led to its closure in the mid-1980s.) It is the task of UNMOGIP to 'observe and report on the quantum of forces' on each side of the Line, but India forbids it to perform its duties in Indian-administered Kashmir (where it 'maintains a presence'), although Pakistan facilitates the 'field tasks' (patrols) carried out by observers on its side of the Line. The problem is that the Mission is only forty-four strong, because of Indian pressure, and does not have enough observers to man its posts all the time, never mind increasing their number to a desirable level.

Pakistan, of course, would not have been happy about United Nations officers sitting in Astore, Skardu, Minimarg, Gultari or Dalunang in early 1999, because they would have detected movement and notified United Nations HQ in New York, whence this information would have quickly reached New Delhi. It is ironic that the very element so vehemently opposed by India, had it been adequately constituted and properly deployed, could have alerted India to the fact that something untoward was taking place in the Kargil-Dras sectors. (The statement by Pakistan's then Foreign Minister that 'no one knows where they [the infiltrators] come from and who they are'[23] is, with respect to Mr Sartaj Aziz, quite unbelievable.) There is also the aspect of 'open-source' information. General Pervez Musharraf visited the Northern Areas/Pakistan-administered Kashmir twice during the winter. Defence attachés (DAs), whether Indian or of other nationalities, generally maintain a log of movements of senior officers in their host country and try to find out what they are doing. (This can pay remarkable dividends.) Disruption to a pattern sends signals, and even if the DA himself cannot determine why a senior officer should make a certain visit, his alerting of other of his country's agencies as to unusual movements can result in closer examination, perhaps leading to interesting revelations.

First reports in the Indian media were optimistic about how the militants were being dealt with during Operation Vijay, as the Indian military action was named. There was talk of 'mopping-up', but the mood soon changed as casualties rose and Indian aircraft were shot down. A Mi-17 helicopter and a MiG-21 fighter were destroyed by missiles, and another fighter crashed through technical failure. The MiG-21 is a singularly inappropriate aircraft to commit to tactical air support in mountains, and it is not surprising that operations had to be scaled back in order to keep up morale-boosting appearances. Contrary to Indian press reports, Mirage 2000 sorties reported to be using laser-guided bombs were ineffective. (It is questionable that such ordnance was used, as there do not appear to have been electronic intercepts of the readily-identifiable procedures that would have been employed.) India's command system was inadequate in many ways, not the least being the inability to use combat air support until the return of the army chief from an overseas visit, when he gave permission. The infiltrators were dug in and capable of maintaining most positions indefinitely because they had a plenitude of rations and other stores, but, contrary to the opinion of some commentators at the time (including myself on BBC radio and other international media), not all of this came over the LoC, because much had been left behind by Indian troops the previous year. There was no point in removing it, as it would have had to be carried back again when the positions were reoccupied, so there were considerable quantities of food and heating oil available. This, and the fact that most of the bunkers were strongly constructed of concrete with metal reinforcement, caused speculation that the operation must have involved much more effort than it did. Certainly it was an impressive and major undertaking, involving much carriage of rations and stores, but most bunkers appear to have been existing Indian positions that had been developed over decades.

The matter of alleged torture of Indian soldiers was important because of its effect within India. I wrote at the time that:

> The temperature in the mountains is zero and below but has risen markedly in New Delhi and Islamabad, in part because Pakistan reported that India has used chemical weapons, and largely because of Indian allegations of torture of prisoners of war. The former claim is nonsense, for many technical reasons, but the accusation of torture is more serious, if only because it has inflamed public opinion in India. There is not an Indian who disbelieves that the half-dozen soldiers whose bodies were delivered to the Indian army (across the Line from the Pakistani side, to the significance of which little publicity has been given) were tortured and put to death after capture. There is no point in attempting to question the Indian version – although any soldier who has seen the result on a human body of concentrated firing from an ambush will know that the victims resemble pulped and messy colanders of meat, with eyes and teeth shattered and bits of flesh torn away by the lacerating impact of point-blank bullets. It was the fact that eyes had been destroyed – 'gouged out' – that particularly upset Indian public opinion.[24]

It has been acknowledged in some quarters in India that the claims were exaggerated, but the damage had been done and it would be a brave Indian commentator who would deny that torture took place. The Kargil episode confounded what little trust India had in Pakistan (as established by the Lahore meeting between Prime Ministers Nawaz Sharif and A.B.

Vajpayee in February 1999), and it was easy to believe what was being retailed in the media as a result of statements by government spokesmen. There may have been hesitancy, later, about the truth of the stories, especially as the matter was not taken up by the international media (which would have been more than happy to expand on such a juicy story had they considered it credible), but tales of atrocities are easier to spread than to deny, even if the originator sincerely wishes to do that.

There was terrible irony in the gleeful description in *India Today* of the body of what might have been a soldier of the NLI:

> He is a prized possession. The sight of him motivates the men and gears them for the next round of battle. Seeing him at the make-shift army headquarters in Dras sends their adrenaline pumping. The dead Pakistani Army regular – hung on a tree before his body was buried and a grid reference made on the map in accordance with the Geneva Convention – was a morale booster. More than 439 Pakistani casualties so far.[25]

This is crass. No soldier worthy of the name would have his morale boosted by the sight of a rotting corpse, and it is ghoulish and macabre to claim that they would. They might – such is the way of soldiers in all armies – have a joke about it to try to reassure themselves that death will never beckon them, but anyone who receives a pump of adrenaline from seeing a dead body is seriously disturbed. And the Geneva Convention does not approve of soldiers' bodies being hanged on trees. That reporter was sick.

At the end of May it was recognized by Nawaz Sharif that the incursion was regarded in the US and elsewhere as a desperate gambit on the part of Pakistan to do something about Kashmir. It did not appear to be understood exactly what Pakistan was trying to achieve, but, then, it seemed not to be known within Pakistan itself what the government wished to do. It is difficult to accept that the operation was conducted without the knowledge of Mr Sharif and his small circle of advisers, if only because the Prime Minister did not deny it (and, after all, the head of ISI, an important man in this affair, was his personal appointee). Sharif had achieved the departure of a president and a chief justice and declined to refuse the resignation of a popular army chief; he was the most powerful prime minister in the history of Pakistan, and if he considered the Kargil venture to be an erratic initiative on the part of the army he was quite capable of dismissing its chief if he so wished. He stated on 2 June that the Lahore process was 'in grievous danger of being derailed',[26] which was ludicrously at odds with reality because the understanding reached at Lahore was already stone dead, but continued that 'The urgent necessity is to defuse the current situation' which nobody would have denied. The problem for Sharif was how to do it, because New Delhi was in no mood to compromise on anything.

India was angry, and had every right to be. The Union Home Minister, Mr L.K. Advani was outspoken concerning Pakistan's perfidy and reflected what was in the minds of many by saying, 'It is a case of an armed intrusion by Pakistan, amounting to armed aggression.'[27] India was determined to evict the invaders, but was finding this difficult. 'The armed forces did not quite anticipate this battle and were unprepared for it,' wrote the respected defence analyst Manoj Joshi in August,[28] and listed some of the major deficiencies that caused the campaign to drag on and cost so many lives. These included lack of cold-weather clothing, protective vests, surveillance equipment, high-altitude helicopters and radios. There was no excuse for the shortages, because the Indian Army has nine mountain divisions and should have had stocks of equipment suitable for operations in their eponymous terrain. The fact that there were no night-vision devices is a reflection of grave incompetence within the procurement system, and Joshi is absolutely right to castigate politicians and senior officers for 'pushing big-ticket items instead of investing in equipping the soldier better'. There is much glamour in the thunder of a Su-30 combat aircraft, but little in a decent rifle, which is badly needed by the Indian Army. There was no lack of courage on the part of Indian troops of all ranks, and, as always happens in good armies, there was a high ratio of young officers killed compared to the number of deaths of the brave soldiers they led so well.

The Northern Light Infantry and other Pakistani troops were brave, too, and casualties were considerable.[29] But Indian soldiers were at a disadvantage in fighting over unknown terrain, for most troops were brought in from elsewhere – which was why they were amazed, initially, at the Pakistanis' dug-in positions, not realizing that many of these were well-established Indian defended localities. The bunkers were small, difficult to locate, bristled with weapons, and had steep and difficult approaches, some of which were mined. Attacking such positions would be a nightmare for any soldier. It was doubly difficult for units that were brought in to the area hastily and whose men were not fully acclimatized, and it is regrettable that some were required to operate at these heights without acclimatization, which is a comparatively long process. They would be fit, of course, and would adjust more readily than most to the demands imposed on them, but committing them to battle before they were ready, and without adequate equipment and clothing (as evidenced by reporters and official photographs), was an act of desperation. It is not known what part was played by prompting from New Delhi in the early stages (and there is little of relevance in the Kargil Commission Report),[30] but it can be surmised that military leaders were under pressure to evict the intruders, in addition to their own natural inclination to get on with the job. It is easy to be critical, afterwards, but there are disturbing facets of this campaign that are reminiscent of the 1962 period, and it is hoped for the sake of the Indian Army that its internal investigations result in forthright recommendations that will be adopted by the politicians and pushed through the moribund civil service system, which is more to blame for equipment deficiencies than either politicians or generals.

One thing for which the bureaucrats in New Delhi cannot be blamed was the shortage of spares for Bofors 155mm guns, which was caused by an embargo that followed bribery in contract negotiations. Depots and barracks in India were scoured, and over a hundred guns were cannibalized to ensure that those hastily moved to and around Indian-administered Kashmir could continue firing. Ammunition was a problem, too, and expensive to acquire at over $1,000 per round.[31] Conversely, Pakistan had few problems with artillery, not only because it had adequate spares, but most of its ammunition is manufactured by Pakistan Ordnance Factories,[32] as are spare parts for many equipments, of which there was a considerable stockpile. It is of course bizarre that these two members of the Commonwealth should have been shelling each other and causing so much destruction and loss of life – but the whole affair was verging on the surreal.

Pakistan kept on talking about talks, and one could not but feel an occasional twinge of sympathy for spokesmen who were trying to defend the indefensible against a growing barrage of adverse observations around the world. Some foreign comment was muted or disguised, with the intention of defusing an ugly situation, but India sometimes claimed support where none was evident, and on occasions damaged international goodwill by putting into headline news a 'spin' on statements that was undesirable from the point of view of those making them. Comments by the G-8 nations were one instance of this, and a source close to their deliberations informed the author that there was no need for India to 'reinterpret' what the G-8 communiqué had said, 'weak as it was', because the Group's critical stance had been made 'crystal clear' to Pakistan. Matters were becoming serious for Pakistan on the political front, although the intruders were difficult to dislodge and Indian casualties continued to rise. A distinguished Indian defence analyst and commentator, General V.R. Raghavan, observed that 'The Kargil aggression has inevitably ended the good faith and trust which was painstakingly built up over the last few years' and that talks were 'an essential medium for understanding each other's needs and demonstrating the willingness to go the extra mile',[33] but understandably, there were political considerations on the Indian side.

Mr Vajpayee was facing elections in September and it would have been impossible for him to appear to be backing down in the face of aggression, especially as public opinion was hardening as time went on, and voices advocating war were raised throughout the land. Bodies were being delivered to families in villages, towns and cities, and resentment against Pakistan was high and growing more intense as the weeks went by. The political problem was to keep channelling this resentment towards the 'enemy' and not to let it be deflected towards the government. Up-beat briefings, playing down equipment deficiencies, infusion of the idea that objective comment was not acceptable because this would be criticizing the gallantry of 'our boys' (a cynical political ploy not confined to India) – all these were important to the BJP's election campaign. At all costs the momentum had to be kept up against the invaders, but the problem was that they were so difficult to dislodge that casualties would undoubtedly increase – which they did, alas, dramatically – and it was difficult to gauge just how much the Indian public would stand.

As it happened, the Indian public would stand a great deal and the government was able to maintain pressure on Pakistan to withdraw without making any concessions itself. The US endorsed a proposed visit by Pakistan's Foreign Minister to New Delhi, and then agreed to further the proposal that Mr Sharif himself should go there for talks, but although this was initially acceptable to New Delhi, the government read the mood of the country otherwise – and correctly. On no account could there be a visit by the Prime Minister of Pakistan. The manner in which the initiative was killed was as Byzantine as might be expected in the circumstances, but Islamabad continued to be optimistic about talks and was living in a dream world, as evidenced by the cabinet's 'serious concern' about 'the unwarranted Indian military operations in the area across the Line of Control involving heavy artillery, helicopter gunships and jet aircraft'.[34] This was ridiculous, as was known by India and the rest of the world. (In fact, there were no gunships: the Indian Air Force's Mi-25 attack helicopters cannot fly above 12,000 feet, and although it was claimed by India that troop-carrier Mi-17s were used as gunships, and there was a photograph of one apparently firing rockets, the official record shows that there were only thirty-one sorties by Mi-17s throughout the whole period.) The US became exasperated, as well it might, but eventually got Pakistan off the hook – and India, too, because in spite of the hype about success, Operation Vijay was a horrible, brutal slog in classic infantry fashion. The operations of 18 Grenadiers in the battle of 'Tiger Hill' (to take but one example) were superb, but were immensely costly against well dug-in and strongly supported NLI troops.

There were unofficial attempts to end the fighting, amongst which was the dispatch of the distinguished Indian journalist R.K. Mishra and a notable diplomat, Vivek Katju to Islamabad, reciprocated by a visit to New Delhi by Pakistan's former Foreign Secretary, Niaz Naik, an admirable emissary of dignity, acumen and experience. Openings to dialogue were effected, but the moves resulted in internal criticism in both countries and, although valuable in establishing a modest approach to future personal contact, had no chance of success.

In the end, Mr Sharif, failing to obtain support of any sort, even from China (whom one would have thought might not be averse to making things difficult for India, given its own little-reported incursion at Daulat Beg Oldi on the Indian side of the Line of Actual Control in Aksai Chin), had to crave audience with the American President to obtain a fig leaf that would enable him to order retreat with a semblance of dignity.

There had been fears that clashes could spread to the point that forces along the border would become involved, and that this might lead to a nuclear exchange. Much pressure was brought to bear on India and Pakistan (in spite of what is claimed to the contrary) to refrain from widening the conflict,[35] and although both sides claim that the 'nuclear deterrent' ensured that their governments behaved 'responsibly', the fact is that existence of basic nuclear devices served to push much of the rest of the world to exert influence on the countries to refrain from taking more aggressive steps.[36] It was assessed that a nuclear war in the subcontinent, especially given the lack of systems for weapons' control, would be a world disaster and not just a local one. It was not deterrence in the classic sense, although Islamabad and New Delhi tried to present their avoidance of conflict-expansion in the context of cold war nuclear theology.

A worrying aspect of the conflict was an increase in attacks by militants within Indian-administered Kashmir, especially against what are considered 'hard targets' – security forces' fighting patrols and well-guarded camps. There were instances of merciless murder of civilians, especially in Hindu villages and hamlets, but the aim appeared to be to demonstrate the militants' ability to extend their fight to debilitate and demoralize paramilitary forces, especially the Rashtriya Rifles who were bearing the brunt of internal security duties in the absence of regular troops redeployed along the Line of Control. Escalation of these operations was disconcerting because India, with good reason, stated that Pakistan was supporting the militants, and there was even further distrust of Islamabad by New Delhi.

In the Kargil affair Pakistan behaved outrageously and contrary to international norms – and, of some importance, inconsistently with the Simla [now Shimla] Accord of 1971.[37] India, in spite of politically motivated bluster and understandable but excessive nationalism, had its confidence shaken by the Kargil debacle. Over 600 soldiers were killed and some 1,800 wounded in a few weeks,[38] as against 1,150 dead and 3,000 incapacitated in almost three years in the disastrous 'peacekeeping' operation in Sri Lanka

(July 1987–April 1990). This is a dreadful toll to be exacted and it would have been very much higher if the intruders had not withdrawn as a result of mediation.

Senior Indian figures stated flatly there was no outside mediation concerning the Kargil affair, but President Clinton spoke with Mr Sharif and Mr Vajpayee at length. While Mr Vajpayee did state bluntly that there was no question of mediation by a third party,[39] he cannot deny that he was informed that Mr Sharif would be going to Washington, that he (Mr Vajpayee) was told he was welcome should he wish to pay such a visit, that Mr Clinton was going to use his good offices to persuade Nawaz Sharif that the bloodstained disaster had gone on long enough and that withdrawal of the Pakistanis had better take place *ek dum* (or words to that effect). And so it happened, after the 4th of July meeting.

The Indian Army's assaults on the heights in the Dras and Kargil sectors cost its gallant regiments dearly. The NLI and other Pakistani soldiers fought well and tenaciously before evacuating the fourteen posts from which they were driven. Withdrawal from the remaining 120 or so defended localities was on orders from the Pakistan side of the Line of Control. Casualties were high, perhaps as many as 400,[40] and many of these know no grave, no honour and receive no acknowledgement of their dedication. May they all, of both sides, rest in peace, and may their families take consolation in the fact that they were doing their duty according to their code and oaths, whatever these may have been, of whatever faiths they espoused. It was not their fault that Kashmir is a disputed territory whose status could have been resolved long ago were it not for the intransigence of successive governments in both countries.

The Indian government issued a statement on 5 July concerning the withdrawal from Indian-administered territory in Kashmir. It is ungracious, as might be expected from an offended party, and had a sting in the tail for those countries who wish both India and Pakistan well, and who would be more than happy to offer their assistance in furthering good relations between them.

> We have seen the US-Pakistan joint statement issued in Washington yesterday. Our US interlocutors have informed us that 'concrete steps' referred to in the statement mean withdrawal by Pakistan of their forces from our side of the Line of Control in the Kargil sector.
>
> We have also noted the sequencing of steps agreed to in the statement, that only after withdrawal is completed will other contemplated steps be initiated. We hope Pakistan will heed this call immediately. We will be watching developments on the ground.
>
> We reaffirm that Pakistan's armed intrusion and aggression has to be vacated.

Our military aggression [*sic*] in the Kargil sector, which has been initiated for this purpose, is making steady progress.

It will continue with full force until the aggressors are cleared out, and the *status quo ante* on the Line of Control fully restored.

One word about the Lahore process. It is direct and bilateral. In this process there is no place whatsoever for any third party involvement. The same is true for any other aspect of India-Pakistan relations.[41]

There was no need for this sort of pietistic stuff (although there may have been chuckles about 'our military aggression') and Washington considered its tone inappropriate. (A US diplomat in Washington informed me at the time that India's attitude of jubilation was 'unfortunate'.) It was regarded unfavourably by the invaders, and a spokesman for the United Jihad Council wasted his breath by stating that 'A withdrawal from Kargil would be detrimental to the freedom struggle for Kashmir and ... the mujahideen will fight to their last breath to free their motherland from Indian forces of aggression'.[42]

India was entitled to be satisfied that the intruders had been withdrawn, but political point-scoring was difficult to resist. The BJP and its allies were determined to be seen as the winning team and the perceptive Dinesh Kumar wrote that 'They are bound to hold celebrations like they did after the May 1998 Pokhran explosions, and would, in keeping with the nature of politics in the country, even seek to capitalize on the "victory" keeping the forthcoming elections in mind.'[43] The interim government did indeed claim that the Kargil 'war' had been 'won' by the all-seeing BJP coalition, and on at least one occasion placed enormous photographs of the service chiefs and an Agni missile on an election platform. The mood of belligerence was fostered in many quarters, and although in Pakistan there was a fair amount of war-talk, there were fears, too, that India might go the extra mile – not towards talks, but towards conflict. The army chief made speeches emphasizing that the country was prepared to defend itself, but the mood in the army seemed to vary from outright bellicosity to fairly strong criticism of the Sharif government for getting the nation into a difficult position.

The government in Islamabad tried to put as brave a face on the debacle as it could, but the mood within Pakistan was largely of confusion. The army was shaken, and young officers, especially, felt betrayed. There was some plain speaking when the Chief of the Army Staff toured military bases, and morale was badly affected in some units. The entire episode seemed so unnecessary and harmful to Pakistan's already shaky image abroad that explanation appeared at best superfluous and at worst mere political ground-shifting. Mr Sharif's national broadcast on 12 July was worth giving,[44] however, even if it was shaky on the aim of the invasion.

He acknowledged that there was 'no secret that the threat of a big war with India is looming, by the way things have deteriorated between India and Pakistan', which he could hardly deny, but then he said that 'I think the basic purpose of the mujahideen occupation of Kargil was to attract world attention to the Kashmir issue ... They have fully succeeded in that objective and they have also practically proved our stand that the Kashmir issue is a nuclear flashpoint.' Of course, no Pakistani troops occupied Kargil but the question must be put as to when did Mr Sharif know of 'the basic purpose'? He approved of it, but did he approve the means of achieving it? There was not much point in 'proving' that Kashmir is a nuclear flashpoint, as many concerned people have been saying this since the time of the nuclear tests[45] – and there is a danger that proof might one day be obtained with unexpected finality.

There is little wonder that Mr Vajpayee's vexation with Pakistan was not diminished by the address, because Mr Sharif stated that 'During talks in Lahore I told Indian prime minister Vajpayee that we have achieved nothing through war, and after every war we moved to another war'. This is mind-reeling stuff, on the same level as India's contention that it exploded nuclear bombs in order to further the cause of nuclear disarmament. Deep talking to deep, obviously. General Talat Masood, sagacious as ever, wrote that:

> The Kargil crisis has once again exposed the bankruptcy of Pakistan's national policy. Events in and around Kargil brought India and Pakistan dangerously close to an all-out war, dealt a shattering blow to the peace process, have done immense damage to the already faltering economy, isolated Pakistan internationally, and proved highly divisive internally.[46]

And Dr Maleeha Lodhi, analysing the affair in a wide-ranging document, included the observations that:

> The failure to objectively assess national strengths and vulnerabilities during the Kargil crisis was in large part a consequence of ... unstructured, personalised decision-making, and led to the avoidable diplomatic debacle ... In using with an international audience the same propaganda techniques and tools, even idiom, that the government believes serves it so well in the domestic sphere proved utterly and predictably counterproductive ...
>
> In the post-Kargil situation, Pakistan faces critical choices on both domestic and external fronts ... Policy clarity is urgently needed about which direction the leadership wants to take the country. Playing holy warriors this week and men of peace the next betrays an infirmity and insincerity of purpose that leaves the country leaderless and

directionless. But if flip-flops and government by muddling through, cum policy reversal continues, the dangers to Pakistan's stability will only mount.[47]

These sobering observations (much resented by the Sharif brothers and their henchmen) are applicable to government direction of the armed forces, and she notes that it was only on the eve of Mr Sharif's visit to Washington that there was a meeting of the Defence Committee of the Cabinet (DCC) which, almost unbelievably, was the first of the year.[48] It is essential that the higher direction of war should be understood by those in government whose duty it is to direct the armed forces (when democracy returns) and that the entire command and control system of the services be restructured, as outlined below.

Later comment and analyses concerning the Kargil episode have been in the main more in sorrow than in anger, at least within Pakistan, but those imagining that the memoirs of President Musharraf would throw light on what happened were to be confused and disappointed in equal measure. *The News* newspaper of 5 October 2006 encapsulated feeling by observing that:

President Musharraf's book[49] seems to have opened up a veritable Pandora's box on many controversial matters. One of them [is] Kargil on which we now have at least three versions – President Musharraf's, prime minister Nawaz Sharif's and India's. Given that all three differ vastly from each other – in India, as was to be expected, the president's version has been dismissed as a pack of untruths – it is only reasonable that there be an impartial inquiry conducted into what happened in 1999 so that the people of Pakistan at least know what actually happened and what the truth is. In his book, the president paints Kargil as a brilliant manoeuvre which from a purely military and strategic point of view was an outstanding tactic which helped bring the Kashmir dispute to the world's attention. Mr Sharif, the Indians and those in among the pacifist and anti-war ranks in this country have a completely different take on this arguing that it was badly executed, needlessly costly in that hundreds died for no eventual strategic gain and that far from bringing India to the negotiating table (on Kashmir), it almost provoked another war between the two neighbours. In other words, those who oppose the president's assessment of Kargil say that the peace process began and continues not because of Kargil but despite it.

One has to say that after Kargil ended, the Indian side did at least hold an inquiry into it and stock was taken of various intelligence blunders. No such thing happened in Pakistan, with people divided, some calling it a major and impressive military tactic while many others saw it as something needless that would unnecessarily provoke a larger and much-better armed neighbour ... Kargil may have been controversial and certainly has its detractors but it was an important episode in this country's history and the people of Pakistan need to know the truth about it. This will also lay to rest all claims and counter- claims of those who wish ill of Pakistan and believe that it has something to hide on Kargil.

The editorial was a reasonable plea for a move to transparency, but is unlikely to have any effect no matter what democratic government achieves power in Pakistan, there being no desire on the part of most people to rock a very sensitive boat. It is strange that those involved at a high level, both political and military, have refrained from divulging details of what went on. This is possibly because there were so few people privy to the affair and so few details to give, anyway.

In 1999, a Pakistani senior officer[50] and his wife stayed with my wife and I in our house. At that time I was writing about Kargil, as was the rather better-known (and, to be frank, much better) author, Victoria Schofield, who was updating her book on Kashmir.[51] We had exchanged news and views on the subject and had come to the conclusion that the official version coming out of Pakistan at the earliest stage – that the force that had crossed the Line of Control was composed of militants – seemed believable. It was, we thought, a strange, perhaps semi-accidental situation that had got out of hand, and I mentioned this to the general. He guffawed ruefully and said that he wished that were true. He had been at a meeting at GHQ chaired by General Musharraf and attended by all of the most senior officers, including the air and navy chiefs, at which it was apparent that almost nobody, not even the heads of the other Services and most of the principal staff officers in GHQ, of whom my guest was one, had been told about the operation before it began. Further, he said, there may have been a few militants involved, but it was almost entirely an army affair although, strictly speaking, the Northern Light Infantry were not regular troops of the Pakistan Army, but in theory subordinate to the Interior Ministry. This was astonishing news; and after our guests went to bed I telephoned Victoria to warn her that we were both in danger of looking a bit silly if we pursued our present line. We could not indicate the source but we had other ways of checking, and it quickly became apparent that the operation had been a nonsense whose tactical execution may have been efficient enough, but whose effect was entirely negative in every way: professionally, politically, strategically and internationally. It is amazing that General Musharraf was able to count on so much military loyalty later in the year when he deposed the government.

After Kargil

In 1999 the country was far from stable: corruption continued on a massive scale, the economy was in tatters and the rule of law was all but defunct. The 'Anti-Terrorism Act 1997 (Amendment) Ordinance' was repressive and reminiscent of the worst periods of martial law. Press freedom was under continuous threat, and it was only international outrage that resulted in the release of the courageous publisher and editor, Najam Sethi, and cessation of harassment of various newspapers, especially the Jang Group. According to Human Rights Watch:

> The government finally charged Sethi on June 1 with sedition, promoting communal enmity, condemning the creation of Pakistan and advocating the abolition of its sovereignty, and violating the Prevention of Anti-National Activities Act. The charges were withdrawn a day later, after the government failed to produce evidence before the Supreme Court justifying Sethi's detention and following international condemnation of the demonstrably illegal manoeuvres by the government. Although Sethi was released on 2 June, the authorities seized his passport and his wife's bank accounts. On 24th June, Zafar Ali Shah, the parliamentary secretary for parliamentary affairs, filed a petition with the chief election commissioner seeking an inquiry into Sethi's religious status. Shah suggested that if Sethi were found to be a non-Muslim, he should lose his right to vote.[52]

It appeared that the government of Nawaz Sharif would go to almost any lengths to destroy those who opposed it or even commented adversely on its erratic performance.

In September 1999, Benazir Bhutto and her husband were found guilty in Pakistan of corruption involving deals with a Swiss company. Ms Bhutto had been overseas since April, and decided to remain out of the country. Her husband was already in prison in Pakistan and remained there until freed on bail in 2004. According to a BBC report: 'Soon after the conviction, audiotapes of conversations between the judge and some top aides of then Prime Minister Nawaz Sharif were discovered that showed that the judge had been under pressure to convict.'[53]

The threats made against the Editor of *The News*, Rawalpindi, Dr Maleeha Lodhi, by a member of the government were bizarre, and resembled those of the Nazis against the German Press in the mid-1930s. There was a nationwide strike caused by proposals to institute a sales tax. Violence against women was actually endorsed by the ruling party, and Human Rights Watch recorded that: 'On August 3, the Pakistani Senate voted to block debate over a draft resolution condemning incidents of violence against women. Only four members of the Senate voted in favour of discussing the draft, itself a substantial dilution of an earlier text that specifically condemned [Ms Samia] Sarwar's murder [a so-called "Honour killing"].[54]

The government's aim appeared to be to enunciate grandiose projects of which nothing more was heard after headlines have been obtained. There was no credible political Opposition, and religious militancy was on the rise.[55] The military were confused, but although resentful of Sharif's conduct it seemed that they were prepared to live with it. Certainly none of the senior officers at the time has indicated otherwise, and one wonders whether there would have been an army takeover had Nawaz Sharif not decided to appoint a new army chief while Musharraf was overseas.

Notes

1. General Karamat to author, 23 August 1999.
2. General Karamat to author, 22 August 1999.
3. The US and several other countries were aware of detail concerning the nuclear programme. It was surprising – and fascinating – just how much was known. The US, in consequence of this knowledge and Congressional requirements, had to curtail all aid. Other countries did not have such legislation and could continue as if there were no nuclear programme, although they conducted a robust diplomatic campaign behind the scenes. The G-8, and especially Japan, were most active. In Canberra the author, on returning from a visit to Pakistan in September 1985 as guest of General Zia, attended an intelligence briefing for the Chief of the General Staff at which US imagery of nuclear facilities was shown.
4. A US definition, as covered in most advanced military colleges.
5. Correspondence with the author, 18 August 1999.
6. 'Pakistan Army Chief quits amidst controversy', Andrew Hill, Reuters, 13:25, 10-07-98.
7. Press Release by the Directorate General of Inter Service Public Relations (ISPR), 6 October 1998.
8. See the excellent chronology in Craig Baxter & Charles Kennedy (eds), Pakistan 2000, OUP, 2001; also Kux, 2001. The IMF cancelled a mission to Pakistan in October 1998 but in November the US leant on the IMF/WB and a $5.5 billion bailout package was arranged.
9. The High Commissioner, through no fault of his own, did not know that the British Prime Minister would call on Sharif to say a few words – but not a speech as such – at a luncheon in Downing Street. Sharif, inarticulate as ever, was furious. The High Commissioner was sacked.
10. From which he was appointed Pakistan's ambassador to the US in 2004, an admirable choice.
11. Conversation with the author.
12. See http://www.presidentofpakistan.gov.pk/Biography.aspx
13. 'Power companies to be handed over to army', The News, 23 October 1998.
14. 'Text of Pakistan Armed Forces Ordinance, 1998', Dawn, 21 November 1998.
15. 'The Constitution of the Islamic Republic of Pakistan', edited and introduced by Makhdoom Ali Khan, Pakistan Law House, Karachi, 1990. The 14th Amendment curtailed the powers of the President, the 15th sought to establish the 'Supremacy of the Quran and Sunnah' (see 'Implications of the 15th Amendment, Asma Jahangir, The News, 13 September 1998), and further restriction was placed on the President on 24 December 1998 (see 'President's powers further curtailed', The Nation, 25 December 1998).
16. 'Pakistan PM bows to ruling against military courts', Raja Asghar, Reuters, 11:12, 01-19-99.
17. 'Pakistan PM calls for Taliban-style laws', Andrew Hill, Reuters, 08:50, 11-17-98.

18. Report of a conversation between a British visitor to Pakistan and two mujahideen in Gilgit in July, supplied to the author on 16 August 1999. They had been in militants' camps in Afghanistan during the US cruise missile attacks and stated that there were 'British Muslims' amongst the mujahideen at Kargil, a claim supported by a senior officer of RAW in New Delhi in a telephone conversation with the author, 24 August 1999.

19. *Delineation of the Line of Control in Jammu and Kashmir Resulting from the Cease Fire Line of 17 December 1971, in Accordance with the Simla Agreement of 2 July 1972* (UN Document dated 11 December 1972. The author has copy No. 14.)

20. Bammi, Lieutenant General Y.M., *Kargil, The Impregnable Conquered*, Gorkha Publishers, Delhi, 2002 is 558 pages of relentless praise for Indian forces, but in the case of Pakistan artillery is perhaps a trifle inaccurate when stating that in August 1998 there were 'Chinese manning Pakistani guns'.

21. *Ibid.*, pp. 492–3. General Bammi points out that Brigadier Surinder Singh was criticized by the Kargil Review Committee in its Report. It appears the Brigadier was the only officer in the entire Indian Army who performed inadequately. Bammi points out that the Committee 'did not comment upon the threat assessments of his higher commanders and how [they were] monitoring [the situation]'. See also 'New Chief for Army' by Praveen Swami in *Frontline* of 18–31 January 2003 at http://www.flonnet.com/fl2002/stories/20030131005403400.htm

22. See, for example, http://www.southasianmedia.net/index_opinion4.cfm?id=38377 for comment by Kanwar Sandhu of the *Hindustan Times*, 4 August 2004.

23. 'Indian jets fire on Kashmir', Arthur Max, Associated Press AP-NY-05-26-99 1256 EDT.

24. 'Kashmir with a capital N', Brian Cloughley, *Canberra Times*, Australia, 5 July 1999.

25. 'Kargil War: Battlefront', Harinder Baweja, *India Today*, 12 July 1999.

26. 'Kashmiri Militants Dismiss Offer', Kathy Gannon, Associated Press, AP-NY-06-03-99 2252EDT.

27. 'Sharif responsible for aggression', *The Hindu*, 3 June 1999.

28. 'The Kargil Syndrome', *India Today*, 5 August 1999.

29. General Bammi states that 'the award [of a decoration] to only one lieutenant colonel of infantry indicates that after initially deploying their units, the Commanding Officers [COs] of Pakistan Army did not come forward to fight or direct operations.' This is not only an unseemly and vulgar insult but is rubbish, militarily. For a CO to come forward and 'fight or direct operations' unless he is mounting a battalion attack is to interfere with his company and platoon commanders. If a CO has to use his personal weapon in a battle, there is something very badly wrong. This sort of nonsense began in Vietnam, when unit and even brigade commanders used helicopters to hover near platoon engagements and thoroughly confuse things by giving orders to hard-pressed subalterns. Pakistani COs were doing what COs ought to do: visiting the troops whenever possible and directing war at battalion level. The standard and credibility of Bammi's book can be summed up in his statement that 'The operations of 9 Mahar and 13 Kumaon ... showed that with adequate planning Pakistani troops can be defeated in any terrain. Unfortunately, operations of 3 Rajput did not go well.' But he doesn't say what happened to 3 Rajput.

30. There are balanced accounts of the Kargil affair in Sawant, Gaurav, *Dateline Kargil*, Macmillan India, 2000, and Baweja, Harinder, *A Soldier's Diary* Books Today, New Delhi 2000. A Pakistani book, Mazari, Dr Shireen, *The Kargil Conflict 1999*, Institute of Strategic Studies, Islamabad, 2003, is on a par with Krishna, Major General (retd) Ashok and Chari, Dr P.R. (eds), *Kargil: The Tables Turned*, Manohar, New Delhi, 2000, which, with Verma, Major General Ashok, *Kargil: Blood on the Snow*, Manohar, New Delhi, 2000, are well reviewed by A.G. Noorani in *Frontline* of 22 November to 5 December 2003 (http://www.frontlineonnet.com/fl2024/stories/20031205000507300.htm). Other essential reading is Sharma, Rajendra K., Sharma, Y.K. and Sharma, R.N., *The Kargil War: A Saga*

of Patriotism, Shubhi Publications, New Delhi, 2000; and Tellis, Ashley, Fair, Christine and Medby, Jamison Jo, *Limited Conflict under the Nuclear Umbrella: Indian and Pakistani Lessons from the Kargil Crisis,* Rand, 2001. Singh, Jasjit (ed.), *Kargil: Pakistan's Fourth War,* South Asia Books, New Delhi, 1999 adds some other perspectives.

31. The scandal over corruption in acquiring equipment continued for years. See 'Kargil Scam: Supreme Court asks Defence Ministry to file status report', *Outlook India,* 13 August 2007. http://www.outlookindia.com/pti_news.asp?id=495462

32. POF is a Pakistan success story. Probably its most outstanding Chairman (of some very high-grade officers who occupied the position), Lieutenant General Talat Masood, who later became Secretary Defence Production, brought the organization to a peak of efficiency. It does not manufacture 'big-ticket' items but concentrates on ammunition, for which it has a significant export market, and spares for all types of equipments. Heavy Industries Taxila (HIT) manufactures and upgrades armoured fighting vehicles.

33. 'The larger purpose in Kargil', *The Hindu,* 5 June 1999. General Raghavan is Director of the Delhi Policy Group and a former DGMO. His columns in *The Hindu* are always worth reading, being wise and succinct.

34. 'Pakistan urges urgent world steps to end escalation', *Dawn,* 6 June 1999.

35. Diplomatic and defence attaché sources of several countries to the author, June–August 1999.

36. General Bammi claims that in July 1998 there was 'Deployment of M-11 missiles at Deosai Plains' by Pakistan. The M-11 is the export version of the Chinese CSS-7, essentially a Scud-B, which has a trailer-erector-launcher 13.36 metres long and 3.03 metres wide. The TEL weights 37,400 kg with missile. In 1999 the approaches to the track across the Deosai plains were difficult for a jeep to negotiate, although they were later improved.

37. One of the interesting items in a telephone conversation during the conflict between General Musharraf (in China) and the CGS, Lieutenant General Aziz, recorded by the Indians (transcript in Bammi, 2002, Annex 15), is that the former is heard to say '[it] is in Simla Agreement that we cannot go for UN intervention', which is not so. There is nothing in the Simla Accord that states any such thing.

38. See http://www.subcontinent.com/sapra/military/kargil11.html quoting the *Times of India* on 6 and 9 July 1999.

39. See, among many other reports at the time, 'Vajpayee turns down Clinton's invitation', by Jyoti Malhotra in the *Indian Express* of 5 July 1999. http://www.indianexpress.com/res/web/pIe/ie/daily/19990705/ige05003.html

40. Sources in Pakistan.

41. Reuters, 08:38, 07-05-99.

42. 'Kashmir combatants make conflicting claims', Reuters, 13:19, 07-10-99.

43. 'Kargil was a lapse. Halt the celebrations', Dinesh Kumar, *Times of India,* 15 July 1999.

44. Text in Reuters report, 12:56, 07-12-99.

45. See, for example, 'Nuclear Risk-Reduction Measures in Kashmir', Brian Cloughley, Stimson Center, Washington DC, November 1998. New edition in Chapter 7 of *Nuclear Risk Reduction in South Asia,* Michael Krepon (ed.), Palgrave Macmillan, 2004.

46. 'Lessons to learn from Kargil', *Dawn,* 17 July 1999.

47. Dr Maleeha Lodhi (former Editor of *The News,* Rawalpindi; former Ambassador to the US; appointed High Commissioner in London 2003), 'The Kargil Crisis', *Newsline,* July 1999. A most important analysis, as might be expected from this gifted public figure.

48. A meeting of the DCC on 25 August 1999 delivered, amongst other banalities, the observation that 'It is noted that India's intention to go ahead with the deployment and operationalisation [*sic*] of its nuclear weapons and delivery systems is fraught with serious risks and dangers not only for the security of the region but the world at large.' Wow.

49. Musharraf, General Pervez, *In the Line of Fire*, Simon & Schuster, 2006. The respected writer Ikram Sehgal welcomed the book but wrote that 'With Humayun Gauhar, having about the best English among Pakistani columnists at this time, helping Musharraf write his autobiography, the book should not suffer for want of lucidity and/or expression. The stating of facts is a different proposition.'

50. Lieutenant General Jehangir Nasrullah, Engineer-in-Chief, who died, alas, in May 2006.

51. Schofield, Victoria, *Kashmir in Conflict*, IB Tauris, 2000. Latest edition 2003.

52. Human Rights Watch *World Report 1999*. http://www.hrw.org/wr2k/Asia-07.htm Other observations included: 'During late 1998 and early 1999, the government persistently tried to prevent the Jang group of newspapers from publishing. The Karachi-based group includes Jang, Pakistan's largest circulation Urdu newspaper, and the News International, the country's second-largest English-language newspaper. The Federal Investigation Agency raided Jang's Rawalpindi bureau in mid-December 1998, the day after Jang published a story on a financial scandal involving the Ittefaq group of companies owned by Prime Minister Sharif's family. Prior to the December raid, the government had frozen the Jang group's bank accounts, placed deadlines upon it to pay large taxes, ceased government advertising, and withheld supplies of government-regulated newsprint. The government's harassment of Jang continued into early February.' This appalling behaviour is ignored by many who support the return to politics in Pakistan of Mr Nawaz Sharif.

53. http://news.bbc.co.uk/2/hi/south_asia/2228796.stm

54. 'The government repeatedly failed to uphold the civil liberties of women or to punish 'honour killings'. In one particularly egregious case, Samia Sarwar was shot and killed in the Lahore office of the AGHS Legal Aid Cell on 6 April by a gunman who had apparently been hired by her family. A resident of Peshawar in the North West Frontier Province (NWFP) and the daughter of Ghulam Sarwar Khan Mohmand, president of a local chamber of commerce and industry, Sarwar had travelled to Lahore the previous month to obtain a divorce, over her parents' objections. Although the First Information Report (FIR) included them in the list of the accused, neither Sarwar's father, mother, or uncle was arrested. And despite strong and credible evidence linking them to the murder, the investigation report submitted by the police concluded that there was no evidence of involvement by Sarwar's family.' Human Rights Watch *World Report 1999*.

55. 'Pakistan Islamic head urges "coward" PM to quit', Ismail Khan, Reuters, 13:16, 08-27-99.

Chapter 5

The Coup, the Borders, and the Army's Capabilities

The October [1999] coup capped a year of increasing discontent with the Sharif administration, stemming from its crackdown on opposition political activity and increasing encroachments on civil liberties, with the courts providing only occasional relief. Leaders of Pakistan's normally fractious opposition announced on September 14 the formation of the Grand Democratic Alliance (GDA) grouping together nineteen political parties with the avowed aim of dislodging Sharif's government. The government responded with overt attempts to suppress opposition political activity. A GDA call for a protest rally in Karachi led to the arrest from September 24 to 26 of more than 1,000 opposition activists throughout the city, including much of the leadership of the Pakistan People's Party, as well as senior leaders of the Muttahida Qaumi Movement (MQM), the Awami National Party, and the Pakistan Tehrik-e-Insaaf party. (Human Rights Watch)[1]

The announcement on 12 October 1999 that Prime Minister Nawaz Sharif had for the second time dismissed an Army Chief led to a coup that confused much of the outside world as much as it was approved by most citizens of Pakistan. It was essential, by tacit international convention, that the government's dismissal be criticized by foreign countries and institutions, in spite of the fact that they were all well aware that 'democratic' Pakistan was thundering downhill morally, socially and economically. The United States imposed more sanctions, the European Union expressed 'deep concern', the United Nations declared that Pakistan must 'restore civilian rule and the constitutional process', the World Bank and the International Monetary Fund muttered about stopping new development aid, and the Commonwealth suspended Pakistan's membership. The future looked bleak.

One intriguing thing about the dismissal of Musharraf was that only two weeks before Sharif took action to get rid of him he had appointed him

Chairman of the Joint Chiefs of Staff Committee (CJCSC), while continuing to hold his army position. He had been made Acting CJCSC on 8 April 1999, when it was announced he would serve in the position for a year, but in a surprising move Sharif confirmed and extended him in the appointment.

The only other officer to have held both posts was his predecessor, General Karamat, and, according to former government figures in office at the time,[2] the reason that Sharif wanted to have one person holding the two appointments was that he thought it essential for his own security to have both in the hands of one pliable individual who would do precisely what he wished. Apparently he considered himself more threatened by the existence of two senior figures than by one who held two appointments. The notion that a Chairman on his own could pose a threat to the government was and is doubtful. He commands no troops, and although undoubtedly a man of stature and personality – otherwise he wouldn't be in the post – it is troops that matter if any physical move is to be made against those holding political power. And, of more importance, the notion that someone like Musharraf, as either COAS or in both posts, would stand aside limply if an increasingly paranoid prime minister was taking the country through constitutional hoops was also questionable. Z.A. Bhutto had thought Zia would be a supine yes-man, and Nawaz Sharif made the same mistake about Musharraf.[3]

It had been thought that Musharraf would serve only a token period as Acting Chairman, thus allowing the Chief of Naval Staff, Admiral Fasih Bokhari, to be appointed at some stage, but when the PM extended Musharraf as Chairman until 6 October 2001 he was making it clear that this would not occur. His action resulted in the understandable resignation of Bokhari, who had had only five months left to serve as navy chief, at the end of which time he would be required to retire were he not made Chairman. His public reason for resigning is interesting, however, and was given three years later in an interview with the *South Asia Tribune*.[4] Sharif's decision about the CJCSC was made on 29 September, and Bokhari stated to the *Tribune* that 'I resigned on October 5, 1999, a week before Musharraf's coup of October 12 because I had come to know that he had decided to topple the Sharif government.'

This is an intriguing statement. If the Chief of Naval Staff had evidence that there was about to be a coup against the government of his country, it is strange that he did not inform the President of the fact. President Tarar was not the most effective head of state that Pakistan has known, and indeed was a mere puppet of the Sharif family, but Admiral Bokhari owed him allegiance as the nation's highest constitutional authority.[5] Every member of the armed forces swears that he or she will 'uphold the Constitution of the Islamic Republic of Pakistan', and the CNS was hardly doing this by quietly resigning rather than telling the President that it seemed the nation's government was about to be overthrown by the army yet again. Bokhari is quite definite about it: when he was asked 'why, in his view, General Musharraf wanted to topple Nawaz Sharif' the Admiral replied, 'Because he feared he will have to face a court martial for master-minding the Kargil (debacle)'. But there is the point that if Bokhari had resigned immediately after the coup took place he might have given a rather more effective message to the nation concerning the disapproval he belatedly registered.

Certainly, there were many rumours about a possible coup. At the Saudi Arabian National Day reception in Islamabad on 23 September, General Musharraf answered a question hinting at the possibility of a serious rift with the Prime Minister by saying, 'We enjoy excellent relations with the government,' but was also asked about a US statement that 'We [the US] would strongly oppose any attempt to change the government through extraconstitutional means.'[6] His reply that 'It's an old story. I don't want to comment. I am a soldier and don't want to enter into any controversy,' was no more nor less than was proper, but it was obvious that something was going on, especially as the PM's spokesman on 29 September referred to 'uncalled for rumours and speculations about change of command in the army' that 'certain vested interests were fanning in pursuance of their political agenda'.

There was a strong element of farce entering the Sharif government's handling of senior appointments, and not just in the armed forces. Over 100 senior civil servants had been moved or reallocated in a large-scale, politically motivated reshuffle; an unforgivable and completely avoidable disruption of the country's administration, economically and socially, in a critical period when their expertise was essential for effective administra-tion of the country's affairs. As observed by Benazir Bhutto, 'He has sought to dismantle democracy, he has been sacking everyone – the chief justice, the president – attacked the press, the foreign investors, the opposition.'[7]

On 9 October 1999, it was announced that the Corps Commander of XII Corps (in Quetta), Lieutenant General Tariq Parvaiz Khan (the gallant officer who had escaped from a prisoner-of-war camp in Bangladesh and walked home over the Himalayas) had been 'asked to retire' by GHQ (i.e. the COAS) as from 13 October. The initial notification was terse, and even a later clarification said only that he had been removed 'for service reasons'. In fact, he had met with political figures without informing GHQ. This might not have been unusual in normal times because the General, who attended staff college in Australia and is thoroughly cosmopolitan, in addition to being a most likeable person, has a first cousin (a retired Major, Raja Nadir Pervez) who was a government minister; but these were not normal times and anyone in the military who had even fleeting contact

113

with Sharif or his cronies was considered to have ulterior motives. Concurrently the Commander of I Corps (HQ at Mangla), Lieutenant General Saleem Haider, was transferred to GHQ, apparently for revealing to persons unknown (but suspected to be in Sharif's circle) the subjects discussed at a recent corps commanders' conference presided over by Musharraf.

These events were strange, to say the least, and created concern throughout the country, as it was obvious that something untoward was afoot. (And it should be noted that it is a thoroughly unhealthy thing for officers to be spied upon. The atmosphere was decidedly rancid.) It appeared that senior officers were becoming at least peripherally involved in politics, which was considered unforgivable. The bizarre series of resignations and dismissals cannot have given neighbouring India much confidence in the way Pakistan was being governed, especially after the Kargil fighting earlier in the year, and it was in this period, according to a highly placed official in Islamabad,[8] that several senior officers decided something was amiss and began to plan for action if Nawaz Sharif decided to move against the COAS/Chairman, which he did on 12 October.

The man chosen by the Prime minister to succeed Musharraf was General Khawaja Ziauddin, one of the Sharif family's close associates, who was not well known for his soldierly qualities.

During the military reshuffle in 1998, when Pervez Musharraf was promoted to become COAS, the PM appointed General Ziauddin as Director General Inter-Services Intelligence, and it soon became apparent that he enjoyed the confidence of Sharif, as he was used in a quasi-governmental fashion to make Pakistan's position on terrorism clear to Washington. This included, and indeed emphasized, Pakistan's commitment to assisting US efforts to kill or capture the infamous Osama bin Laden of the al-Qaeda organization which was based partly in Afghanistan and was held responsible by Washington for several terrorist attacks on US personnel and facilities well before the 9/11 outrages.

Ziauddin's appointment as COAS was a major turnaround for the Pakistan Army, which had never before had a chief from the Corps of Engineers.[9] All former chiefs have been from a fighting arm, either infantry, armour or artillery, and from what could be gathered from telephone calls by the author to Islamabad at the time, and in later discussions with senior officers, the army was unhappy with him as a person and a leader. He had been due to retire on 2 February 2000, but received an extension of service when appointed DG ISI. He did not enjoy the confidence of his peers or the trust of the army as a whole.

When the Prime Minister made the announcement of his army chief's dismissal, Musharraf was in Colombo, having attended Sri Lankan Army

114

ceremonies marking its fiftieth anniversary, along with several of his international counterparts including those of India and Bangladesh.

The fact that General Musharraf had gone to Sri Lanka at all was an indication that he was not intent on taking action against the Prime Minister. Indeed, before boarding his scheduled PIA flight to return to Pakistan he played a round of golf in Colombo, which was hardly an indication of a man in the middle of preparations to overthrow a government. He seemed to be completely relaxed.

His attitude changed when PK 805 did not land immediately after arriving in Karachi airspace on time. It circled for almost an hour, with the pilot being ordered by PIA's chairman, Shahid Khakan Abbasi,[10] who was in the control tower, to divert to Dubai. It is presumed the order came from the Prime Minister. The pilot protested that he did not have enough fuel to make the trip safely (that is, to divert to Dubai and still have enough fuel to divert to another airport if for some reason it was not possible to land there), and Abbasi told him to fly to Nawabshah, about 220 km north of Karachi. Musharraf was told of the problem and patched in by telephone from the cockpit to the commander of V Corps (Karachi), Lieutenant General Usmani, who sent troops to the airport and went there himself as soon as he could. Abbasi and his deputy, Nadir Chaudhry, were apprehended by troops and later arrested. One mistake was to have failed to place obstacles on the runway, or to have otherwise rendered it unusable, but even if the aircraft had flown to Nawabshah, the army would have been there before it landed and would have made sure the COAS came to no harm. It was unbelievably irresponsible of the Prime Minister and the Chairman of PIA to order an aircraft to stand into danger. Had the pilot been forced to divert to Dubai after circling Karachi for fifty minutes he would have been extremely short of fuel, and it is quite conceivable that the aircraft could have crashed. The affair characterized the entire Nawaz Sharif regime: inadequate planning, followed by hasty decisions, resulting in chaos.

There have been several accounts of the affair, each no doubt as accurate as the other, but one in particular gives the atmosphere of the drama. A PIA pilot, Captain Tariq Baloch, wrote that:

In October 1999 Captain Sarwat of Pakistan International Airlines, an old buddy, and I went to Colombo for the Air Lanka Golf classic tournament. On 10th October, returning from the 18th hole I saw General Pervaiz Musharraf teeing-off with the Bangladeshi COAS for a friendly match. On the 12th October we were to return back to Pakistan and our flight route was Colombo–Male–Karachi. The flight time between Male and Karachi was almost three and a half hours. Capt. Sarwat was Commander of the flight (PK 805) and I was travelling as a passenger, but being PIA aircrew I could visit the cockpit with the consent of the captain. The first officer was Mr Shami and the flight engineer Mr Amir. General Musharraf and his wife were seated in the front right hand side seats and the PSOs occupied the last two seats in the same row. There were 198 persons on aboard, of whom almost 50 were children from the American school [in Islamabad] with six foreign teachers.

[The aircraft landed first at Male, from which] departure was un-eventful. The airplane was cruising at 29,000 feet. I was sitting in the cockpit jump seat and occasionally would stand up to stretch and walk in the cabin. Captain Sarwat also came through from the cockpit to greet the VIP.

After two and half hours of flight and now cruising at 33,000 feet, we established contact with Karachi air traffic controller. [He] started asking how much fuel was on board? What was our alternate airfield? And how many passengers were on board? I was standing behind the flight engineer's seat and listening to the conversation through the cockpit speakers. On hearing this I said to Captain Sarwat 'Isn't it strange for Karachi to be asking this?' to which he nodded 'yes'. It was a clear night and probably the third [quarter] of moon but we could later on see Karachi very clearly from around 40 miles. The initial approach given to us was direct Marvi (shortest route) but after a while Karachi changed the clearance via Nansi (the longer route) and gave us descent clearance to 10,000 feet. As the airplane reached almost within 60 miles, the Karachi tower said 'PK 805 you are not cleared to land at Karachi.' 'Can we proceed to Nawabshah?' Captain Sarwat asked after pondering for a little while as to what must be going on down below. 'Nawabshah is also closed' came the reply. 'But Nawabshah is our alternate!' said Capt Sarwat forcefully. Karachi ATC said 'you will land at your own risk, you cannot land in Pakistan. All airfields are closed.' Captain Sarwat replied 'We do not have fuel for any other field!' but there was complete silence from the ATC. The Karachi ATC was questioned thrice but it was all in vain – there was no answer. During the ATC conversation it seemed obvious that someone behind the controller was passing the instruction because more than three or more persons could be heard in the background of the reception. KLM flight crews listening to this conversation also shouted in its typical accent, 'Karachi why don't you give the reason to PK?' While the commotion was on, Capt Sarwat assumed that perhaps it may be due to the VIP sitting aboard. Sarwat, knowing my air force background, asked me and the other crew 'partner, what do you think, should I tell the general about this?' I immediately said 'why not, let's get whatever help we can!' The Captain called the purser and asked him to inform the personal staff officers of the general. Both PSOs came rushing into the cockpit. After listening to the Captain they went to tell the General. Meanwhile Capt Sarwat asked the flight engineer how much fuel was left, and if we could make it to Muscat. 'No way, we have only five and a half tons of fuel left at this 10,000 feet altitude,' he calculated. Meanwhile General Musharraf had entered the cockpit. During the discussion between flight crew members, two other alternate airfields for diversion were considered. Chahbar in Iran and Ahmedabad in India. After a little discussion with the flight engineer regarding remaining fuel and new airfield and night landing facility, Chahbar was not considered as an alternate airfield. 'Do we have the approach and landing information on Ahmedabad? Please open and consult Jeppesen [the flight crew bible] immediately,' Sarwat asked the co-pilot. General Musharraf was listening to the conversation and he commandingly asserted 'We will not go to India,' to which Capt Sarwat said 'okay General, as you say.' Now the General said he wanted to talk to the Corps Commander Karachi, immediately. After a while the PSO gave the mobile telephone [numbers] to the flight engineer and wrote down the telephone number of the Corps Commander Karachi. The flight engineer Amir tried many times to dial the telephone but there was no dial tone. Then Amir said we are not getting the connection through and it seems as if the telephone lines have been cut. The general then asked why we couldn't speak on the long range radio – the high frequency. The flight engineer tried to establish contact through company high frequency phone patch but it was all quiet, and no answer was received.

Other airplanes flying in the Karachi vicinity were instructed by Karachi ATC to divert because Karachi airport was closed. An aircraft of the Pakistan Air Force which was in inbound to Karachi from Islamabad was instructed to land at Nawabshah, immediately. But the PAF Captain was not willing to accept this order and asserted that the PAF flight would go back to Islamabad. While the argument between the PAF aircraft and Karachi ATC was going on Captain Sarwat changed the radio frequency. However I later found out that it was a Boeing 737 VIP aircraft on a routine maintenance trip to Karachi but was forced to land at Nawabshah airfield. The police at Nawabshah, with some special instructions, were in fact waiting for a twin-engine jet aircraft. Since it is difficult for a [layman] to distinguish between a Boeing 737 and an airbus A-300 the Nawabshah police cordoned off the aircraft after parking. But as the doors were [about] to open, [along] came a Pakistan Army soldier and shouted at the police to buzz off otherwise they would be shot at. The police dispersed and the army took over the charge of the aircraft. The door opened and the army officers entered the aircraft. To their dismay they found the wife and children of the PAF Captain [pilot] inside, 'where is the general?' inquired the army officer. 'What general?' asked the crew, who told them that they were going to Karachi from Islamabad. 'But we were told that you are coming from Colombo,' said the officer.

In the air at the very same time, the first officer of our aircraft saw two blips on the traffic collision avoidance system and shouted 'we are being intercepted; probably there are two fighter aircraft.'

The conversation in the cockpit of our plane had become tense [but] I noticed that at no point [did] any of the crew or the VIP [Musharraf] loose their cool. The general insisted more than twice that we land at Karachi. He also inquired as to why we couldn't land at the air force runways at Karachi. But probably due to the fighter aircraft and no knowledge as to what was happening below on the ground, with no runway lights landing at [a] PAF airfield was considered as the last option. If we could not land at Karachi or at Nawabshah due to runway blockade with tractors and bulldozers etc then Shahrah-e-Faisal or Masroor was the last option anyway. At this point Capt Sarwat changed to [the] PIA company radio channel. [He was asked] about the remaining fuel. Someone at the company channel directed PK805 to proceed and land at Nawabshah, then refuel the airplane with 30 tonnes of fuel and once again get airborne and wait for further instructions.

After a few minutes, Karachi ATC cleared PK805 to divert to Nawabshah. Capt Sarwat then sighed with relief and said 'let's go to Nawabshah.' The airbus climbed like a missile to 20,000 feet in no time since there was hardly any fuel left and the aircraft was light. About 60 miles north of Karachi PK805 was redirected to come and land at Karachi by Karachi ATC. A quick turnabout and descent was initiated. Someone from ATC asked about the general [and said] that he wants to speak to the general. Captain Sarwat gave his microphone to the general and said, 'Sir, please speak.'

'This is Pervaiz, who is there?' the general inquired very assertively. 'I am General Iftikhar, sir, your retirement was announced two hours before but we have control, please land at Karachi.' 'Where is the corps commander?' the general asked. 'He is in the next room waiting for you' was the reply. Both PSOs were listening and the younger PSO (a major) shouted, 'Sir, ask him the name of his dog.' Probably he wanted to be sure in recognizing the GOC, but the general who had kept his cool all along said confidently, 'he is my man, don't worry!' [Later on this officer, a friend of mine, told me that General Musharraf had given him (the corps commander) two puppies and that's how the PSO wanted to confirm his identity.]

Meanwhile the plane was getting to its final approach. Suddenly the low fuel warning light of the right wing fuel tank came on with an audio chime. The cockpit was dead silent and everyone was hoping for touch down as soon as possible. We had waited almost one hour and ten minutes in the air. The remaining fuel of 1.2 ton in the wing tanks, if [the gauge was] reliable, was only enough for approximately ten minutes of flight time. Twelve miles short of landing, the left wing fuel tank warning light also appeared, with chime.

After touch down PK 805 was told to park in a remote area (bay 66) and was informed that no other person than the VIP will come out of the aircraft. After the engine shut down, soldiers who were almost two hundred cordoned-off the aircraft. The general was looking out from the cockpit window and seemed relaxed.

Before disembarking from the aircraft the general shook hands with all of us and said, 'thank you, don't worry, he is my man.' And he immediately passed his very first order through his PSO, 'tell them I don't want anyone to leave the country.'

The general, his wife while trying to control her tears, and the two PSOs disembarked from the plane and were greeted by the corps commander and the GOC with some super salutes from the soldiers.

They all went inside a building for a short conference, which took almost 15 minutes after which the whole contingent drove away at a very high speed ... During the whole episode, I was the quietest and closest observer in the cockpit and was thoroughly impressed [by the] total professionalism of Captain Sarwat and his crew. Not to mention the way [the] general carried himself, who remained confident and totally composed through out the whole episode.[11]

Musharraf then conferred with Lieutenant General Usmani and other officers at Malir barracks, and future action was planned. Obviously Nawaz Sharif was behaving erratically to the point of endangering the country as a whole, and something had to be done. The President was entirely in the hands of Sharif and his group of intimates, and was power-less to act as a neutral adviser or broker, even if he so wished. Reluctantly, Musharraf concluded that the only course open to him was to dismiss Nawaz Sharif and his associates. He issued orders to that effect and then flew to Islamabad in an air force plane.

In Islamabad/Rawalpindi, the commander of X Corps (HQ at Chaklala, a Rawalpindi suburb), Lieutenant General Mehmood, arranged for the SSG detachment at GHQ, and 111 Infantry Brigade, located at Westridge in Rawalpindi, to secure the television and radio stations and to move troops close to government centres in Islamabad. While these deploy-ments were being carried out, Musharraf gave orders to place the Prime

Minister and other prominent figures under house arrest. Throughout the country there were several detentions, including those of the Governor of Punjab, the Chief Minister of NWFP and various provincial ministers known to be Sharif ultra-loyalists. The short-reigning army chief, General Ziauddin, was confined to his house only a few hours after having his new badges of rank pinned on by Sharif (recorded for posterity by government-controlled Pakistan TV). General Tariq Parvaiz and the Prime Minister's military assistant were also detained. The operation was over quickly.

Pakistan's army coups have taken place in essence because there was direct confrontation between the most senior government and military figures, fuelled by public dissatisfaction with governmental corruption, warping of the constitution and gross economic inefficiency. All four seizures of power by the army were without bloodshed and attracted almost total support from a long-suffering citizenry, but the trouble was that military rule went on for too long and made returning to democracy extremely difficult. The inability of politicians to accept probity as a requirement of governance contributed directly to the 1999 takeover, and the country's poor economic situation had been worsened by the Sharif government's terminal corruption. Shady characters made millions from tax-avoidance, strangely contrived loans from various banks, and favours granted by the Sharif brothers and their immediate advisers, which were repetition of the sleaze and shameless venality so evident during the two governments of Benazir Bhutto. Sharif was the most powerful Prime Minister in the country's history but made no attempt to alleviate poverty, provide a decent education or health system, or even run a reasonably efficient administration. The decision to hold nuclear tests, following those by India in May 1998, was internationally disastrous and resulted in painful embargoes by most of the world, and there was no economic plan to cope with the consequences, of which Sharif was warned by President Clinton and many others.[12]

The plight of the average person was pitiful, as they saw their savings decline in value and their quality of life deteriorate week by week, and off-the-cuff price increases penalized only the middle classes and the poor. The exit of the Sharif brothers was welcomed by almost the entire population and took place on the day that, by coincidence, Mr Moeen Qureshi, a former and most competent interim Prime Minister, was quoted by *The News* newspaper as saying that there should once again be a caretaker government. This time, he said, 'The caretakers should be given at least two years instead of only three months so that they could introduce reforms with far-reaching effects.'

But there was to be no interim government of carefully chosen, apolitical, incorruptible economic experts with a strong sense of social justice. It was to be the army again, albeit with modifications to the practices of previous military regimes. Although the country benefited as a whole and was relieved to be rid of the squalid soap opera that had been playing for so long, it wasn't democracy by any means. The new management, which was run, appropriately enough, by the 'Chief Executive', as General Musharraf dubbed himself before deciding to assume the presidency, had many problems to resolve, and it is relevant to the story of the army to describe one of them, to indicate where the army fitted in with foreign policy and resolution of domestic problems that were in danger of affecting the stability of the country.

Afghanistan and Pakistan's Border Areas

Allegations have been made that the Pakistan Army was involved in the Taliban takeover of Afghanistan in the mid-1990s and in furthering its members' aims in that savage, unhappy and divided land. So far as can be determined, there was indeed direct military support of the Taliban by the army,[13] although they were already well-supplied with weapons, most of which were left over from the CIA's cornucopia of arms that was showered on the various mujahideen organizations in the 1980s. In 1985, while visiting an Afghan guerrilla group near Dalbandin in Balochistan, I was shown and photographed an enormous arms kote, with AK rifles, anti-personnel mines and anti-aircraft weapons, all in heavy care and preservation, and hundreds of thousands of rounds of ammunition, along with countless boxes of grenades. These, I was told, were being kept for the 'real war' against other bands after the Russians were driven out. Doubtless there were many caches of this nature, but in any event the country was awash with weapons. Pakistan's Inter-Services Intelligence Directorate was deeply involved in Afghanistan, and connived at sending ill-trained fanatics (especially Swatis) to join the Taliban, and – according to the excellent *Ghost Wars* by Steve Coll,[14] who drew on a plenitude of impeccable sources – aided them in many other ways. According to several observers and analysts, including Human Rights Watch, the Saudi Arabian government was deeply involved in providing weapons for the Taliban.[15] The CIA had been informed in 1994 and 1995 that the 'principal patron' of the Taliban was Major General (retired) Nasirullah Babar,[16] Interior Minister in the government of Benazir Bhutto and a long-time Bhutto family loyalist (from the time of Zulfiqar Ali Bhutto in the 1970s, to 2007 when he was deeply involved in negotiations between Ms Bhutto and President Musharraf). In August 2007, official documents acquired by the National Security Archive in the US indicated that substantial aid was given to the Taliban by Pakistan in 1996 and 1997.[17]

The Taliban were militant religious zealots, but not soldiers in the normal sense of the word, being totally unfamiliar with even the low-technology equipment they acquired. In their advance throughout the country they needed artillery support, for example, and while the guns could be manned at least in part by former soldiers of the Afghan Army, their technical direction was provided by Pakistanis who, along with most of the many other advisers, were eventually evacuated in night-time Pakistan Air Force C-130 pickups from Afghan airstrips at the time of the Taliban collapse. Some were left to be captured and were either murdered or thrown in jails run by the Northern Alliance leaders who were (and are) every bit as brutal as the Taliban.

Washington was heavily involved in fostering criminal mayhem in Afghanistan in the 1980s through its support of vicious and villainous mujahideen whose human rights awareness was zero. America washed its hands of Afghanistan once the cold war was over, and its revitalized concern was based on the Taliban's shielding of the terrorist Osama bin Laden, and thus solely on self-interest. It was in no way the result of benevolent ideals concerning peaceful development of the country. Had this been an imperative, the US would have striven to encourage stable government there many years before, and would have provided the wherewithal for an advance to stability. (Even its de-mining efforts in Afghanistan were perfunctory and involved special forces soldiers receiving short-term in-area familiarization and language training, rather than engineer mine specialists.)[18] At a meeting of the UN Security Council on 27 August 1999, Pakistan was castigated by the US and others for 'supporting Afghanistan's Taliban militia and helping fuel its recent offensive with weapons and warriors'.[19] This criticism by the US can be described only as deep humbug, especially as it changed completely when it was realized that Pakistan could once again be useful in implementation of US foreign policy.

A disturbing aspect of Taliban influence, in addition to their appalling human rights abuses and especially their subjection of women to disgusting privation, was their recruitment of hundreds of semi-educated youngsters from madrassas (religious schools)[20] in Pakistan and elsewhere. These youths have been rendered unemployable in other than persecuting those who do not follow the Taliban's warped interpretation of the Quran and the Hadith, and following the law of the gun. They represent some of the brainwashed raw material from which 'guest militancy' in Indian-administered Kashmir is forged, and although their sense of purpose may be confused, as they appear to regard fighting almost anybody as a holy duty, this does not make them any less dangerous; the reverse, probably. The remnants of the Taliban and, it is alleged, al-Qaeda, were driven to the borderlands between Afghanistan and

Pakistan where troops began searching for them on both sides. Army and paramilitary operations by Pakistan in the border regions in pursuit of supposed aliens were unpopular, and in March 2005 I wrote in Jane's *Terrorism and Security Monitor*[21] that:

> In September 2004 a news report about Pakistan's military operations in Waziristan, which involved aircraft attacks, stated that 'until now, aerial bombing has never been used to crush an armed insurgency in [Pakistan].' But in 1929 the British bombed exactly the same area. Bombing did not subjugate the tribes then, and will not do so in the future.
>
> In the tribal region of Pakistan, known as the Federally Administered Tribal Areas (FATA) of North West Frontier Province (NWFP), the government in Islamabad is as alien as was the British Raj. South Waziristan is the southernmost of 7 Agencies in FATA, and like the others its inhabitants are largely illiterate (the literacy rate for men is 18%; for women, negligible), and as profoundly ignorant of the outside world as it is of them. They are devoutly religious; devious and aggressive; bound by a code of honour incomprehensible to most westerners; and implacably opposed to development that might alter their way of life. They are loosely contained by the Frontier Crimes Regulations (1901) which are based on collective responsibility in that the authorities, if they dare, can detain members of a law-breaking fugitive's tribe or quarantine his village should he fail to surrender or if tribal punishment is not administered.
>
> The troubles of 2004–2005 began when Washington insisted that Pakistan take action against tribes sheltering Taliban adherents and possibly (indubitably, in the US assessment) members of Al Qaeda. The writer was told in December 2003 by a US general in Pakistan that 'the Paks aren't doing enough' to assist America and that the government must drive out or kill those to whom the tribes were affording sanctuary.
>
> Concurrently officials in Islamabad said that increased pressure on President Musharraf to strike in FATA was resisted by explanation that the area was most sensitive in domestic politics and that NWFP was controlled by (democratically elected) fanatics of the Muttahida Majlis-e-Amal (MMA; a group of six religious parties) whose retrogressive policies were exceedingly difficult to counter. Military action would result in greater support for the MMA, which was against the interests of Pakistan as a whole. It was observed that attempts were being made to introduce reforms in FATA, and that the process would collapse should there be confrontation. None of these arguments succeeded. Nor did the military operations that followed.

Two operations in South Waziristan in 2002–2003 were intended to eradicate foreign militants. They caused much reaction against the government and the United States, as it was claimed by the tribes that there had been participation by the US military. No matter what might be announced by Islamabad or Washington it is firmly believed in NWFP and the rest of the country that US forces were involved and continue to be involved in operations along the frontier. This belief was given impetus by a 3 hour visit to Wana on 14 January 2005 by five US senators, accompanied by the US defence attaché in Islamabad. (She was not wearing uniform, but was recognized.) The official handout stated: 'The elders of the Ahmadzai Wazir tribe profusely praised the Pakistan Army during the meeting [with the senators] ... They stressed that military operations against foreign militants enjoyed the support of the tribes.'

The Ahmadzai Wazir and the Mahsud tribes are the most prominent in the Agency. The Zalikhels, a sub-tribe of the Ahmadzai, gave sanctuary to militants fleeing Afghanistan following US bombing and Northern Alliance massacres in 2001–2002. There are Wazirs on both sides of the Pakistan-Afghanistan border, and kinship bonds are close.

On 14 March 2004 units from the army and the Frontier Corps (FC; a militia force under the Home Ministry but with officers from the army), began an operation in South Waziristan to 'flush out Al Qaeda and Taliban activists and arrest tribesmen who harbour them.' Some 7,000 troops took part, using artillery and mortars. Over 40,000 people were driven from their homes, some hundreds of houses were demolished, cattle were killed, orchards destroyed, and an unknown number of civilian casualties inflicted. The army lost forty-three killed and the Frontier Corps seventeen, eight of whom were murdered after being taken prisoner. The operation was declared a success. (There were Mahsuds among the FC dead, which served to further Wazir-Mahsud enmity. In former days it was unusual to have FC units, which are tribally manned, pitted against tribes in the same general area as tribal members of the unit, as blood feuds are inevitable if there are deaths on either side.) It was stated that 215 'fighters' had been captured, of whom seventy-three were foreigners. No independent observer has sighted these captives.

At a jirga (assembly of prominent tribesmen) at Shakai, near Wana, on 24 April it was agreed with representatives of the Pakistan government that there would be an amnesty for foreigners handed over. On 3 May the US commander in Afghanistan, Lieutenant General Richard Barno, stated 'Our view is that there are foreign fighters in those tribal areas who will have to be killed or captured.'

Further negotiations resulted in a tribal committee being formed to rid the area of foreigners. It reported in May that there were none. The authorities refused to believe the claim, and continued disbelief when a tribal lashkar (army) of some 2,000 men were said to have conducted an unproductive search. As a result of perceived non-cooperation a policy of collective punishment was invoked. On 29 May hundreds of Ahmadzai Wazirs' shops in and around Wana were closed, as was the hospital. Salaries to state-employed Ahmadzais were stopped, and seventy tribesmen were imprisoned, including a dozen maliks, or tribal elders, thus effectively ending negotiations.

From 11 June military operations again began, involving more air strikes, and a popular local brigand, Nek Mohammad, was killed by a heliborne missile. Official loss figures were nine FC and six soldiers killed. In August and September there was further bitter fighting, and it was announced on 14 September that four 'foreigners', suspected members of Al Qaeda, had been killed. They were no such thing, and on 29 September the bodies were handed over to the Pakistani tribes to which they belonged, and their burial was attended by thousands of tribesmen. After further fighting it was announced in December that 'militants' were no longer capable of 'regrouping and attacking security forces', that 200 soldiers had been killed, and that 'several hundred' fighters had been killed or captured.

For the moment [March 2005] FATA is fairly quiet. A 'peace plan' has been drafted and promises of development 'uplift works' have been made. No foreign fighters have been seen by independent witnesses and none has been put on trial. The tribes are alienated from one another and their suspicion and dislike of the government have turned to distrust and hatred while support for Islamic extremism and militancy has grown.

Military operations confirmed the inhabitants of North West Frontier Province and much of the rest of the country in their belief that the US was responsible for the decision to invade the tribal areas. As forecast by officials in Islamabad in 2003, the operations worked against national harmony. Further, they did not achieve their aim, and it is unlikely future operations will do so, either. But the hatred will last for decades.

Deployment of the army into the tribal areas was impossible to avoid if Pakistan were to continue to be considered a supporter in President Bush's 'war on terror' and receive economic and political support from Washington for maintaining that stance. The Corps Commander in Peshawar from October 2001 to March 2004, Lieutenant General Ali Mohammad Jan Aurakzai, had tried to avoid direct military confrontation, although in late 2001 he ordered troops into what had been termed 'No Go' parts of the Federally Administered Tribal Areas (FATA). His conviction was that development and education were the answers to tribal alienation from mainstream Pakistan, and to that end he made

> a plan for development projects in FR Kurram, Orakzai and Khyber Agencies. We have been allotted Rs 80 million by the President for these projects which will be released to us after submission of details to MO [Military Operations] Directorate. Essentially, we are concentrating on a road network to reach out to the inaccessible areas to connect various tribes/agencies through roads, construction of school buildings and dispensaries etc. We will construct tracks to start with, which will be metalled (hopefully) by the provincial government utilising ADP [Association for the Development of Pakistan] and KPP [Khushhal Pakistan Programme, a rural development organization] funds which run into hundreds of millions of rupees. Regrettably, due to the inept, inefficient and irresponsible attitude of the bureaucracy, no work has started yet despite the fact that the financial year is coming to a close in four months. Anticipating allotment of Rs 80 million to us for these projects, I have already hired six civilian dozers, two compressors and drilling machines etc. during the last week of December 2001 and work on various tracks in FR Kurram and Khyber Agency is progressing well.[22]

US representatives in Pakistan and Afghanistan insisted that action be taken and would not agree – could not even begin to understand – that the last resort should be employment of the military on what would be seen by the tribes as a punitive expedition. Anyone familiar with *The Pathans* by Sir Olaf Caroe,[23] and especially his chapter on Waziristan, would realize that little has changed in the Frontier over the last century, and that military force, while an attractive solution in the short term, is certain to produce long-lasting resentment.

Use of all the paraphernalia of hi-tech warfare against tribes and their villages, especially armed helicopters firing missiles, looks very good on television and undoubtedly kills many people. Inevitably, some of these are the wrong people and, equally inevitably, the rage and resentment that follow far outweigh any military or social benefit achieved by blasting a few outlaws. The fact that over 200 army and Frontier Corps soldiers were killed (and double that number wounded)[24] in operations against the tribes is not surprising, especially as several of the army units had been redeployed from I Corps in the east of the country where their training had been almost solely for highly mobile, fully mechanized, 'strike' operations against Indian forces. The lesson is simple: nobody can expect soldiers and their leaders to be instant experts in all types of warfare. Fighting through every defile, every nala – 'every rock, every hill'[25] – demands very different skills to those required in an armoured advance. They can be acquired, of course, because that is what soldiering is all about, but not overnight; and it was extremely unwise to commit troops to footslogging, ambush-prone, classic frontier warfare without intensive and lengthy preparation. It takes an ordinary battalion at least eight months of concentrated training to be prepared for operations in terrain and conditions that are utterly different from those with which it is familiar. Little wonder there were problems of morale in some units.

Military operations in FATA have never succeeded in permanently imposing the authority of the central or province governments on the region, and never will. The most effective means of capturing or killing dissidents being shielded by the tribes is through a combination of deviousness, patience, threat of force and bribery, and to make this work requires a deep knowledge of the region and long familiarity with personalities, dialects and customs. The maliks of the Ahmadzai Wazirs (and of other tribes, clans and sub-clans) will say all the right things when US politicians drop by on one of their earnest, well-meaning and absurdly unproductive junkets, but it is remarkably ingenuous of anyone to believe they mean what they say, especially after their lands, their houses, their people and their pride were so savagely assaulted. Kipling summed it up well when he wrote of a fictional but all too believable Afridi outlaw that

'Tis war, red war, I'll give you then,
War till my sinews fail,
For the wrong you have done to a chief of men
And a thief of the Zukka Khel.

Thieves they may be, when the opportunity arises; and they are cruel, predatory and selfish, without any regard for what foreigners consider to be social justice. But they have their own codes of law and equity with which they are content. The Pakistan Army was well aware of what it was taking on when it began its operations in Waziristan, but both it and the government in Islamabad were not only outmanoeuvred by the tribesmen, but by Washington. It is the goodwill of the United States that is so important for the equipment status of the armed forces – for the navy and air force more than the army, but nevertheless of considerable consequence to the latter in acquiring such items as helicopters, communications systems, ground surveillance radars, air-platform anti-tank missiles, counterinsurgency and riot-control equipment, and night-vision devices. The effects of US co-operation and its impact on Pakistan's defence budget and capabilities have been considerable. As discussed in Chapter 7, operations since 2005 have varied from employment of tribal jirgas, talking with the tribes in the hope of persuading them to co-operate with the authorities, to full-scale military action, growing to a peak in early 2008.

US Weapons' Supplies and the Defence Budget

As a result of their nuclear tests the US imposed sanctions on India and Pakistan that adversely affected both countries' military capabilities, but those of Pakistan more than India's.[26] Pakistan was even further penalized following the army takeover of 1999, and, naturally, sought closer links with China. President Musharraf's declaration of support for the US after the 9/11 attacks spurred the Bush administration to reconsider its stance, when it became apparent that the Pakistan Army and US access to Pakistan's military facilities were essential components of what Mr Bush called the 'war on terror'. United States' laws and principles were subordinated to Washington's focus on al-Qaeda, and the result was re-establishment of defence connections with Pakistan and the opening of an equipment cornucopia. The Federation of American Scientists explains how this was effected:

> The Pakistan-only waiver was put into a separate bill (S. 1465, sponsored by Senator Brownback), which became law on 27 October 2001. This law waives the military coup provision (no arms or aid to countries that have undergone a military coup until democracy is restored) from Foreign Operations Appropriations bills for FY 2002 and 2003; allows for greater flexibility on sanctions related to MTCR [Missile Technology Control Regime] or Export Administration Act violations; and exempts Pakistan from restrictions on aid relating to loan defaults. It also shortens the congressional notification period for transfers of weapons from current US stocks from 15 to 5 days and transfers of excess US weapons from 30 to 15 days for all countries if the transfers would respond to or prevent international acts of terrorism. In June 2003, the State Department formally ended the ban on arms transfers to India and Pakistan, announcing that henceforth all requests would be considered on a standard case-by-case basis.[27]

Pakistan's defence expenditure has historically been opaque and only briefly outlined in annual budget papers. Lack of detail is justified officially by references to the imperatives of national security, but in practice flows from long-term, deeply rooted military influence on the country's governance and an ingrained proclivity for secrecy about almost everything to do with military matters. Even during Pakistan's brief periods of democracy, civilian governments have not provided other than the blandest statements relating to military spending, and there has been no indication that transparency might be favoured, no matter the nature of government in the foreseeable future. Official figures for overall defence expenditure are:

Financial Year	2000–1	2001–2	2002–3	2003–4	2004–5	2005–6	2006–7	2007–8
US$ (billions)	2.41	2.68	2.78	2.81	3.37	3.69	4.13	4.54

Defence spending accounts for about 20 per cent of the national budget of some PRs 903 billion and, as declared, is about 3 per cent of gross domestic product. Budget documents provided little information on division of expenditure other than to note allocations to 'defence administration' and 'defence services'. It is probable that appropriations for missile programmes and nuclear weapons are disguised in these, and other line items and under other budget headings. It's known as creative accounting.

The figures do not include allocations for military pensions or paramilitary troops (in common with many other countries' budget statements), or funds spent on procurement made on credit. This last figure is not revealed officially even to economic aid donors such as the International Monetary Fund or the World Bank, although it appears both have been quietly pressuring Islamabad for more transparency. It is probable that as much as US$7 billion of Pakistan's foreign debt in 2007 was related to defence procurement, excluding such arrangements as may have been made in 2006–2007 for the purchase of further F-16 aircraft. Foreign debt relief, although not intended for defence purposes, is likely in some fashion to serve to reduce amounts owing for foreign defence procurement. The military related debt, including the part funded through foreign loans, is not indicated in the debt figures released as part of the national budget. It is not known if earnings from such diverse enterprises as the Pakistan Ordnance Factories, military farms, land rentals and the National Logistics Cell are accounted for as income or offset against individual outlays.

Defence expenditure statistics are meaningless in the context of military capabilities. On 31 March 2004 the Finance Ministry informed the National Assembly that Pakistan had received some US$5.776 billion in aid from the US in the past four years, including a US$3 billion package announced while President Musharraf visited Washington in 2003. Of this, the Ministry indicated that US$1.38 billion had been granted for 'security and the fight against terror', but function allocations within that amount were not revealed. Provision of defence matériel from this military assistance, and generous transfer of spares, systems and equipments under terms of existing regulations and 'major non-Nato ally' status cannot be counted in national budgetary calculations.

US Military Assistance to Pakistan, FY2001–FY2008 (in millions of dollars)

Programme	2001	2002	2003	2004	2005	2006	2007	2008 (Request)
Foreign Military Financing	nil	75	225	75	299	297	297	300
Other Security Related Aid	4	102[a]	32	38	50	75	81	99
Coalition Support Funds	nil	1.169[b]	1.247	705	964	845	996[c]	1.785

Notes:
a. Includes $73 million for border security projects that continued in FY2003.
b. Includes $220 million in Peacekeeping Emergency Response Funds reported by State Department.
c. Congress authorized $1.1 billion in FY2007 CSF funds for 'Pakistan, Jordan and other cooperating nations'. CSF reimbursements to Pakistan averaged $83 million a month for the first four months of FY2007. The FY2007 estimate is a CRS extrapolation based on that average and in line with Pentagon projections.

Source: Adapted from a paper by Alan Kronstadt of the US Congressional Research Service, 24 August 2007[28] with figures updated on 18 October 2007. It is of note that the CRS Table, which includes development aid amounts, is headed 'Direct *Overt* US Assistance to Pakistan' (author's emphasis).

It can be appreciated that declared defence outlays are but an unknown fraction of actual expenditure on military equipment and provide no indication of the market or replacement value of equipment obtained from foreign sources. The situation regarding acquisition of weapons and associated systems has been made more complex by declaration of Pakistan as a 'Major Non-Nato Ally' (MNNA) by the US, which was welcomed by Pakistan, although regarded in India as having been handled in a singularly inept fashion.

In March 2004, then Secretary of State Colin Powell visited India and Pakistan. In Islamabad he announced that the US would confer MNNA status on Pakistan, without having hinted at such a major decision to the government in Delhi, and on 19 April the State Department notified the Senate Committee on Foreign Relations of the President's intention in a letter indicating exactly where the US-Pakistan nexus now hinges:

We wish to inform you of the President's intention to designate Pakistan as a Major Non-Nato Ally (MNNA) pursuant to 22 USC 2321k (Section 517 of the Foreign Assistance Act of 1961, as amended). Pakistan is one of our most important partners in the Global War on Terrorism. The GOP[29] has stepped up its counter-terrorism activities along the Afghan-Pakistan border and has firmly warned tribesmen in the area that they must stop harbouring foreigners. It has also captured and handed over to the US more than 550 suspected al-Qaeda operatives, including the group's senior commanders Khalid Sheikh Mohammad and Abu Zubaida as well as September 11 conspirator Ramzi bin al-Shibh. Currently [April 2004] there are 70,000 Pakistani troops deployed in the border region, and they have encountered stiff resistance. On March 17 alone, 16 Pakistani paramilitary personnel were slain in an encounter with groups that appear linked to terrorists and Taliban remnants. President Musharraf has accompanied his actions with important efforts to lead the public away from extremism. On February 18, for example, he delivered a nationally televised address calling on foreign extremists in Pakistan to leave, and urging the public to adhere to a moderate course.

The United States has had an important relationship with the Islamic Republic of Pakistan since its creation over 50 years ago. We intend to maintain it in the future and demonstrate our support for the firm actions Pakistan is taking in the Global War on Terror. It is in the US interest to seal our friendship with Pakistan; granting Pakistan MNNA status would signal our continued commitment to strengthened military-to-military ties.[30]

In fact, the status of MNNA does more than signal a commitment: it confers on allies so designated a considerable number of tangible benefits:

- Eligibility to receive US-owned war reserve stockpiles on its territory (22 U.S.C. 2321h) and obtain US foreign assistance to purchase depleted uranium ammunition (22 U.S.C. 2378a); [The latter is judged to be extremely unlikely.]
- US Foreign Military Financing (FMF) may be used by the country for the commercial leasing of certain defence articles (not including Major Defence Equipment, with the exception of helicopters and certain types of aircraft) (Consolidated Appropriations Act, Fiscal Year 2004, Foreign Operations, Sec. 510);
- Entitlement to enter into agreements with the US government for the co-operative furnishing of training, on a bilateral or multilateral basis, provided the agreements are based on financial reciprocity (22 U.S.C. 2761);
- The right to loans, by the secretary of defence, of materials, supplies, or equipment for purposes of cooperative research, development, testing, or evaluation (22 U.S.C. 2796d);
- Expedited US export license approval, as appropriate, for US companies to deliver commercial satellites, their components, and systems (22 U.S.C. 2778); and
- For those MNNAs located on the southern and south-eastern flank of NATO – priority delivery of excess US defence articles (22 U.S.C. 2321j).[31]

After making the announcement, Powell stated that 'in some instances [MNNA status] is more symbolic than practical ... I don't know if Pakistan [will] be able to take great advantage of it,' but in fact Pakistan has thus far benefited greatly from conferral of MNNA status, and will continue to do so. The flow of equipment and especially spares for existing inventories has been considerable, and even before MNNA included provision (or provision notification) for the army of forty Bell 407 helicopters, 2,000 TOW-2A anti-tank missiles and 3,270 manpack and vehicle-mounted Harris radios (interoperable with US Army and Special Forces' systems). The navy and air force did well, too, with P-3C and Hercules aircraft and Phalanx systems. Then, in March 2005 it was announced in a remarkably clumsy fashion by Washington that Pakistan would receive an unspecified number of F-16 aircraft, probably of the latest type.[32] It appears that for the foreseeable future Pakistan's armed forces will continue to receive quantities of surplus and advanced weapons systems from the US, to complement its inventories of equipment from other foreign suppliers and from its own manufacturing establishments, which have proved remarkably efficient in producing many items.

Defence Production and Procurement for the Army[33]
Defence procurement and production in Pakistan have been affected by the swings and caprices of Washington's policies regarding the subcontinent. Although the overall procurement plan is well structured and realistic, it has been recent practice to accept what is on offer from the US rather than to abide strictly by assessment of sequential requirements as is done in the relationship with the PRC.

Pakistan has a history of corruption in defence acquisition matters, and there has been influence by political figures and service officers on procurement decisions in the past. Former President Farooq Leghari stated in 1998 that the Prime Minister during his tenure, Benazir Bhutto 'and her husband were involved in efforts to buy Mirage [2000] aircraft from France. This whole deal reeked of corruption from day one, and I insured that [the] deal should not go through because [of this].' (The unit cost had increased markedly and for no apparent technical reason in the course of preliminary negotiations.) Given this and other highly publicized instances of improbity, particularly the scandalous conduct of Admiral Mansoor-ul Haq,[34] it can be expected that domestic and international media scrutiny of future major contracts will continue to be intense.

The three services are receiving and about to receive large quantities of weapons and ancillary items from the US under various programmes, and Pakistan is in a position in which it may be able to balance US largesse against the financial commitment required to obtain equivalent technology systems elsewhere. Its domestic military equipment programmes are

132

effective, especially in armoured vehicle and ammunition production, and it has co-operation agreements with China, France and Ukraine that are expected to expand.[35]

The views and intentions of weapons-exporting nations other than the US and China as regards supply of weapons and associated systems to Pakistan are regarded as important but subordinate to these two countries' foreign policies. Pakistan wishes to obtain high-technology equipment from almost any source but realizes and accepts that some countries cannot or will not engage in co-operation because of Indian commitments or US disapproval. So far as the army is concerned the main technology focus is on mobility, armour and local air defence, which is consistent with doctrine.

The best tank in the army's inventory is the T-80UD, bought from Ukraine, but the Al Khalid, manufactured by Heavy Industries Taxila (HIT), and developed with much Chinese input, is also an effective fighting vehicle – mainly because it now has a Ukrainian diesel power pack. The story of the Khalid goes back to 1988, when Aslam Beg took over from President Zia as Chief of Army Staff and decided, quite rightly, that the flirtation with the US Abrams tank had gone on too long, and that it was far too expensive and complicated (and, at that time, performed poorly in desert conditions) to justify purchase. This was a remarkably prescient decision for many other reasons, but the outcome was closer co-operation with China and joint development of MBT 2000, otherwise Khalid, from original Russian designs via the PRC's Type-90.

In the early 1990s I was taken round the factory at Taxila, not then named HIT – it was the Heavy Rebuild Programme – and shown the shop floors (where coy Chinese figures kept peeping round pillars) in addition to the plan for the future of Pakistan's tank and APC development and production; and most impressive it was. It covered almost all four walls of an office, and the detail, from year to year, of much of what was intended for the future has been kept to schedule as far as practicable. (It is now, of course, entirely computerized.) The delay in the projected M-113 armoured personnel carrier programme was caused by US withdrawal of support because of its sanctions, and Khalid production was delayed in the main by prolonged discussions about the engine – whether to continue with the desert-unfriendly turbine or move to diesel. The results were that the army's programme for mechanization of infantry battalions almost came to a halt, and it became obvious that in spite of the rebuild and upgrade programmes for existing tanks (shown in great detail in the Taxila production plot) there was a pressing requirement for a modern tank. During a visit to HIT in 2006 I toured production lines and was briefed on current projects, which appeared effective and flexible. Querying the comparatively slow rate of output of the Khalid, and remarking on the high level of human rather than computer-guided mensuration, I was informed that there was no foreseen requirement to increase the rate, but there were plans for acquisition of more hi-tech equipment should that be necessary.

The T-80 was first trialled in Pakistan in 1993, and a firm order was placed for 320 in August 1996, with deliveries from Ukrainian army stocks beginning the following year. The initial batches (seventeen and eighteen) were unsatisfactory because not all systems could be provided as agreed. Russia, for a combination of reasons,[36] attempted to derail the contract by denying Ukraine access to some components. Ukraine eventually overcame the difficulties and resumed provision of new and fully updated tanks. Concurrently, the rebuild and upgrade process was expanded to refurbish the Type 59 fleet by a combination of improving its armour and fire-control systems while fitting a more powerful engine and a 125 mm smooth-bore gun whose ammunition would be usable by the T-80 and Al-Khalid, and, of considerable importance, manufactured by Pakistan Ordnance Factories. Al-Zarrar, as the rebuilt machine is named, is practically a new tank altogether, and, from accounts by two non-partisan sources, is impressive not only in firepower but in mobility, although I am not convinced of its survivability against India's T-90S tanks from Russia. The Kharkiv Morozov Machine Building Design Bureau (KMDB) of Ukraine is a major contributor to its development, and it appears that defence association with Ukraine will continue. The Zarrar programme modifications include:

- Up-gun to 125 mm;
- Upgraded engine;
- Improved suspension;
- Improved Bottom Plate armour (anti-mine);
- New Fire Control System;
- Autoloader;
- Explosive Reactive Armour;
- Fire/explosion suppression; and
- Electronic Tracking System.

Standardization on the 125 mm smooth-bore gun was essential, but older tanks in the inventory cannot be modified, so retain the 105 mm gun which is of little use in modern armoured operations. Phased-out M-48s, non-modifiable T-59s and all T-69s have been and continue to be replaced by a combination of the NORINCO T-85 II-AP (manufactured at HIT under licence with some components from other suppliers), Khalid, Zarrar and T-80, for a probable total of about 1,500, which should maintain a balanced force structure.

HIT manufactures and refurbishes M-113 (Talha) armoured personnel carriers which, although not infantry fighting vehicles (IFV) as such, give infantry greatly increased mobility and thus, among other advantages, contribute to flexibility of armoured operations. The temptation to use lightly armoured M-113s as IFVs instead of fast and fairly well-protected battle taxis appears to have been resisted, as it is recognized that they could not survive in an armoured battle in spite of some being TOW-equipped, but in the HIT model there have been some major design improvements that include, of great importance, better troop comfort.[37] Consistent with the gradualist approach to improved capabilities, manufacture and rebuild/upgrade will continue until at least until the end of this decade, during which time the army will continue to have many responsibilities, including major UN commitments.

Although HIT has the capability to rebuild 155 mm self-propelled (SP) artillery pieces (M-109s) there is a requirement to replace these because of age. There do not appear to be reliable 155 mm SP suppliers other than United Defence LP of Arlington, owned by BAE since March 2005. It is possible they could offer the new International Howitzer which is based on the M109 A6 Paladin, or they could suggest the A5 version (still in production), or Paladin itself, but all would involve large sums. The International Howitzer can probably be ruled out by reason of cost and complexity, and it is more likely the A-5 would be the solution, especially if it could be provided under favourable financial terms.

In general the army's equipment and other systems are adequate for its tasks, although there continues to be a requirement for modernizing tactical command links and for more surface-to-air missiles, which are inadequate in both quantity and quality. Given its present capabilities, however, it is apparent that it could not only withstand an Indian attack but probably take and hold ground in Punjab and Rajasthan. Fortunately it is becoming less and less likely that it will be put to the test, as the process of rapprochement with India continues.

Peacekeeping

In September 2007 Pakistan had 10,629 people serving in UN peacekeeping missions. Details are shown below, and it is of note that of the 103 countries contributing to twelve peacekeeping missions worldwide, Pakistan ranks first, with Bangladesh and India not far behind. (Western nations are more modestly represented, with the United Kingdom, for example, fielding 371 personnel (275 in the former colony of Cyprus), and the US, which for national reasons does not place military personnel under foreign command, having nine soldiers and twelve military observers in five missions, with 220 contract police in Kosovo.)

Pakistan's UN Contributions – September 2007

Operation	Observers	Troops	Civilian Police
BINUB (Burundi)	1	0	0
UNOCI/ONUCI (Cote d'Ivoire)	11	1,123	127
MINURSO (Western Sahara)	7	0	0
MINUSTAH (Haiti)	0	1	249
MONUC (DR Congo)	56	3,579	0
UNIOSIL (Sierra Leone)	1	0	0
UNMIK (Kosovo)	2	0	181
UNMIL (Liberia)	15	3,402	31
UNMIS (Sudan)	20	1,569	39
UNOMIG (Georgia)	11	0	0
UNMEE (Ethiopia/Eritrea)	5	0	0
UNMIT (Timor–Leste)	4	0	195
Totals	133	9,674	822

Source: UN Department of Peacekeeping Operations.

Almost all peacekeeping missions to which Pakistan has contributed troops have been successful in contributing to stability in countries riven by internal conflict, but the main exception was Somalia in 1992–1995, from which lessons were learned concerning command, control and co-operation. It was unfortunate that the lessons were learned in circumstances involving the slaughter of Pakistani soldiers.

The Somali operations were a humiliating failure for all concerned – except the Somali thugs and warlords who drove out the peacekeepers – and their ineffectiveness was due almost entirely to a convoluted and gravely inadequate international command structure. Pakistan's forces were at the bottom of the chain of confusion and suffered accordingly. In consequence, the main lesson learned was more political than tactical: do not commit troops to a mission in which their safety is placed at hazard equally by armed opposition and structural deficiencies.

Pakistan was involved in contributing troops from the beginning of the debacle, and it is appropriate to examine just how and why it was placed in a situation that cascaded into chaos.

In 1991 Somalia was ungoverned and ungovernable (it still is). Food aid was being provided, but was looted by gangs of criminals who roamed round the country in 'Technicals', pick-up trucks with machine guns mounted on the back, killing each other, menacing aid officials and, as UN Secretary-General Boutros Boutros-Ghali put it, engaging in 'a war of all against all'. Eventually in 1992 the Security Council was shamed into approving 'United Nations Operation Somalia', or UNOSOM I, which involved deployment of a security force of 500 troops to protect delivery of food and other assistance in the country. The trouble was the troops were not permitted to use force and its entry was dependent on permission of the strongest warlord, who at the time was Mohammad Farah Aideed. Although authorized by the UN to arrive in April 1992, they were not accepted by Aideed until September. The UN official description of developments is banal:

> On 23 June, the Secretary-General informed the Security Council that both principal factions in Mogadishu had agreed to the immediate deployment of the unarmed observers. The Chief Military Observer, Brigadier-General Imtiaz Shaheen of Pakistan, and the advance party of UNOSOM observers arrived in Mogadishu in early July 1992. On 12 August, the Secretary-General informed the Security Council that, after considerable delays and difficulties, agreement had been reached with the principal faction leaders in Mogadishu to deploy 500 United Nations security personnel in the capital as part of UNOSOM. The Government of Pakistan had agreed to contribute a unit for the purpose. The first group of security personnel arrived in Mogadishu on 14 September 1992.[38]

Pakistan's soldiers were confined to the airport (where the aid material and food arrived) because UN rules of engagement forbade them to take physical action to carry out their mandate to protect its distribution. The Security Council authorized a further 3,000 Belgian and Canadian troops for the mission but they did not arrive, which was extremely unfortunate as both country's armies are experienced in peacekeeping missions. Lawlessness and extreme violence continued, and foreigners were harassed and humiliated. In December the Security Council accepted a US proposal to contribute to and command a force to establish order. The Unified Task Force (UNITAF) was a mission of 'armed humanitarianism' and was referred to by the US as Operation Restore Hope. The US contingent was authorized to participate until 4 May 1993, when the task would be handed back to the UN. When the first Marines waded ashore in the full moonlight of 9 December 2002, apparently expecting an opposed landing, they were met by reporters and cameramen, at least one of whom they arrested.[39] The operation, involving 28,000 US troops and 9,000 from twenty-three other nations was initially successful in terms of providing starving people with sustenance. Much aid was distributed, but the country remained chaotic, with no semblance of government emerging. The changeover to UNOSOM II was when the real trouble began.

There were three quite separate military chains of command in UNOSOM II: one in the hands of the UN and two of the US. The UN Force Commander had no power over US forces, which operated entirely separately (apart from a logistics element), and although the UN Deputy Force Commander was an American (Major General Thomas M. Montgomery), he was also Commander US Forces, Somalia. He, however, had no control over Task Force Ranger, which consisted of Rangers and Delta Force personnel, and was responsible solely to the Commander of US Special Operations Command in the US. The operation's command arrangements would be regarded with derision by a first-year military cadet. The overall commander of UNOSOM II, 'the Special Representative of the Secretary-General', was retired US Admiral Jonathan Howe, and the military commander was Turkish Lieutenant General Cevic Bir. Howe, in the words of William J. Durch[40] of the Stimson Center, 'might have been an ideal *Deputy* [emphasis added] Special Representative'.

The major problem for the Pakistani contingent began on 4 June 1993 when another US/UN representative, April Glaspie, authorized two US officers to undertake weapons inspections of installations controlled by the Somali National Alliance (SNA), headed by Aideed. The SNA asked for time to consider the matter and, when this was refused, informed the UN that if the inspections went ahead it would mean 'war'. Next day, Friday, the Muslim day of rest, a singularly inappropriate choice for operations by any troops, inspections went ahead, with the two officers being accompanied by a contingent of Pakistani troops who had not been informed of the SNA's unmistakable threat, and were in soft-skinned vehicles. Immediately after the inspection the lightly armed Pakistanis were menaced by an angry crowd of about 200, but were able to withdraw.[41] Groups of Pakistani soldiers at humanitarian feeding stations and other posts were less fortunate and suffered full-scale attacks by SNA forces amongst large mobs of civilians, many of whom were also armed. They requested support from the Italian contingent, but the Italian helicopters that responded strafed the Pakistani positions and wounded three soldiers, while the armoured vehicles that had been requested at 11.00 am did not arrive until 4.30 pm, when they found only dead soldiers at the food distribution area. That day the Pakistan Army suffered twenty-four dead and fifty-seven wounded.

These attacks led to aggressive operations, and on 12 June US AC-130 Spectre gunships and attack helicopters strafed the headquarters of Radio Mogadishu and other sites suspected of being Aideed stockades, following which the overall situation deteriorated alarmingly. The US placed a price on the head of Aideed and increased strikes by gunships; his supporters became even more violent. There were many more attacks on all contingents that involved the killing of soldiers from Malaysia, Italy, Morocco, India, Nepal and Nigeria, and the shooting-down of US helicopters. On 3 October 1994 US Special Forces launched an air-landing assault on a suspected Aideed stronghold. The operation had been authorized by Special Forces Command in Florida, and neither Admiral Howe nor General Bir was informed of it until immediately before the attack, which was a disaster. It resulted in the killing of eighteen American troops and the well-publicized dragging of a US soldier's body through the streets of Mogadishu. Several hundred Somalis were killed. Two days later the US President announced that the US would withdraw its forces, which it did, in small batches, in February and March 1994. Others followed, with the Pakistani contingent being the last to leave, in February 1995. The entire mission was a failure.

The lesson for Pakistan (and others) is that UN peacekeeping operations should not be supported unless there is a clear task and a well-defined chain of command. Neither applied in Somalia, and the Secretary-General said there were important lessons to be learned about the 'theory and practice of multifunctional peacekeeping operations in conditions of civil war and chaos and especially about the clear line that needs to be drawn between peacekeeping and enforcement action'.[42]

UN operations since that time have been conducted under UN command, and have been successful in subcontinent terms as well as in a wider context, to the point of involving close co-operation between Indian and Pakistani forces. The Pakistan Army will continue to provide troops for UN missions, and both it and the missions will benefit.

Problems in the Army

The report by Pakistan's Auditor General for 2002–3 (released in March 2005)[43] showed that there was gross mismanagement of defence funds by almost everyone who had any control over them. There was incontrovertible evidence of inappropriate letting of contracts, cost overruns of absurd proportions and general inefficiency in management of public monies. Worse, from the point of view of the army's standing and honour, were the cases of hanky panky over construction of married quarters and guest houses, and such grubby antics as ripping-off rickshaw drivers. The *Nation* newspaper's editorial of 10 March 2005 summed things up very well:

> The army remains outside the ambit of the National Accountability Bureau because the military hierarchy believes their internal justice system is better suited and more efficient. The question presents itself then: if their internal mechanism is so strong, why did it fail to detect these financial discrepancies? The army's continuous interference in the political process has definitely played a part in inducing indiscipline within their ranks. As the army became politicised, it resorted to increasingly undesirable practices to prolong [and] cement its position in the power circles of Islamabad. With such political considerations, it is difficult to understand how the military can focus on its primary objective to defend the motherland. That the military machinery has become corrupt is therefore not incomprehensible. Any

process of reformation must commence with its quitting politics and sticking to the job it was created for.

These are strong words, but increasingly reflect the public's gradual swing to considering that it is time the army became less prominent in the country's management. Involvement of the army (any army) in financial matters of any sort is the way to perdition. As a rule, soldiers do not relish professional involvement in economics. Little as many soldiers (including myself) revere those who are pejoratively referred to as 'defence civilians' or 'bean-counters' (and much worse), there is no doubt that civilian bureaucrats have an important role to play in financial management, acting not only as advisers but as brakes, checks and balances and, if necessary, whistle-blowers. The image of the services as a whole suffered badly from the revelations about Admiral Mansoor-ul Haq. Who would have thought that a Chief of Naval Staff could have behaved so disgustingly? It was all very well for the armed forces to look down their noses at the corruption of Benazir Bhutto and her squalid gang, and to express similar revulsion and contempt for what Nawaz Sharif did in his flamboyant and amoral looting of the country's coffers, but what answer can there be to the sheeting home of undeniable financial chicanery to some of the most senior citizens in uniform?

There are even worse instances of the army using its influence in the country to obtain financial gain. The scandal of dispossession of poor peasant farmers from lands near the border with India in the Okara region of Punjab is a blot that cannot be expunged by claiming it is the responsibility of the Pakistan Rangers. The Rangers are a para-military force, certainly; but its officers come from the army and its persecution of the peasants could not take place without army approval. The report by Human Rights Watch (*Soiled Hands: the Pakistan Army's Repression of the Punjab Farmers*)[44] makes sad reading. The facts are readily available to anyone with access the Internet, but I never imagined I would read anything like this about an officer in the modern Army of Pakistan:

> We were arrested at six in the morning. We were blindfolded and kept in a vehicle for about forty-five minutes while twenty-five others were arrested. We were brought to Rangers Headquarters. We were made to sit at a cold and dusty place in freezing temperature. Major Tahir Malik ordered us to start doing push-ups. We carried on like that for one hour. Major Tahir then made us stand with our arms raised for hours. If anyone's arms fell, they were beaten. He asked us to sign up and pay the contract money to secure our release. We were also forced to pressure our families to pay contract money. We were kept at Rangers' Headquarters for seven days. During this time, we were whipped and beaten with sticks as well.

Human Rights Watch states that:

Major-General Shaukat Sultan, the Director General of Inter-Services Public Relations [ISPR, the public relations wing of the Pakistan Armed Forces], succinctly summarized the views of the Army: 'The needs of the Army will be decided by the Army itself, and/or the government will decide this. Nobody has the right to say what the Army can do with 5,000 acres or 17,000 acres. The needs of the Army will be determined by the Army itself.'

This is indeed a novel approach to democracy.

After I wrote the above section in draft I sent it to several friends in Pakistan and to some foreigners who know Pakistan well. The reaction from almost every one of them was words to the effect that 'I thought you were a friend of Pakistan and admired the army very much, so why are you so critical?'

Quite so: I am a friend of Pakistan and admire the army greatly. Which is exactly why I wrote what appears above. There is a virus attacking the army and it is time it was dealt with. As with most viruses, the cure is a dose of antibiotics, and in this case the best antibiotic would be a stiff dose of democracy mixed with an injection of accountability.

Notes

1. Human Rights Watch World Report 1999 – http://www.hrw.org/wr2k/Asia-07.htm
2. In conversations with the author, November 2002, April 2003.
3. It is interesting to speculate on what might have – or might not have – taken place had Ali Kuli Khan been appointed COAS, as he deserved. There is no doubt Musharraf was a well-above-average officer, even a brilliant one, but Ali Kuli had star quality and a great deal of influence outside the military, which is probably why Sharif was frightened to appoint him. One thing is certain: had Ali Kuli been COAS there would have been no Kargil operation. He told the author on 29 May 2005 that the Kargil affair was an appalling mistake by the army.
4. Mohammed Shehzad, *South Asia Tribune*, 7–13 October 2002. http://www.satribune.com/archives/oct7_13_02/P1_fasihbokhari.htm
5. Article 42 of the Constitution states inter alia that the President 'will preserve, protect and defend the Constitution of the Islamic Republic of Pakistan'.
6. Reuters, 14:39, 09-23-99.
7. 'Pak PM ousted by army, in custody' Scott McDonald, http://www.rediff.com/news/1999/oct/13 pak1.htm
8. In several meetings with the author.
9. This is not in any way to denigrate that Corps. The best army chief and Chief of Defence Force that Australia ever had was the redoubtable, wise and highly intellectual General Peter Gration, late Royal Australian Engineers, who had never heard a shot fired in anger or commanded a fighting formation.
10. Later Chief Executive of Air Blue International, a private venture airline formed in Pakistan in 2006.

11. I am indebted to Captain Baloch for giving me permission, in October 2007, to publish his memoir.

12. Dennis Kux describes the period admirably in *The United States and Pakistan 1947–2000*. The US Senate was forced by the powerful farmers' lobby, however, to 'water down' sanctions to avoid loss of grain sales to Pakistan.

13. In an interview broadcast by [Australian] ABCs *Lateline* on 17 July 2002, Ms Bhutto was asked to comment on the observation that 'After all, it was during your second term as PM that Pakistan sponsored the birth of the Taliban, sent them into Afghanistan' to which she replied, 'Yes, that's partially true and certainly there is a perception. In retrospect, having seen what the Taliban did, I would say that was a wrong decision by our part.' http://www.abc.net.au/lateline/stories/s609909.htm. See also Eweres, Martin, *Afghanistan: A New History*, Curzon, 2001, pp. 182–3.

14. Coll, Stve, *Ghost Wars*, Penguin Press, 2004. An outstanding account of Afghanistan's vicissitudes up to 10 September 2001 by an author with a deep knowledge of the sub-continent.

15. Human Rights Watch World Report 2001. http://www.hrw.org/reports/2001/afghan2/Afghan0701-02.htm

16. See The National Security Archive, *The September 11th Sourcebooks Volume VII: The Taliban File*, Documents 4 and 5. http://www.gwu.edu/~nsarchiv/NSAEBB/NSAEBB97/index.htm

17. 'US documents show Pakistan gave Taliban military aid', *Guardian* (UK), 16 August 2007. http://www.guardian.co.uk/pakistan/Story/0,,2149588,00.html

18. Official despatch written by the author following five visits to the de-mining instruction camp at Risalpur.

19. 'Pakistan blamed for Afghan fighting', Nicole Winfield, Associated Press AP-NY-08-27-99 2145EDT.

20. See Cloughley, Brian, 'Pakistan's Religion and Madrassas' in Jane's *Islamic Affairs Analyst*, January 2005.

21. My thanks to Jane's for permission to reproduce the piece.

22. 'Aurakzai Diaries', 9 February 2002. The author is editing the diaries for publication. They cover the periods 2001–4 when Lieutenant General Aurakzai was Corps Commander in Peshawar, 2005–6 as secretary Defence Production, and 2006–8, when he was Governor of NWFP.

23. Macmillan and Company, 1958; now available in the Oxford Historical Reprints series, 1983, with a new Foreword and Epilogue by the author.

24. Private sources indicate that 254 army and Frontier Corps troops were killed in calendar 2004.

25. An apt phrase used by Winston Churchill, and the title of a superb book on the area by Victoria Schofield (Tauris Parke Paperbacks, 2003).

26. The Pakistan Army's mechanization process was almost halted because the M-113 programme could not continue, and the PAF's F-16s were running out of spares. The army's helicopters, too, suffered from lack of parts and no upgrades were possible, while the navy's frigates had inadequate close-in protection. It was fortunate for Pakistan that it had not chosen the Abrams tank.

27. http://www.fas.org/terrorism/at/

28. CRS report RL 33498, *Pakistan-US Relations*. With thanks to the CRS, and especially to Alan Kronstadt whose personal assistance is much appreciated.

29. The Government of Pakistan; not the Republican Party of the United States.

30. See the Federation of American Scientists' site at http://www.fas.org/terrorism/at/docs/2004/PakMNNAdesignation.pdf

31. See the Center for Defense Information: 'US Arms Transfers to America's Newest "Major non-NATO Ally"' at http://www.cdi.org/program/document.cfm?documentid= 2443&programID=73&from_page=../friendlyversion/printversion.cfm

32. The Secretary of State, Dr Condoleezza Rice, visited India, Pakistan and Afghanistan from 16 to 18 March 2005, and was asked repeatedly about possible provision of F-16s, with India reiterating its considerable concerns. The announcement was made a week later, prompting official criticism in New Delhi.

33. For a well-researched and comprehensive history of Pakistan's defence procurement, see Siddiqa-Agha, Ayesha, *Pakistan's Arms Procurement and Military Build-up 1979–99*, Palgrave, 2003, and Sang-e-Meel (Pakistan), 2003.

34. Convicted of corruption associated with acquisition of container ships and Agosta submarines.

35. The United Kingdom has almost lost Pakistan as a partner in defence and other matters because the 'New Labour' government made it clear it favoured India. The diplomatic skills of individuals and their rapport with senior figures in Pakistan cannot counter what is perceived in Islamabad to be British government policy. The result has been a diminution of British influence. In 2005 I called on President Musharraf immediately after he had a visit by the British High Commissioner; his comments were dismissive.

36. Russia is the main supplier of armaments to India, and the T-80 is operated only by Russia, Ukraine and Pakistan. Commercial loyalty to India and a general desire to disoblige Ukraine whenever practicable resulted in the Moscow government denying some components made only in Russia, forcing Ukraine to agree to penal terms for their supply and then to manufacture as many as it could.

37. There is no point in being able to speed around the battlefield if all that happens is fast delivery of disoriented and travel-sick soldiers. The old M-113 and its international equivalents were excruciatingly uncomfortable. Much practice is required if APC-borne soldiers are to be properly trained for operations, but exercises use up a great deal of fuel and few armies can afford to conduct prolonged realistic training. One problem with APCs is that during exercises their young commanders sometimes imagine themselves to be latter-day Guderians and try to take on AFVs, which tendency is to be deprecated.

38. See http://www.un.org/Depts/dpko/dpko/co_mission/unosomi.htm which is 'Not an official document of the United Nations. Prepared for the Internet by the Information Technology section/Department of Public Information (DPI). Maintained by the Peace and Security Section of DPI in co-operation with the Department of Peacekeeping Operations.' It should be noted that in the Pakistan Army the correct rank description is 'brigadier' and not 'brigadier general'.

39. Description by reporter Richard Dowden (http://www.somaliawatch.org/archivedec/ 01/011218201.htm) in which he states the Marines made a considerable mistake when they ordered the arrested people to separate, with 'Whites over here; Somalis over there'.

40. See Durch, William J., *UN Peacekeeping, American Politics and the Uncivil Wars of the 1990s*, Macmillan, 1997, an admirable collection of essays, edited by Durch, who himself wrote the chapter on Somalia titled 'Introduction to Anarchy: Humanitarian Intervention and "State-Building" in Somalia', a penetrating analysis which should be required reading on every course of instruction concerned with peacekeeping. Another valuable reference is Shawcross, William, *Deliver us from Evil, Warlords and Peacekeepers in a World of Endless Conflict*, Bloomsbury, 2000, especially Chapter 4.

41. Information from a Pakistani officer.

42. The US State Department account is somewhat different. 'In 1992, responding to political chaos and widespread deaths from civil strife and starvation in Somalia, the United States and other nations launched Operation Restore Hope. Led by the Unified Task Force (UNITAF), the operation was designed to create an environment in which assistance

could be delivered to Somalia suffering from the effects of two catastrophes – one man-made and one natural. UNITAF was followed by the United Nations Operation in Somalia (UNOSOM). The United States played a major role in both operations until 1994, when US forces withdrew.' See http://www.state.gov/r/pa/ei/bgn/2863.htm

43. See *The Nation*, 9 & 10 March 2005, for a news item at http://nation.com.pk/daily/mar-2005/9/index12.php and an editorial at http://nation.com.pk/daily/mar-2005/10/editorials3.php
44. Human Rights Watch HRW vol. 16, No. 10 C, July 2004. At http://hrw.org/reports2004/pakistan0704/

Chapter 6

How the Army Looks After its Own

In 2004 Dr Rehmat Ellahi wrote a scientific treatise with the catchy title 'Unsteady periodic flows of a magneto hydrodynamic fluid due to non-coaxial rotations of a porous disc and fluid at infinity'. A notable academic achievement, as the readers of Volume 40 of *Mathematical and Computer Modelling* would no doubt consider. And this paper, with many others written by Dr Ellahi, is indeed a distinguished accomplishment, made possible not only by the outstanding (and somewhat daunting) intellectual abilities of the author, but the interest and actions of one of the army's welfare organizations, the Fauji Foundation.

Professor Brian Straughan of the University of Durham's Department of Mathematical Sciences commented that Rehmat Ellahi's PhD thesis 'represents a significant contribution to mathematical knowledge' because it is 'of the finest quality'; and the words 'significant contribution' and 'finest quality' are equally appropriate in describing the Fauji Foundation's charitable enterprises, and the commercial interests that fund them.

Rehmat's father served in the army and retired to run a small business in the tiny village of Bamla in southern Punjab. As with all retirees he was considered a 'beneficiary', and when Rehmat displayed more than usual interest in his studies the Fauji Foundation was alerted and began to subsidize his education. From schooldays to university he and many others were taken under the Fauji wing, and he showed his gratitude for sixteen years of assistance in his studies by dedicating his PhD dissertation to the Foundation. In a matter-of-fact fashion, as befits a scientist, he says he regards the organization as a second father, and there can be fewer deeper tributes than that.

In India a similar position obtains. The Indian Army Welfare Education Society[1] runs 116 army schools throughout the country, attended by over 100,000 students. There are seven vocational institutes with an annual intake of 730 students and a total capacity of 2,350. Each year 9,000 scholarships are awarded to 'promising children of all ranks of the army', and the Army Institute of Hotel Management and Catering Technology in Bangalore offers a four-year Bachelor's degree course 'exclusively for children of serving army personnel or retired army personnel with pension' and the 'wards of war widows in receipt of pension'. In Kolkata the National Institute of Management provides sixty MBA places and thirty for a Master's degree in Computer Applications with the same beneficiaries in mind. Also provided are degree courses in dentistry, law, mechanical engineering, information technology, electronics and teaching. The difference between systems in Pakistan and India is that in the latter these benefits are funded through government revenue and not by private profit-making organizations like the Fauji Foundation and the Army Welfare Trust.

The Fauji Foundation has the aim of providing or assisting in 'quality education and medical care to beneficiaries through investments in profitable ventures ensuring earning growth compatible to our demands for providing high quality services', which is one way of saying they improve access by pensioners and their families to education and health by running businesses. This practice has attracted some criticism, domestically and internationally, apparently because it is considered that undue influence might be wielded by the military on the country's economy. One critic wrote in mid-2007 that the armed services' association with business (called 'Milbus'):

> perpetuates the military's predatory style. The defining feature of such predatory capital is that it is concealed, not recorded as part of the defence budget, and entails unexplained and questionable transfer of resources from the public to the private sector, especially to individuals or groups of people connected with the armed forces. Second, the military's economic predatoriness increases in totalitarian systems. Motivated by personal gains, the officer cadre of the armed forces seeks political and economic relationships which will enable them to increase their economic returns. Third. The military's economic predatoriness, especially inside its national boundaries, is both a cause and effect of a feudal, authoritarian and non-democratic political system.[2]

Given the charitable nature of the Fauji Foundation and the Army Welfare Trust, the allegations that they are predatory and form part of an 'illegal military economy' intent on avoiding 'laws which are detrimental to their personal interests and that of their civilian cronies'[3] attracted some resentment in the army, and especially in the organizations that provide, through profit-making in business, a range of social services that benefit former members of the forces and their families, and thus the country as a whole. The allegation that there are 'unexplained and questionable transfer of resources from the public to the private sector' is not and cannot be substantiated, but it engendered headlines round the world, especially in India.

The Fauji Foundation has over 9 million beneficiaries, increasing at an annual rate of about 2 per cent. It generates income through seven fully owned industrial/commercial enterprises and nine associated companies in which it has shareholdings of from 12 to 52 per cent. All pay tax at normal rates and are quoted on the Stock Exchange.[4] The financial accounts are open for any citizen to inspect, and total tax paid in the financial year 2005/2006 was 32 billion rupees (US$528 million). It employs 12,500 people, of whom 4,500 are ex-service.

In an interview with *The Times of India* published on 16 September 2007 Dr Ayesha Siddiqa, a vocal critic of the Pakistan army and the Fauji Foundation, stated that:

> unlike India which relies on state benefits for its officers, Pakistan has set up a number of organisations to look after its officers. The Fauji Foundation is the oldest and most powerful. Set up in 1954 to look after the needs of ex-servicemen, the foundation has assets worth Rs 9.8 billion ($169 million). It runs 25 industrial projects, 18 of which are fully controlled by the foundation. Around 80–90% of people employed in these projects are army personnel.[5]

The Foundation's welfare expenditure in 2006–7 totalled $46 million in a ratio of 8:4:1 in medical care, education services and training of family members of ex-service personnel and some civilians. One sector of particular interest is vocational training, which takes place at sixty-five centres.

The Vocational Training Centre in Rawalpindi, as with others (in every province), has the aim of 'educating and training [female] beneficiaries (widows/wives/daughters) of deceased pensioners and retired personnel in tailoring, cutting, embroidery, first aid and education' in order to improve their earning capability. Although 'education' appears at the end of the list it is higher in practice, and not only is there instruction in English language but the thriving computer class is over-subscribed. The beauticians' class is probably the most popular after English instruction, mainly because knowledge of hairdressing and cosmetics is a sure way to financial independence. Of the 150 women at the Rawalpindi VTC in August 2007, only two were illiterate before joining the course, although education standards were in general not high. Ages ranged from fourteen to fifty, and the main age group represented was fourteen to twenty-four (ninety-six), with only a handful aged forty to fifty. In other centres the literacy rate is lower, sometimes much lower, and in rural areas the emphasis is more on handicrafts than computers or beauty classes, although there is still interest in, for example, instruction in how to decorate brides' hands preparatory to marriage. This is hardly the stuff of an 'illegal military economy' although, inevitably, it is claimed that there is some baleful purpose behind the enterprise. One commentator states that:

> The available literature on welfare recognises the presence of special interest groups taking responsibility for the welfare of their own members [quoting a single study of 1988]. However, the literature also talks about the representation of the otherwise incommensurable[6] needs of individuals by a relatively small group of people chosen as representatives, or a local elite. The decision-making structure of the Fauji Foundation and other military foundations is highly elitist. Post retirement benefits are decided exclusively by the military high command, without the participation of the *jawans* [soldiers]. Consequently, there is no system of feedback within the military regarding client satisfaction by the personnel for whom the welfare system is intended and to whom the various packages are offered. Colonel (retired) Bakhtiar Khan claims that the actual beneficiaries of the welfare system are the officers and not the ordinary soldiers.[7]

Tell that to Dr Rehmat Ellahi, son of a soldier, and to the women benefiting from vocational training, almost all of whom are relatives of soldiers. And tell it to the limbless soldiers who have received prosthetic limbs and attentive care from the Fauji Foundation's hospitals.

So far as can be determined there is no military oriented retirement benefits scheme in the world in which settlements or remuneration are decided upon with participation of private soldiers, however desirable such a system may be. As to the Fauji Foundation's 'highly élitist system of decision-making, it is well to consider the meaning of 'élite', which is defined as 'the most powerful, rich or gifted members of a group', or in other words, the leaders. It appears that most organizations in most countries, be they profit-making, political, civil service or military, are headed by those who are best qualified to do so, and that the Fauji Foundation (and other institutions wishing to survive) would be unwise to adopt alternative means of managing their affairs.

Most military associated commercial enterprises have come under attack from various quarters, but evidence of malpractice is rarely provided by critics. In a study conducted by the author in August 2007, the Fauji Fertiliser Company was examined in detail.

Following the Enron scandal it became obvious worldwide that creative accounting – a phrase conveying the company's intention to defraud its investors – was effective in lining the pockets of the fortunate few who were privy to that company's machinations. There were undoubtedly incidents of 'questionable transfer of resources' at Enron, but on examining the accounts of Fauji Fertiliser (and the Fauji Foundation as a whole) there is no evidence of 'off-balance-sheet' transactions or similar jiggery-pokery. Audits are carried out internally and by independent accountants. It would be unlikely that the firm KPMG would welcome assertions of impropriety or illegality in the manner that Fauji Fertiliser carries out its business and might even be tempted to take action were any to be made, as KPMG Taseer Hadi & Co are the auditors.[8]

Fauji Fertiliser is a medium-sized company employing 2,916 staff of whom 536 are ex-service. In 2001–6 it paid some Rs 45 billion (US$740 million) in taxes and other government imposts, paid dividends of over 9 billion, and contributed almost 2 billion to the Workers' Welfare Fund. It runs technical training centres for its employees, and has five mobile laboratories whose scientists conduct soil analysis throughout the country and advise farmers on how best to manage their land (using, of course, Fauji Fertiliser's products). It is hardly 'Business in Jackboots' as one headline had it.[9]

In 2006–7, when it became fashionable in Pakistan to criticize the army, there came other and equally pejorative headlines and articles. The author of 'Pakistan: The Army as the State' pronounced that '[The Army Welfare Trust] is the second-largest private conglomerate in Pakistan. The largest is the Fauji Foundation. But the word "private" is something of a misnomer here as both these (and other conglomerates linked to the navy and air force) are run by serving army officers, and some were set up with public funds. Today, their combined assets could be as high as $20 billion.'[10] Certainly the Army Welfare Trust and the Fauji Foundation were set up with public funds.[11] The Foundation, for example, was 'incorporated under the Endowments Act of 1890 out of the Post War [Second World War] Services Reconstruction Funds' which were then allocated to India and Pakistan at the time of Independence in 1947. None of the organizations is 'run by serving army officers', and the assertion that the assets 'could be' up to $20 billion is backed by neither facts nor figures, although it would be neither illegal nor undesirable were this true. There are certainly retired officers heading the Foundation and the Trust, but the notion that they are part of some vast conspiracy to plunder the nation is risible.

Pay, Pensions and Plots

Pakistan is a poor country (although its economy appears to be growing in the macro sense), and cannot yet afford to pay its public servants on anything like the scale of those in more developed nations. Neither can it afford to provide pensions at all comparable with those arranged by private pension funds that have sprung up since the early 2000s. But it has been claimed in a widely publicized book[12] that retired service personnel in Pakistan enjoy 'a comparatively sizeable pension' and it is of interest to examine this pronouncement in the light of fact.

The monthly pension of a Pakistan Army lieutenant general (who, like others, is allowed to 'commute' part of his pension and thereby receive a lump sum of US$28,178 on retiring) is US$509 a month when he leaves after a minimum of thirty-two years' service. The pension may be thought of as 'comparatively sizeable' when placed beside that of a retired major, who gets about half that amount, or a naik (corporal), who exists on Rs 3,129, or US$51 a month, but it is open to question if it is appropriate remuneration for a person who has left the army with high rank after over three decades of service.

Sixty-five per cent of Pakistan army officers retire as majors, usually in their forties, an age at which employment is hard to find in any country. The rank pyramid then narrows even further, and chances of promotion beyond colonel, even for extremely well-qualified officers, are remarkably slim. Out go the passed-over colonels and brigadiers and major generals, to exist on monthly amounts that would barely buy an air ticket from Karachi to Lahore to attend a job interview. Soldiers, junior commissioned officers and non-commissioned officers are not exactly in the lap of luxury, either. (In the tables below the Rupee-US$ exchange rate is as at mid-September 2007.)

Rates of pay and pensions for the rank of Sepoy (private soldier) to Sergeant Major are:

Rank	Years of service	Monthly Pay and Allowances		Monthly Pension (after minimum service (varies))		Retirement lump sum	
		Rupees	US$	Rupees	US$	Rupees	US$
Sergeant Major	30	21,960	362	7,167	118	622,505	10,263
Subedar	22	17,727	292	6,169	102	577,010	9,513
N/Subedar	20	16,463	267	5,090	84	547,357	9,024
Havildar	18	12,612	207	3,911	64	492,195	8,115
Naik	14	11,233	185	3,129	52	429,084	7,074
Sepoy	9	9,624	158	2,656	43	384,485	6,340

Rates of pay and pensions for officers:

Rank	Years of service[1]	Monthly Pay and Allowances[2]		Monthly Pension (after minimum of 23 years service)		Retirement lump sum	
		Rupees	US$	Rupees	US$	Rupees	US$
Lieutenant General	32	64,290	1,057	30,913	497	1,768,817	29,092
Major General	31	58,809	967	28,457	468	1,863,644	30,652
Brigadier	27	49,706	817	25,580	420	1,867,078	30,708

Colonel	26	46,439	763	19,596	322	1,900,202	31,253
Lieutenant Colonel	21[1]	40,238	661	19,192	315	1,862,133	30,627
Major	16[1]	33,366	548	15,043	247	1,949,621	32,066

Notes:
1. This length of service is applicable only to pay rates. Pensions are payable after twenty-three years of service.
2. In an attempt to discourage officers of the Indian armed forces from seeking premature retirement, the Indian Pay Commission has proposed the granting of a year's salary after serving for specified periods.[13]

By some standards, a sergeant major's monthly pension of $118 and a brigadier's of $420 might be regarded as 'comparatively sizeable' (although not to be compared with that of the British equivalent of the latter, who receives about $7,500 a month), especially as the average annual income in Pakistan is tiny,[14] but it is not an appropriate amount for a retired senior executive who has occupied a position of considerable responsibility in either a staff or command appointment. (All brigadiers, even those not fortunate enough to be selected to command a brigade of some 5,000 soldiers, are selected on the basis of overall capability.) For retired officers and soldiers to maintain a decent standard of living they must, most of them, find further employment after retiring from the army. For specialists (pilots, engineers, IT and other communications experts), there is not too much of a problem. And there are some, an unknown but obviously substantial minority, who do not need a further income, having their own family assets. My former bearer, an old soldier, lives contentedly on his army pension in the hills of North West Frontier Province. He is surrounded by his large family, some of whom work or have worked in the Gulf and therefore contribute substantially to the joint family income. But for many others, soldiers and officers alike (and especially generalist officers), no matter their expertise in what is now called 'human resources' and decision-making, the future can be bleak. Therefore it is realistic and humane to make alternative provisions that will not be a drain on the national exchequer. The World Bank examined pensions worldwide and commented that:

> Military pensions that begin to be paid while retired soldiers are young do not seem to have the same objectives as national and civil service pension schemes that are set up to deal with old age. In an integrated system, these soldiers could continue accumulating pension wealth until old age. A separate benefit or other form of assistance for reinsertion into the labour force might be granted to deal with this issue.[15]

In Pakistan there has been institution of alternative means, and it is this that in many cases has meant and continues to mean that retired members of the armed forces are able to live in dignity and reasonable comfort for the many years that lie ahead of them following retirement at a necessarily early age. As noted in a study by David R. Segal and Mady Weschler Segal,[16] published in December 2004:

> Most people who enter the American armed forces serve for fewer than 10 years. Many express patriotic reasons for joining the armed forces, but their motivations for serving also include the desire to learn a skill applicable in the civilian labor force, or to earn educational benefits that will enable them to go to college. Even the relatively small proportion of personnel who serve for a military career return to civilian life in their late 30s or early 40s, too young to truly retire, and with a pension too small to support a family. What happens on their return to the civilian labor force?

One thing that happens in Pakistan *before* return to the civilian labour force is the dawning of fear about the future. Here, for example, is a diary entry by Lieutenant General Ali Aurakzai on 22 January 2004:

> I could get a loan ... and cut down certain expenditures during my post-retirement life to get some breathing space until my house is rented out, and maybe I could get some job after retirement which will place me in a relatively comfortable financial position ... I decided ... to construct a modest house in Pindi. I cannot afford to live in the Karachi house. The rent recovered from it will be my only income after retirement to sustain me as it is not possible to live on Rs 15,000/– per month pension.[17]

General Aurakzai's construction of a small house in Rawalpindi was intended to be funded from his savings through a central fund which was described to me by another senior retired officer in somewhat rueful terms:

> The DSOP or Defence Services Officers Provident Fund is the equivalent of GPF or General Provident Fund of civilian departments. Contributions are voluntary above a certain minimal level. On being commissioned I like many others contributed Rs 20 which was the minimum possible as I wanted to spend every penny! However when I got married I wanted to increase but did not have the money! The returns are very good, better than most investments, and vary, but towards the end of my service it was about 17% compound interest. It may have fallen since. Had I invested sensibly through my service I could have walked away with close to Rs 10 million! [USD 165,000.] Instead, in spite of [having had a posting overseas] and later [being able to save more] as a general I saved [only] about 1.8 million [USD 26,000].[18]

In the context of post-retirement employability the Indian Army website on welfare[19] notes that:

Approximately 1,200 officers and 50,000 men retire every year from the [Indian] Army. They constitute a disciplined and trained force. The Officers generally retire in their early fifties, the Junior Commission[ed] Officers and other ranks retire in the age group of 34–45 years. Being in the prime years of their life and having been groomed over the years with a result oriented culture, they acquire skills, potentials and expertise in various fields. This trained and disciplined force would be an asset to any industry.

Given India's enormous industrial base there are many opportunities for post-retirement employment for all ranks who have served in the armed forces. Similarly, in Europe and the US there is little problem in this regard, especially for senior officers. The boards of defence contractors in Britain and America are bulging with retired generals. In the UK 'Between 1984 and 1994, 2,002 officers in the armed forces received approval to take up [post-retirement] employment with companies in military industry. Figures are not available for 1995 to 1998, but between 1 January 1999 and the end of June 2004, 614 officers received such approval.'[20] The situation in the US is similar.[21] There are also resettlement boards which cater for all ranks and manage to place many of those who apply to them for assistance.[22] But none of this applies in Pakistan. What does apply is an informal system whereby some retired personnel are provided with employment by such organizations as the Fauji Foundation, and by government agencies as civil servants.

Pakistan's energetic and forthright (and totally independent) media organizations do not ignore such arrangements, having the public interest at heart. In *The News* newspaper in April 2006 there was a scathing critique of the practice of employing retired senior officers in government appointments which,[23] in fairness, noted that 'there are a few posts like that of the Wapda [the Water and Power Development Authority] chairman or those in the Pakistan Railways which were earlier held by generals but they are today occupied by civilian officers.' To which could be added the head of Pakistan International Airlines (formerly an air marshal) and other positions; but the point is made, and is a reasonable one, that there are more former military officers in government posts than there are in many other countries. According to *The News*, there are nine retired military officers serving as ambassadors, out of a total of ninety-four heads of mission.[24] This does not represent a serious distortion of the promotion pyramid, as occurs, for example in the US State Department, where forty-three of 162 ambassadors are non-career individuals who contributed to political campaigns,[25] but undoubtedly there is resentment on the part of those career officials in Pakistan's foreign service who see their prospects limited by appointment of outsiders to senior posts.

Although continuing its offensive against the army in September 2007, and further criticizing 'bloated bureaucracy' (see below), *The News* did note that:

> Unlike the distortions that are characteristics of the civilian bureaucracy and which furthered [sic] during the last eight years, the systems in the military have not been played with. While in the civilian bureaucracy no top mandarin gets retired and is generously allowed extension in complete violation of the law and rules, the Pakistan Army, during the last eight years, has seen just three cases of extensions.

In August 2007, the *Daily Times* carried an exposé of what it considered to be a disproportionate number of retired military personnel employed by power distribution companies:

Retired military officers dominate power companies

ISLAMABAD: Serving and retired military personnel dominate nine out of the 12 power distribution companies working under the Water and Power Development Authority (WAPDA), according to official documents procured by Daily Times. According the documents, a total of 3,002 military people are working in the nine companies, three of which they head as well. The highest number of military people is in the Faisalabad Electricity Supply Company (FESCO) where 647 of them work, with a retired colonel and retired major in senior positions. The lowest ratio is in the Tribal Areas Electricity Supply Company (TESCO) where only three junior retired military men serve as security guards. A total of 496 retired military officers work at IESCO [responsible for the Islamabad capital territory and outlying areas] which is headed by a retired brigadier. As many as 493 work at the PESCO [Peshawar], two of them at senior posts. Five hundred and twenty-five work at HESCO [Hyderabad], and one of them is at a senior post. MEPCO [Multan] has two retired brigadiers working at the top posts and three retired officers at less senior – important nonetheless – posts. The rest of the 326 retired military men work at junior positions in the company. As many as 218 work at GEPCO [Gujranwala], with a retired colonel and major serving at senior posts. In total, 114 retired military officers work at QESCO [Quetta]. A retired colonel with 28 years of experience in power companies and the military works at a senior position. The LESCO [Lahore] employs a total 176 retired military officers, two of them in senior positions.[26]

Independent verification shows that the figures are accurate (although it is nonsense that there are 496 retired *officers* at IESCO – the writer means all ranks), and the total of '3,002 military people' is a large number in almost any context. But some numbers were not mentioned in the analysis. There are, the paper says, 647 'military people' employed by FESCO, the Faisalabad Power Company. Indeed there are: 647 out of a total of 15,635,[27] or 4.1 per cent. Hardly, one might think, a cause for alarm that the army exerts a stranglehold on the 2.1 million customers for electricity in the Faisalabad region.

In IESCO, the company that looks after power distribution in a large area round Islamabad, the CEO is a retired brigadier, and there are three retired officers shown in the list of eighty-four senior and managerial personnel.[28] According to IESCO the Board of Directors 'consists of a blend of very experienced persons from government/WAPDA and [the] private sector'. The Chairman is Mr Tariq Sadiq and the Directors are Messrs Mohammad Aslam, Mian Habibullah, Salman Iqbal, Abdullah Shah and Mohson Khalid, who are unlikely to feel menaced by the presence of fellow board member Brigadier Shahbaz Alam at their deliberations.[29]

In QESCO (the company in Quetta, capital of Balochistan province) the situation is equally unexciting. It is stated that 114 military officers (in fact, all ranks) are employed, but not that the strength of the organization is 5,826.[30] There are 15,931 employees in MEPCO.[31] The Chairman is Mr Tanvir Ahmad Sheikh and of his five directors one is a retired brigadier.

This newspaper piece is indicative of the attitude of much of the media to the army. The facts and figures in many articles criticizing civilian employment of retired service members are presented in such a manner as to create and bolster anti-military sentiment. Similarly, reports on allocation of land to military personnel concentrate on those fortunate souls who have been able to sell their plots at a considerable profit.

The practice of allocation of plots of land to officers and soldiers excites much criticism, which may be understandable, given that the scheme is better run than those of other organizations such as Pakistan Railways and Pakistan International Airways. The system is simple. In answer to my questions a retired senior officer emailed me that:

> Allotment of plots in DHAs [Defence Housing Authorities] are called 'Benefits' in the Army. A total of four benefits can be given to an officer depending on rank and completion of required service. So a Gen/Lt Gen gets 4 benefits, Maj Gen/Brig gets 3 benefits, Col/Lt Col gets 2 benefits and Majors get 1 benefit ... Also the COAS can give benefits to families of officers killed in action or as a welfare measure.

In an examination of Defence Housing Authorities and allocation of plots, titled 'The New Land Barons'[32] it was stated that:

> The perks and privileges provided to senior officers, including land grants, have progressively resulted in increased corruption in the armed forces. This has not remained exclusive to real estate. A number of reports are coming into the fore [sic] of officers involved in financial kickbacks related to weapon procurement, and other cases of corruption. [A footnote here reads: 'Following the sacking of the naval chief in 1997/98 on corruption charges, there has been a spate of stories regarding alleged kickbacks in various procurement deals. Some of the stories were published in the South Asia Tribune. For instance see M.T. Butt's 'Army's budding Mansurl [sic] Haq pays extra $21 million in hush-hush French deal', South Asia Tribune, 30 June 2005. The government did not deny the story.] This could be as a result of the greater aggressiveness of the media, or it could simply indicate increased corruption amongst the officer cadre. The questionable involvement of senior army officers behind the real estate-related scandal in the DHA, Lahore has raised quite a few eyebrows. The scandal concerns the DHA entertaining more applications for the sale of plots than the actual number of plots. It must be noted that to buy a plot in a DHA scheme it is necessary to pay a certain percentage of the total cost of the plot, so there is an obvious financial advantage to the DHA if too many deposits are accepted. Reports indicate [no reference or other detail provided] that senior generals involved with the development scheme were aware of this scandal.

The Defence Housing Authority Lahore is refreshingly direct concerning applications for plots of land under its control, and there is no mention of non-returnable deposits in its laconic website advertisement to the effect that:

> *If you want to buy, we will offer you variety of plots. On striking a deal, transaction will take place as under:*
>
> 1. *You will be required to pay 25% as advance money.*
> 2. *Balance amount will have to be paid within a week.*
>
> *On final payment and completion of necessary documentation, property will be transferred to the buyers name by DHA Transfer Branch as under:*
>
> 1. *Plot will be transferred on same day.*
> 2. *House will be transferred in 4 days.*
> 3. *Rental services will be provided by DHA Property Exchange subsequently.*[33]

There have been other allegations of dishonesty in DHA Lahore, and *Dawn* newspaper reported in June 2007 that:

Opposition members of the National Assembly on Friday alleged that senior army officers were involved in serious 'irregularities and financial corruption' in the Defence Housing Authority (DHA) scheme in Lahore and a provincial minister was acting as a front man for them ... Speaking at a news conference at the Parliament House cafeteria, Liaqat Baloch and Farid Ahmed Piracha of the Muttahida Majlis-i-Amal (MMA), Khawaja Mohammad Asif of the Pakistan Muslim League-Nawaz (PML-N) and Syed Khurshid Shah of the People's Party Parliamentarians (PPP) alleged that the DHA administration was causing billions of rupees loss to the national exchequer in connivance with senior army officers and government-backed private developers ... Farid Piracha said that billions of rupees had been stuck up in DHA, Gwadar and Bahria projects. He said that people knew name of each and every general who were involved in these scams. Syed Khurshid Shah said that the country had been run by several mafias such as stock market, sugar and cement for the last eight years. These mafias, he said, were present all over the country and operating under the regime's patronage.[34]

Undoubtedly there has been a great deal of money involved in the various DHAs, and considerable profits have been made by those fortunate enough to have possessed plots that greatly appreciated in value. There could well have been corruption; indeed it would be most surprising if were there no corruption, with so much cash swilling round. According to Transparency International in September 2007, Pakistan is 138 out of 179 on its corruption index, but in its research results there is no indication that military officers were in any way involved.[35] This does not mean to say that there were no military officers mixed up in chicanery: one has to be realistic about this and accept the fact that many of us might take easy money were it dangling before us, and that army officers in Pakistan or anywhere else might well succumb to temptation. Allegations abound, but evidence is scant.

The BBC explained in September 2006 that:

The huge interest of investors in this [DHA Lahore] and other well-to-do areas is typical of the unprecedented surge in real estate businesses in big cities like Lahore and Karachi following the attack on the World Trade Centre. Since then, the value of one plot in the Defence Housing Authority has shot up from about $65,000 before 11 September to in excess of $1.5m after it. In the town of Johar, another affluent middle class locality, average prices have risen on an equally spectacular basis

157

– from about $35,000 to more than $132,000. The boom has led to a mushrooming of Pakistan's middle class housing suburbs, often at an unprecedented speed. The growth of Lahore's Defence Housing Authority is so phenomenal that it has announced five new building phases since 2002.[36]

It is market forces that have spurred the growth in land prices in Pakistan, just as they have in other countries. As the BBC's reporter noted: 'Poor farmers with small pieces of land in villages close to the municipal limits could hardly make ends meet. But with the fast expansion of the city's frontiers, they sold off their property, pocketing millions of rupees overnight.' Nevertheless one critic holds that:

> These housing schemes create opportunities for the elite to make money rather than generate employment opportunities for other social classes. The elite town schemes are primarily residential areas with no provision for industrial or business infrastructure. Moreover such schemes do not solve the shortage of six million houses presently required in the country, but denote financial investment aimed at filling the pockets of those who have money to invest.[37]

The argument that building houses fails to help solve a housing shortage is an interesting viewpoint, but it can hardly be denied that construction projects of any nature, even those associated with Defence Housing Authorities, must 'generate employment opportunities for other social classes'. In the wider scheme of things it is apparent from seeing the outskirts and centres of large cities in Pakistan that industries and businesses are thriving, although internationally imposed restrictions (such as those of the EU on imports, especially cotton manufactures) are matters for concern. This is hardly the fault, however, of Pakistan's military or organizations like the Fauji Foundation.

Capitalism is alive and working in Pakistan, and there is no doubt that pockets are being filled. Some of them may be the wrong pockets, especially in the judgment of those whose pockets are not being filled, but it cannot be denied that, as with the Fauji Foundation's commercial enterprises, management of land by the various Defence Housing Authorities has resulted in creation of wealth. Whether or not this is a good thing is an interesting academic or ideological point – or even an ethical one – but in practical terms the benefits are widespread. These organizations contribute to improvement in the living conditions of many millions of citizens. It will continue to be contended that there is some sinister undemocratic purpose behind these commercial ventures, but it is difficult to equate such conspiracy theories with the reality of commercial success and consequential rewards for private investors, retired members of the army and their families, and the economy as a whole. In a September 2007 interview with *The Times of India*, Dr Ayesha Siddiqa declared that:

> If you allow the military to run industries … then you won't get the best or most efficient product. This is because you have non-professionals running the show, which often leads to mismanagement. The costs of this inefficiency of the military are then often passed on to the government. The other problem is that to justify the military economy, the army has to justify its role as protector of the state. This can often lead to the creation of a threat perception, a fear of India. Solving Kashmir is just getting rid of an existential issue. It does not mean the rivalry is over.[38]

The military does not 'run industries'. There are retired military people involved at all levels of many businesses that contribute to national growth and individual benefit. During their service military officers have been involved in all facets of administration, general management and decision-making. As noted above, they have been 'groomed over the years with a result-oriented culture, they acquire skills, potentials and expertise in various fields'.[39] It is condescending nonsense to declare that army officers who have been responsible for the organization, command, management and direction of thousands of men and millions of dollars' worth of facilities, stores and equipment are incapable of transferring their skills to civil industry in both public and private sectors. Their involvement in such enterprises as the Fauji Foundation leads to national economic rewards that are quantifiable, and the overall benefits to the community of employment of retired service personnel are demonstrably significant. The army does the best it can to look after former soldiers and officers in the way of pensions, post-retirement benefits and employment; and the enterprises that support them, far from being sinister predators, are transparent organizations that are accountable to both market forces and the community at large.

Notes

1. http://indianarmy.nic.in/arwelf3.htm#Educational%20Facilities
2. Siddiqa, Ayesha, *Military, Inc*, Pluto Press, 2007. I must declare an interest here: Dr Siddiqa stayed with my wife and I in our house in November 1997 and wrote in our visitor's book that 'I am glad I came and had the chance to meet two terribly wonderful people and educate myself. I am sure I will never be able to repay your hospitality.'
3. *Ibid*.
4. 'The armed forces' direct or indirect involvement in the economy and its parallel control of power politics allows it access to privileged information which, in Pakistan's case, has allowed two welfare groups, the AWT and the Fauji Foundation, to become two of the largest business conglomerates in the country. Besides access to strategic economic information, these business groups have been given tax breaks as well. For instance, the

Fauji Foundation was exempt from taxes during the 1960s, and the AWT did not pay any taxes until 1993, when tax was levied on it during the first regime of Prime Minister Nawaz Sharif.' Dr Ayesha Siddiqa, *Newsline* December 2006. http://www.newsline.com.pk/NewsDec2006/cover1dec2006.htm. The point that full taxes have been paid since 1993 is passed over. Where and how the Fauji Foundation gets its 'strategic economic information' other than by normal research by its employees is not explained.

5. 'Military Inc: An Economy Within an Economy'. Interview with Dr Ayesha Siddiqa by Ashwin Ahmad, *Times of India*, 16 September 2007. http://timesofindia.indiatimes.com/Opinion/Sunday_Specials/Special_Report/Military_Inc_An_economy_within_an_economy/articleshow/2373041.cms

6. In plain English – 'incapable of being judged or measured'.

7. Siddiqa, *ibid.*

8. KPMG in Pakistan is represented by KPMG Taseer Hadi & Co., the Pakistan member firm of KPMG International. KPMG Taseer Hadi & Co. was established in 1969. It has twenty-nine partners and directors, and some 800 professional staff.

9. *Newsline*, December 2006, http://www.newsline.com.pk/NewsDec2006/cover3dec2006.htm, which observes, inter alia, that 'It is interesting how the army has evolved for itself a comprehensive system to look after its own, which is sadly missing in the civilian sector.' Indeed it is. There was not a move, in the years of rule by Ms Benazir Bhutto and Mr Nawaz Sharif, from 1989 to 1999, to implement any system of social welfare.

10. Masood, Ehsan, 'Pakistan: The Army as the State', 12 April 2007. http://www.opendemocracy.net/globalization-india_pakistan/pakistan_military_4519.jsp

11. A main criticism of the AWT is that when it experienced financial difficulties in 2001 it was aided by a government loan. In exactly the same manner as enterprises elsewhere in the world are on occasion assisted by governments or central banks.

12. Siddiqa, *ibid.*

13. 'To check the growing number of officers seeking premature release from service, the armed forces are seeking a 'service incentive allowance' (SIA). The allowance is proposed to be paid after completion of the stipulated period of service. According to recommendations sent to the Sixth Pay Commission, excerpts of which are available with The Tribune, the service headquarters have recommended that one year's gross salary be paid as SIA on completion of 15, 25 and 30 years of service.' *The Tribune*, Chandigarh, 25 August 2007. http://www.tribuneindia.com/2007/20070826/main5.htm

14. It is impossible to assess accurately the average income per worker. Gross National Income figures in the context of Purchasing Power Parity indicate that the average income equates to $2,567 (http://www.nationsonline.org/oneworld/GNI_PPP_of_countries.htm); on the other hand it has been estimated that the figure is $420 (http://www.caat.org.uk/caatnews/2006_08/cover-story.php). The latter is more realistic.

15. *Civil Service Pension Schemes Around the World*, May 2006. This is a remarkable study by the World Bank, whose recommendations are compelling. See http://siteresources.worldbank.org/SOCIALPROTECTION/Resources/SP-Discussion-papers/Pensions-DP/0602.pdf.

16. *America's Military Population* www.prb.org/Source/ACF1396.pdf

17. The diaries of Lieutenant General (Retd) Ali Aurakzai, former commander of XI Corps in NWFP and, from 2006, its Governor. The diaries are being edited for publication by the writer.

18. August 2007. The officer does not wish to be named. Being in the same boat, as it were, I have every sympathy for him.

19. Indian Army, at http://indianarmy.nic.in/arwelf4.htm#Management

20. See *Unicorn Against Corruption*, http://www.againstcorruption.org/BriefingsItem.asp?id=13093

21. Including:

'New York, June 26, 2007 (Reuters) – Boeing Co. on Tuesday named retired Marine Corps Gen. James Jones, the former head of U.S. and NATO forces in Europe, to its board. The appointment is the latest in a line of retired senior armed forces and Pentagon leaders joining defense contractors, underscoring the tight relationship between U.S. arms makers and buyers. In 2006, Northrop Grumman Corp. appointed retired Air Force Gen. Richard Myers, former chairman of the U.S. Joint Chiefs of Staff, to its board. The U.S. No. 3 defense contractor has had retired U.S. Navy Admiral Charles Larson on its board since 2002.' http://www.reuters.com/article/companyNewsAndPR/idUSN2635768320070626

'Fairfax, VA (Marketwire – August 17, 2007) – WidePoint Corporation, a leading provider of information technology assurance and identity management services, today announced that Lieutenant General (Retired) Otto J. Guenther has been appointed to the company's board of directors.' http://www.marketwire.com/mw/release.do?id=761720&sourceType=3

'Last December [2006], Lt. Gov. Beverly Perdue announced the launch of the North Carolina Military Foundation, which aims to boost the state's share of both defense dollars and jobs. The foundation's board boasts several retired generals, including former Supreme Allied Commander William F. Kernan, as well as high-powered business executives.' http://www.mountainx.com/news/2007/081507defense

22. 'As a Service leaver you should already be aware of the vast array of transferable skills you possess. But very few of the 20,000 people who leave the Armed Forces each year don't feel apprehensive at the prospect of starting a new life. Regardless of how you view the future, there is much you can do to make the transition a positive one.' http://www.forcesrecruitment.co.uk/skills.html

23. *The News*, 6 April 2006, 'Retired, serving military officers still all around', by Ansar Abbasi. http://www.jang.com.pk/thenews/apr2006-daily/06-04-2006/metro/i16.htm

24. See Pakistan Ministry of Foreign Affairs at http://www.mofa.gov.pk/Green_Book/GREEN_BOOK.htm

25. See the US State Department list at http://www.state.gov/r/pa/ei/biog/c130.htm and http://www.opensecrets.org/bush/ambassadors/index.asp. Campaign contributors included the ambassadors to The Netherlands and Belgium, both of whom gave over a million dollars to the Republican Party.

26. The item is at http://www.dailytimes.com.pk/default.asp?page=2007%5C08%5C20%5C story_20-8-2007_pg7_3.

27. Details given by FESCO at http://66.102.9.104/search?q=cache:htSMZ_SxiugJ: www.privatisation.gov.pk/PDF-Files/FESCO%2520PIM%25202006.pdf+Pakistan+FESCO&hl=en&ct=clnk&cd=4&gl=uk&ie=UTF-8

28. http://www.iesco.com.pk/contact.php?nRndId=391

29. The composition of the board and other information can be found at http://www.iesco.com.pk/aboutus.php?nRndId=573

30. http://www.qesco.sdnpk.org/

31. http://www.mepco.com.pk/htmls/sanctionstrength.asp

32. Siddiqa, *ibid.*, Chapter 7.

33. http://www.dhalahore.org/index.php?p=116&a=guideline_for_transactions

34. *Dawn*, 23 June 2007. 'Army officers accused of irregularities, Defence Housing Authority Scheme', by Amir Wasim. http://server.kbri-islamabad.go.id/index.php?option=com_content&task=view&id=772 & Itemid =46

35. Transparency International Corruption Perceptions Index 2007: www.transparency.org/sur

36. BBC, 21 September 2006. 'Pakistan's Post 9/11 Economic Boom', by Adnan Adil in Lahore: (http://news.bbc.co.uk/2/hi/south_asia/5338402.stm) who also noted that 'Many wealthy Pakistanis in America have responded to increased monitoring of wealth and assets, particularly owned by Muslims, by sending a substantial part of their savings back home.'

37. 'Pakistan's Generals Emerge as the New Land Barons', by Ayesha Siddiqa, *New Pakistan*, Issue No. 5, 13 October 2006. http://www.naya-pakistan.com/issue%205/Pak%20 generals%20new%20land%20barons.htm

38. 'Military Inc: An Economy Within an Economy'. Interview with Dr Ayesha Siddiqa by Ashwin Ahmad, *Times of India*, 16 September 2007. http://timesofindia.indiatimes.com/ Opinion/Sunday_Specials/Special_Report/Military_Inc_An_economy_within_an_ economy/articleshow/2373041.cms

39. 'Indian Army', at http://indianarmy.nic.in/arwelf4.htm#Management

Chapter 7

The Modern Army and its Challenges

International Complications

Cessation of overseas individual and collective training arrangements by Western countries as a result of their disapproval of Pakistan's nuclear tests and the ejection of the corrupt Nawaz Sharif in 1999 did not adversely affect the army's professional knowledge or standards. On the other hand, an entire generation of officers was denied exposure to the wider social and political horizons offered by travelling and living overseas. Western influence was reduced to the point of creating significant resentment, especially among junior officers. This anti-Western feeling was encouraged by a small number of zealots within and outside the armed forces in attempts to attract adherents to more rigid forms of Islam than desired by military leaders. President Musharraf's embrace of 'enlightened moderation' was regarded with approval by the army (although there were jokes made about 'frightened moderation'), but derided furiously by many religious figures.

Many Australian foreign service and civilian defence officials had long wished to sever the connection with the Staff College at Quetta that existed since its founding in 1905, and relished the opportunity to diminish such ties as existed.[1] Britain, ever intent on the Thatcher era dogma, embraced by Blair and Brown, that Commonwealth students' countries (including, ironically, Australia) must pay full-fare for attendance of their brightest young brains at British instructional institutions, gave an old ally the message that its citizens were not welcome in any capacity. This was especially hurtful to those army units having strong British connections, although it has to be said that individual British regiments paid no attention to the hypocrisy of political grandstanding, and continued their association.

If it was the purpose of those imposing sanctions to drive Pakistan to rely more on Islamic partners, with attendant consequences of alienating a

163

large number of gifted students (military and civilian) from the Western world, they did not wholly succeed, but much work has to be done to correct the damage that was inflicted. The West's short-sighted and even spiteful reaction to the ousting of Sharif will be remembered for a long time, and although those responsible for damaging their country's relations with Pakistan may have rejoiced in their satisfying demonstration of principle, they did not serve their countries well. Realpolitik triumphed in the end, as it always does, and those who were most fulminatory about the horrors of the coup were made to look silly humbugs when they reversed their position at the behest of President Bush.[2] There was a similar performance in November 2007 when the Commonwealth foreign ministers suspended Pakistan's membership following Musharraf's imposition of a state of emergency, thereby creating further resentment at a time when, by unfortunate coincidence, an Indian diplomat was selected as the next Secretary General.

China cemented its association as regards provision of defence equipment and technical co-operation, but although this would probably have happened anyway, irrespective of coups or nuclear tests, the prevailing feeling in the armed services appears to be that there is only one country that can be trusted to maintain military supplies irrespective of Pakistan's internal developments. Musharraf went to China in 2000, in the period of his leper-like treatment by the West, and there were subsequent exchanges of high-level visits, of which the most significant was that of the PRC's Prime Minister, Wen Jiabao, to Pakistan in 2005, when twenty-one agreements were signed, including accords on nuclear energy, defence co-operation and a 'Treaty of Friendship, Cooperation and Good Neighbourly Relations'. Co-operation accelerated in provision of warships, combat aircraft and tank technology in addition to considerable Chinese investment in major projects such as Gwadar port and Saindak copper/gold (and perhaps uranium) mines. The Chinese are in Pakistan to stay, and can be expected to expand defence and economic collaboration irrespective of the form of government that obtains, except in the unlikely event of an ultra-Islamic dispensation.

The US military training co-operation agreement[3] was resurrected when Pakistan once again became a valuable consort (which had happened during the Zia years), as were Commonwealth and European programmes, and it seems that for the foreseeable future at least some Pakistani officers will be permitted to experience other social environments – and it is this, more than purely military knowledge, that is so important for Pakistan's overall development. But there have been lasting consequences, not least being a surprising degree of anti-American and anti-British feeling in senior officers who had attended courses of instruction in the US or the UK before the embargoes. This has been evident in the post 9/11 era in a manner that would not be apparent to some Western interlocutors for, while officers in high-ranking posts were ostensibly or even sincerely supportive of the Western allies' 'war on terror' and, as ever, courteous to their foreign colleagues, some did not extend themselves in enjoining or offering co-operation. It became obvious to me in discussions with senior officers in early 2007 that co-operation with United Kingdom forces in Afghanistan's Helmand Province was at best grudging and that there was no intention to go further than minimum or even lip-service support. London's realization of this resulted in energetic efforts to persuade GHQ that the US/Nato war in Afghanistan was in the interests of both countries. Following this it appears that there was at least some diminution in opposition to the British presence, although the conviction remains that it is largely the result of American operations in Afghanistan and within Pakistan that the Federally Administered Tribal Areas have become even more anarchic than previously applied.

Much of the reluctance to work energetically and unconditionally with the main Western nations involved in Afghanistan stemmed from the patronizing and sometimes even arrogant attitude of some foreign military officers, senior and junior, who gave the impression that they and their countries were impatient with Pakistan's seeming lack of urgency in pursuing Western objectives. As noted in March 2003 by Alan Kronstadt of the Congressional Research Service, 'During 2002, the United States took an increasingly direct, if low-profile, role in both law enforcement and military operations being conducted on Pakistani territory. These operations have led to favourable results in tracking and apprehending dangerous Islamic militants, but the activities of U.S. personnel in the country have led to increasing signs of anti-American backlash and Pakistani sovereignty concerns.'[4]

The high-profile killing or detention of Osama bin Laden and his henchmen was a major priority for the US administration (in spite of presidential comment to the contrary),[5] and their military representatives were under pressure to do all in their power to produce a body. Sometimes this sense of urgency manifested itself in unusual proposals.

In June 2002, General Tommy Franks, Commander Centcom, visited Pakistan. In the course of discussions at GHQ he suggested that the US be permitted to infiltrate US citizens of Afghan origin, Pushto speakers, into the tribal areas to gather information. Pakistani senior officers heard him out politely, as always, but told him that for good (and to most people obvious) reasons his scheme would not work. In private their reaction varied from astonishment to hilarity, but the consensus was that the idea was preposterous.[6] Unfortunately it appears that the US went ahead, with predictable results, as indicated by a *New York Times* report in January 2003 that 'The three said they knew of six men who had been murdered in South Waziristan in the last three months because they were suspected of being American informants. The killers in one case daubed a message on the nearby bridge. "We have killed a spy of America, he had dollars, an expensive watch and a G.P.S. finder".[7] In the next two years there appeared to be a decline in such murders, perhaps because there was a reduction in the number of agents sent to the tribal areas, but in April 2006 four men were killed in Waziristan, two of them beheaded, with notes placed beside their bodies alleging association with the US.

Later in 2006 a further ten suspects were killed in ones and twos in similar fashion, and in private a Pakistani senior officer asked rhetorically, 'What did they [the Americans] expect?' He went on to say that it was probable only some of those murdered had actually been spies as such, the others having been pro-American or not anti-American enough to satisfy the extremists, and had therefore been denounced, with the inevitable consequences.[8] One cannot but admire those Pushto-speaking American citizens of Afghan or Pakistani origin who agreed to assist the US by entering NWFP or the Afghan border region, and reporting what they might learn of suspicious activities, because they would be well aware of their fate should they be detected. Some were infiltrated in the guise of Afghan refugees, by first entering refugee camps in Pakistan with cover stories of having been elsewhere in the country but now wishing to take advantage of the UN's programme of assistance for those wishing to return to Afghanistan. Unfortunately their cover was not in some instances good enough to withstand questioning by genuine refugees, and the consequences were that they were either quietly murdered or denounced to Pakistan's authorities who may not have regarded them sympathetically.

The killings continued and the BBC reported in February 2007 that:

Pro-Taliban militants have killed two men they accused of spying against them in a Pakistani region near the Afghan border ... Villagers found the bodies just east of Miranshah town in North Waziristan region late on Monday, [Pakistani] officials said. They were riddled with bullets, with their hands tied behind their backs. There have been a number of such killings in Pakistan's tribal areas in recent months, which local officials blame on pro-Taliban militants. No one has admitted killing the men, who officials said appeared to be Afghan refugees. They have yet to be formally identified. 'Their bodies were riddled with bullets and the throat of one of the bearded men was slit,' a local resident, Mohammad Ayub, told Reuters news agency. He said a note found nearby said: 'Those spying for America will meet the same fate.' Last week, the headless body of another Afghan refugee was found dumped near Miranshah with a similar note.[9]

Other cases included a similar example of brutality in September 2007, when:

> Suspected Taliban militants killed an Afghan national and a settled district resident for being 'US spies' in North Waziristan, as a military convoy escaped two improvised-explosive device attacks, officials said on Wednesday. Wazir Badshah hailed from Hangu district and the Afghan was a resident of Khost province in Afghanistan, who went missing some four months ago. A letter found near the two bodies close to a military check-post east of Miranshah charged the two executed men with 'spying for the United States,' the officials told Daily Times. The militants slit the throat of Badshah, in his 30s, on Monday night and left the body on a road near Mir Ali town, a stronghold of foreign militants in North Waziristan. 'He (Wazir) was a hypocrite and American spy. Such people deserve such treatment,' the letter read. In the same area, the authorities also found the body of refugee Maulvi Shamsuddin, 45, who was kidnapped by militants three months ago on accusations of spying, the officials added.'[10]

The effects of the information-gathering project on tribal perceptions of the US has been slight, as the degree of hatred of America and the West in general was already intense and could hardly be much increased by detection and exposure of a few low-level agents. But it has served to reinforce distrust, and confirmed the widely-held view that most foreigners (and not a few Pakistanis, it has to be said) do not understand tribal society. In early 2007 this was explained to me by Lieutenant General Kiyani, then Director General Inter Services Intelligence (appointed Chief of Army Staff on 28 November 2007), when he described the incident of the performing monkey.

A tribesman acquired a monkey and decided to try to make a living by training it to do tricks. Then he travelled round the tribal areas visiting villages and having his monkey perform. In one village in 2005 he attracted an audience (all men, of course) in a semi-circle, turban-clad and rifle-bearing. The monkey did his act, which was spotted by the cameras of a drone. The controllers in Florida considered the scene to be that of a weapon-training session or a military-style briefing, perhaps having intelligence that indicated the presence of some undesirable in that particular area. A missile then killed many of the audience. This, said the General, was an example of lack of cultural understanding that produced results that were entirely counter to what was intended to be achieved. The monkey incident and other attacks by the US within Pakistan, some of which are examined in Chapter 8, have convinced the population of North West Frontier Province and a disturbing number of other citizens, including many in uniform, that there is nothing to be gained by supporting the

United States, which they consider to be overbearing and imperceptive in its engagement with their country.

Force Structure and Manpower

The basic structure of Pakistan's army is sound and its equipment is adequate, but GHQ should be transformed to a 'raise, train and provide' organization, with operational functions being the responsibility of a Joint Headquarters which perforce would be army-heavy (see below). Following restructure at the higher level, there should be two main subordinate air-land HQs formed: north and south, and a tri-service HQ should be based in Karachi. If this 'jointery' does not eventuate, the army and the air force (not so much the navy) will not be capable of conducting operations to best effect. There has been discussion and some movement concerning formation of three geographic army commands, but a combination of operational requirements, especially in North West Frontier Province, officer shortage and economics have made this restructuring a lower priority. There is a Joint Operations division in GHQ, headed by an air vice marshal, but although this is a step in the right direction it does not go far enough towards establishing the type of overall command HQ that Pakistan (and India) so badly needs.

The Army has rarely had difficulty in recruiting soldiers, who enlist largely because they will be in secure employment, although of course liable to the dangers experienced by most soldiers worldwide. During their years in uniform they will be educated and in many cases taught a marketable trade while drawing a wage that is comparable with that of most civilian workers (see details in the previous chapter). Following their service they will be eligible for retirement benefits from such organizations as the Fauji Foundation and the Army Welfare Trust whose profits are directed largely to the welfare of former soldiers and their dependants. There appears to be a problem with circumcision, or, rather, the lack of it, because uncircumcised youngsters usually cannot pass the entry medical examination. In most cases those refused enlistment are from the tribal areas, and especially from the Mahsuds of South Waziristan, one of the most troubled agencies, where it is estimated that there are some 80,000 males aged between eighteen and twenty-five, most of whom are in dire need of legal employment.[11] Nevertheless, recruiting levels remain satisfactory, although enlistments from Balochistan and NWFP have fallen since major unrest began in 2004.

But there is a shortage of officers, and in August 2007 the Chairman of the Joint Chiefs of Staff Committee, Lieutenant General Ehsan ul Haq, himself the father of two boys who eschewed a military career, explained the problem to me in terms of what he saw as the current attitude of many young people. He said that many of those fortunate enough to have received a good education have always been able to consider going on to university or into the army, but the divide between salaries in civilian professions and the military had become acute to the point that young people were becoming less attracted to a life of service in uniform, especially if they had an opportunity to study or take up employment abroad.

On the same lines another senior figure told me that his eldest daughter, working in America, was paid much more than he was earning, which, although gratifying, was to him a bit hard to accept in cultural terms. He was immensely proud of his daughter, but there was distinct inner confusion concerning the propriety of a young woman earning more than her father. This appears to be one of these social developments that is personally difficult for families and even painful to acknowledge by some of those most directly affected, but it is the type of thing that is having a profound effect on national life, as, bit by bit, family bonds are becoming less cohesive. As in so many countries (including India, the UK and the US), growing prosperity in Pakistan has influenced many high-grade young people against choosing military service. One solution would be to raise military salaries significantly, but the cost would be prohibitive. The only thing to do, said General Ehsan, is to increase salaries modestly, but regularly, while improving conditions of service and retirement benefits.

In 2003 there were instances of three outstanding candidates for the Pakistan Military Academy being rejected by specially-appointed religious members of a selection board because of alleged secular tendencies within their Westernized families. It appears this policy was emplaced at low level and has been discontinued, but the incidents were disconcerting and in later years there was some evidence that junior officers are indeed being influenced by extremists, as are soldiers and some members of the air force. The nine (known) attempts on the life of President Musharraf have been disturbing, but the most disquieting aspect is that there must have been leakage of information concerning his movements to those responsible for the assassination attempts as such. Their motives have not been revealed, as the various courts martial have been held in secret, but one general has stated that 'the percentage of religious zealots in [the] PAF is alarmingly large and they become easy targets for terrorists to cultivate for such tasks.'[12]

It is not unusual for commentators to remark adversely on the numbers of senior officers in the army. For example, *The News* newspaper in September 2007 announced that there was 'Steady growth in Army Bureaucracy':

> The Pakistan Army has presently more than 125 general officers in its strength. While a lot is said and written about the civilian bureau-

cracy, not many know about the military bureaucracy, which is today far more bloated compared to what it was a few decades back.

Today we have three full four-star generals, 30 three-star generals also called lieutenant generals, while the number of two-star generals – major generals – is said to be almost 100. This number, however, includes those serving generals who are also presently occupying civilian posts including the Presidency.[13] [There were three.]

The number of senior officers increased because the strength of the army 'a few decades back' – let us say in 1980 – was 400,000,[14] and is now some 550,000, a little larger than that of the United States. The US Army has an authorized strength of 151 major generals, lieutenant generals and full (four-star) generals, which number can be varied by presidential decree. Similar ratios of senior officers to total numbers apply throughout the world, for good reason, and it is unfortunate that domestic commentators do not take into account best practice in other countries. All organizations have fixed costs that cannot be avoided, although these can be kept under review with the aim of reducing them when opportunities arise. But in armies the main fixed cost is leadership; and irrespective of whether the strength is 100,000 or half a million, the same requirement remains to direct operations, logistics, personnel and the plethora of military activity. And so far as can be determined from frequent contact with officers of the Pakistan Army for over twenty-five years, they do what is required of them very well. Of course, there are some clots about whom one wonders how on earth they got to be where they are, but that happens everywhere, and not only in armies. And naturally there are failures in leadership, as there are in every field of human endeavour, from governments to banking, from cricket to commerce, but the claim by one critic that officers are inefficient during their service because their aim is to be given post-retirement employment in civilian enterprises is offensive nonsense. Dr Ayesha Siddiqa wrote in 2006 that in Pakistan:

> commercial ventures, even if they do not use serving officers, do, unarguably, have an impact on the professional mindset. Senior officers, who are quite aware of the rewards that await them after retirement in terms of extension of perks and privileges as a result of jobs in these companies, tend to compromise on the quality of their work during service.[15]

There is no evidence produced to justify the assertion that the quality of service of any officer has suffered because he (or she) has planned to seek a job after leaving the army. It is possible that there could be some degree of decline in an individual officer's attention to duty should they be offered attractive civilian employment while still in uniform, but it would require a most sophisticated survey to determine if it existed and, if so, to what extent. It would be extremely difficult to measure the comparative efficiency of a brigadier's plan to attack a Taliban fortress in Waziristan should he be expecting a job with a civilian firm when he retires, as against his plan should he have no such employment to look forward to. And it is questionable if an officer's staff paper on any subject, or his day-to-day decisions on personnel matters, or his orders concerning convoy organization (for example) could be affected by the lures of civilian affluence. The assertion that future 'perks and privileges'could encourage officers to 'compromise on the quality of work' is as untenable as it is insulting.

In August 2007 the Adjutant General, Lieutenant General Imtiaz Hussain,[16] was understandably vexed when asked about such allegations, although he stated that personal domestic discipline in the army had improved measurably in the past few years, mainly, in his view, because 'dallying with other people's wives' was becoming less acceptable. Not, he assured me, because of ultra-Islamic tendencies. Some disciplinary action and administrative dismissals, he said, had been effective in reducing the number of social offences, such as adultery, and there was no doubt that the threat of losing both pension and the possibility of future employment played a part, but the notion that the thought of retirement benefits could influence an officer to the extent that his efficiency would suffer was ridiculous. The army's watchwords, he said, were 'We will look after you', and this was known by all ranks. The Welfare Directorate's staff (and the many regimental welfare organizations) work hard, he said, to ensure that soldiers and officers are provided with their entitlements, and although it was obvious that the army would like to do more, there were financial limits.

Of course any Adjutant General would have to say all this. He would be a strange individual if he did not. But experience of the army and discussions with officers of all ranks over many years have convinced me that the welfare and retirement systems are as good as can be expected, given the AG's caveat about expense. The problem for the army is that the country cannot match the salaries and benefits of civilian executives. The long-term adverse consequences are that many intelligent young people will be reluctant to commit themselves to any of the armed services, which are just as competitive in promotion and selection as civilian enterprises, simply because they would not earn enough to enjoy a lifestyle comparable with that of their peers. It is likely, too, that events on the Frontier in 2004–7 have not been aids to officer recruitment.

The Nuclear Factor

The professional challenges presented by nuclear developments in India and Pakistan are immense, and in both countries the services co-operate to

171

the extent that joint doctrine is being considered within a military if not, yet, a national context. Examination of training in Pakistan has shown that it is adequate for conventional war and, indeed, is more than satisfactory in armour tactics, but that the nuclear factor is yet to be fully appreciated. Costs of even elementary protective measures are prohibitive: to acquire and maintain two million protective suits and masks, for example (for the three services and para-military troops, with a 50 per cent reserve), would require an initial outlay of at least $300 million,[17] and annual turnover/attrition/storage costs of about $20 million.[18] There appear to be no plans for decontamination centres or mobile decontamination teams in either country, which makes sense because were there a nuclear exchange there would be few people and very little equipment left to decontaminate. Nuclear and counter-nuclear tactics are discussed and on rare occasions practised, and during the 1999 and 2002 confrontations with India there was some evidence that defensive measures were being considered, but neither country is capable of fighting a nuclear war on the battlefield.

The North Atlantic Treaty Organization and the Warsaw Pact eventually, after four decades of improvements, evolved advanced systems for command and control of nuclear weapons, but even then they were far from foolproof. India and Pakistan are in the nascent stages of such development. Moreover, in Europe, Confidence Building Measures (CBMs) and command and control systems grew together (the OK jargon word for this is 'symbiotically'). In the Subcontinent, India and Pakistan cannot assess with confidence how far their neighbour can go before there may be pressing or even irresistible internal demands to threaten the use of nuclear weapons. Furthermore, it is not clear whether, as one commentator mused, Indian and Pakistani leaders 'can avoid using Kashmir as a bargaining chip in domestic politics – and nuclear threats as a lever in Kashmir'.[19] A paper by Bruce Riedel published in May 2002 by the Centre for the Advanced Study of India, drawing on recollections of his period as special assistant to President Clinton,[20] describes possible nuclear preparations at the time of the Kargil crisis in 1999. Mr Riedel provides insight to US perceptions of the nuclear threat at the time, and states that Mr Clinton asked the Prime Minister of Pakistan, Nawaz Sharif, if he knew 'his military was preparing their nuclear-tipped missiles?' This is an intriguing revelation, although the nuclear expert George Perkovitch and the Indian Army chief of the time, General V.P. Malik, stated they doubted Pakistan had gone so far.[21] I raised the matter during many discussions with senior Pakistan officers of all services in the period 2002–7 and was told that there had been no nuclear mobilization in 1999, although, as one general put it 'We wouldn't have stood still if the Indians had moved, but we had no way of knowing if they did.' (Which is itself an alarming scenario.) It may be that the US did indeed have satellite and other intelligence indicating some degree of nuclear preparedness, and that those with knowledge of it have been admirably discreet, but the disturbing aspect of the affair is the very fact that two nuclear-armed countries were completely in the dark about the other's possible intentions at a time of extreme confrontation.

Opacity concerning nuclear objectives continues, exacerbating regional and international disquiet about the possible direction of nuclear developments in the Subcontinent, although in 2006–7 the Bush administration appeared comfortable with a policy of encouraging civilian nuclear programmes in India, which, whether or not a desirable development, reinforced distrust of the US among educated citizens and especially in Pakistan's defence forces. One often expressed Western fear is that by some means religious extremists could illegally obtain a nuclear weapon, but both physical security and inherent checks are such that this would not be practicable (the downside being that activation is comparatively clumsy and time-consuming, especially given the separation distances of warheads and missiles). In November and December 2007 many items appeared in the Western and Indian press conveying the impression that Pakistan's nuclear programme was at risk from fundamentalists and that, for example, 'The US has long had contingency plans in place under which American Special Forces operatives would deploy to Pakistan to secure nuclear-weapons sites in the event of an Islamic takeover.'[22]

The notion of groups of US troops attempting to gain access to closely guarded nuclear sites is an intriguing one, and the method by which they would 'secure' the facilities once they got there is not explained. There may well be such a plan, for there have been some bizarre schemes conjured up in the Pentagon, but the practicability of US 'Special Forces operatives', or anyone else, being able to take over installations guarded by the Pakistan Army is remote to the point of risibility.

Development and command of nuclear weapons, including the initial release decision and subsequent targeting, is the responsibility of the National Command Authority, which is chaired by the 'head of government' who, under Pakistan's current (December 2007) system, is the President. The NCA was approved in February 2000 by the National Security Council (see below) and has ten members: the President, Prime Minister, Chairman of the Joint Chiefs of Staff Committee, the three service chiefs, the ministers of Defence, Finance and Interior, and the Director General Strategic Plans Division. Science and defence experts are generally invited to meetings to present papers on specific discussion topics. (It is of interest that a meeting of the NCA on 2 August 2007 was attended by the then Director General of Inter Services Intelligence (and, from 28 November 2007, Chief of Army Staff), General Ashfaq Kiyani.)[23] It is of note that the NCA does not confine itself to deliberations and decisions concerning nuclear weapons, but is also concerned with negotiations on disarmament involving the Fissile Material Cut-off Treaty, IAEA safeguards, the US–India nuclear agreement and non-proliferation matters in general. It remains to be seen, under civilian governance, whether this wide remit will continue to apply.

Chemical and Biological Weapons[24]

Pakistan appears to have abided by its commitment to refrain from developing either a chemical or biological weapons' capability, but does have the ability to manufacture chemical agents and to expand biological research. It possesses ground-to-ground and air-to-ground means to deliver non-standard munitions, and could produce chemical agents for delivery by artillery carrier-shells on the battlefield within days of a decision being made to implement a programme.

It is improbable that manufacture of biological weapons will ever be undertaken, largely for reasons of cost and complexity. Even were a biological weapons' project to be approved, with maximum military, financial, industrial and scientific support, it is unlikely that the product could be weaponized in a timely fashion or in quantities sufficient to influence the outcome of a regional conflict. Should an India-Pakistan war reach a level at which employment of non-standard weaponry might be considered a realistic option (e.g. should there be an Indian advance as far as the Karachi–Lahore highway), it is most probable that nuclear attack would be the preferred choice.

In the course of production, storage and movement it is probable that safety standards would be consistent with or closely approaching those applying in developed countries, as is evident in known plants and establishments currently manufacturing legitimate chemicals or undertaking chemical or biological research. An increase in activity associated with production of weapon-specific agents or combinations of dual-use chemicals could be expected to attract appropriate safety precautions. It should be noted, however, that in existing chemical plants not subject to industrial regulations or inspections (by reason of corruption or inefficiency) there is little if any protection against accidents or sabotage. In September 2003 two people died following a major leak of chlorine gas from a plant owned by Ittehad Chemicals Ltd near Lahore. Given the generally chaotic state of law enforcement it is probable that there are other factories with unsatisfactory or no controls, but it is assessed that facilities associated with government programmes, academic institutions and reputable commercial enterprises have adequate safeguards.

The policy of Pakistan's successive governments has been stated as opposing production of military oriented and other illegal chemical and biological material. The country's membership of the Executive Council of the Organization for the Prohibition of Chemical Weapons is generally accepted as an indication of probity regarding adherence to the purpose and letter of current international accords. On 20 July 2007 the then Foreign Minister, Mr Khurshid Kasuri, stated in a letter to the Director General of the Organisation for the Prohibition of Chemical Weapons that Pakistan 'attaches great importance to the promotion of the objectives of the Chemical Weapons Convention'. At a meeting of international experts on *National Implementation of the BTWC* in Geneva on 20 August 2007, Pakistan reiterated that it 'remains fully committed to strengthening the Biological and Toxin Weapons Convention including the establishment of a compliance regime through a legally binding instrument'.

CB Treaties ratified by Pakistan are:

- The UN *Convention on the Prohibition of the Development, Production, Stockpiling and Use of Chemical Weapons and on their Destruction* (A/RES/47/39) of 30 November 1992, Ratified by Pakistan January 1993; short title: Chemical Weapons Convention (CWC);
- The *Biological and Toxin Weapons Convention* (1972), ratified by Pakistan in 1974; short title: Biological Weapons Convention (BWC); and
- The *India-Pakistan Agreement on Chemical Weapons* (1993), ratified by India on 3 September 1996; by Pakistan on 28 October 1997.

Pakistan is prepared to accept inspections but reserves its position 'to exercise its rights under paragraphs 2 and 4 of the verification Annex [to the CWC] to indicate its non-acceptance of inspectors and inspection assistants as it deems appropriate'. (This caveat is most probably India-specific.) Inspections took place in 2001, 2002 and 2003. Results of the first two were not made public, but it is apparent they were not adverse. The April 2003 inspection was of the Fauji Jordan Fertiliser plant near Karachi, the country's largest such facility, and the inspectors made no unfavourable findings.

There have been no incidents of use of either chemical or biological weapons by Pakistan's armed forces. It has been claimed by India that chemical agents were used in the Siachen region, where there has been low-level conflict since 1984 (although an unofficial ceasefire has applied since 2002), based on reports of discoloured snow following impact by artillery shells on the rock base many metres below the snow surface. It is assessed that the phenomenon was caused by normal HE/smoke effect in such terrain and climatic conditions. India has also alleged that Pakistan is involved in illegal activities connected with chemical and biological weapons, based on reports that items of protective clothing, including respirators, have been imported and manufactured.

While there is instruction and discussion on CBW during courses at defence force schools and academies (e.g. the Army Staff College at Quetta, the School of Military Engineering at Risalpur, and air force and navy establishments) it appears that inclusion in studies is a matter of convention, in that the subject is required knowledge on the part of all officers, as in other nations' armed forces. There appears to be no emphasis given to CBW during normal military exercises.

As noted in Chapter 5, international condemnation of Pakistan's nuclear tests in 1998 included imposition of sanctions on all identifiable institutions and organizations linked with or likely to be connected to production of nuclear weapons, or to be involved in even a peripheral fashion with associated technology. Following Pakistan's support for the United States after the terrorist incidents of 11 September 2001, the sanctions imposed by Washington were lifted. Other nations and international organizations such as the IMF followed suit. Although no official sanctions now apply, it has been observed that in the case of Pakistan (although not of India) there is continuing denial of co-operation with any entity having connections with nuclear research. It is considered that this pertains, albeit unofficially, to organizations, businesses and establishments having likely dual-role capability in regard to CB development.

The Interior Ministry is responsible, through the Directorate General Civil Defence, for planning and execution of a co-ordinated response to natural and man-made disasters. There is no national plan for combating an enemy CB (or nuclear) attack, nor guidance at a national level as to how to cope with a domestic CB disaster. Government and private electronic media have no standing instructions concerning crisis response, and reaction to incidents is on a case-by-case basis as advised by the Interior Ministry.

The Directorate General Civil Defence prepares and conducts CD courses, mainly at its HQ in Lahore, but also in varying degrees of efficacy in Rawalpindi, Karachi, Quetta and Peshawar. The emphasis is on firefighting, relief measures and related subjects (although the Bomb Disposal Unit conducts courses in IED neutralization and anti-terrorism), but five four-week courses are conducted in Lahore each year in 'Civil Defence Basic Nuclear, Biological and Chemical Warfare'. While the content appears satisfactory in broad terms it is not claimed that the programme represents anything but an approach to elementary knowledge of the topics.

It is apparent that Pakistan has neither the capability nor intention to develop chemical or biological weapons, and that preparedness to counter their use, in the most unlikely event of India ever employing such weapons, is minimal.

Command and Control

Given that India and Pakistan have a nuclear capability and appear hell-bent on continuing development of nuclear-tipped surface-to-surface missiles, aerial delivery systems, and, in India's case, breathtakingly expensive and complex maritime equivalents, it is important that their command and control systems be scrutinized. This is not to endorse the nuclear weapons race, which is a disaster for the Subcontinent and will keep hundreds of millions in excruciating poverty; but if the countries are to establish a practicable nuclear doctrine – a labyrinth of intellectual contradictions through which even long-established nuclear powers continue to seek their way (and stumble from time to time) – there must be rationalization of their higher defence structure. The first step, in both countries, should be establishment of a Joint Commander.

For the purposes of modern war it is imperative that the armed services of Pakistan be placed under a single officer, with a high-quality staff to assist him in his command and other functions. The present Joint Staff Headquarters would be a start, but is physically far too small and lacks the number of officers required to function properly as a command HQ. The duty statement of the Chief of Defence Force (CDF) should be simply: 'To command the armed forces of Pakistan'.

There should be no equivocation about this, and the words 'chairman' 'committee' and 'staff' should be eschewed in the title as well as in practice. Senior officers would give advice (especially concerning employment and deployment of their own services), which is what they are there for; they may even argue their positions to whatever extent the CDF might consider reasonable; but decisions are for the CDF and him alone. His is a non-executive board, save when he delegates action to be taken.

So far as the higher direction of war is concerned, the CDF should be the primary adviser to government on strategy, which is where a National Security Council (NSC) is important. As retired Lieutenant General Talat Masood wrote:

> The argument that the Defence Committee of Cabinet can serve the same purpose as a National Security Council is inherently flawed ... The DCC generally addresses issues at a time when a particular crisis has already become intractable or the policy has failed to deliver. The NSC, on the other hand, meets at regular intervals and can be convened at any time in event of an emergency. There has to be continuous flow of information ... on the basis of which sound policy options can be evolved and implemented. This can only happen if there is institutional back-up of the NSC.

A National Security Council was established by Act of Parliament in April 2004,[25] but it appears it was not in quite the form recommended by

177

General Masood. It first met on 24 June and the *Pakistan Observer* of 2 July recorded that:

> [The] meeting addressed Pakistan's deteriorating law and order situation, the weeks of killings in Karachi, and anti-Al Qaeda operations on the Afghan border, Karachi turmoil, Sui explosions, WAPDA towers blown [up], Christina Rocca's Congressional hearings, ongoing confidence-building talks with India, agreement between India and Pakistan to open consulates in Karachi and Bombay, and the lingering Kashmir entanglement.
>
> Pakistan's top civil-military body including the then Prime Minister Mir Zafarullah Khan Jamali, National Assembly Speaker Chaudhry Amir Hussain, Chief Ministers of Punjab, Sindh and Balochistan, Joint Chiefs of Staff Committee Chairman and the Services Chiefs attended the meeting as its Members while Ministers for Interior and Foreign Affairs, the NWFP Governor and Vice Chief of Army Staff attended the meeting on special invitation. They vowed to rid the country of terrorism and religious militancy that has claimed more than 60 lives since May. 'If there is a threat to Pakistan it is from (the) internal security environment,' said President Pervez Musharraf, chairing the first meeting of the National Security Council (NSC).[26]

It is for the senior figure in government to decide how much influence the NSC should have – and at that time in Pakistan it was the President – but it is essential that a system be put in place that will be applicable to any future civilian government, whatever form that may take, including that of an executive presidency. The discussion points for the first meeting, noted above, are daunting and far too all-embracing to produce Talat Masood's 'sound policy options', and refined procedures should reflect this. In the context of the direction of defence matters, the deliberations of the NSC should result in overall strategic objectives, naturally including nuclear imperatives, being conveyed to the Chief of Defence Force. It is then up to him to translate these into operational concepts. He must be undisturbed by government and bureaucracy once the national strategy has been spelled out. (There is nothing politicians love so much as being pictured as decisive commanders. When they are involved in military matters, they take on a particular look of macho determination for the cameras and do their best to combine a furrowed brow, jutting chin and steely eyes.) Deployment and command of forces are the CDF's responsibility, although he will discuss matters with the NSC. All of this takes many years to hone to efficiency, but the government of Pakistan should work towards creation of a CDF and a Joint HQ. It will be costly, but there is no point in having expensive weapons and large forces if they cannot be directed properly. The manpower would come from the existing Service head-quarters – from which source much resistance can be expected.

General Ehsan ul Haq took over as Chairman of the Joint Chiefs of Staff Committee in October 2004 (from being Director General ISI). In 2005 he tried to extend the Chairman's authority and proposed to General Musharraf that the service chiefs should work through him, as Chairman, rather than having direct access to the President. Musharraf considered the suggestion and in turn proposed, no doubt with his tongue firmly in his cheek, that General Ehsan confer with the chiefs and come up with recommendations. Predictably, the chiefs (including the army's vice-chief) were having none of it and told Ehsan forcefully that there was nothing doing, which is understandable because in the Joint HQ/CDF concept the service chiefs would have responsibility only to 'raise, train and provide'. They would not be in the operational chain of command, but would be single-service advisers in what might be called the CDF's Advisory Council. Their own headquarters would shrink accordingly, for there would be no requirement for all of the staff branches that now exist. Single-service operations branches, these sacred bodies to which the best and the brightest aspire, would be disbanded and reconstituted within the tri-service HQ, and this is why there is so much opposition within the services. Using the well-tried strategy of divide and rule, the bureaucrats (whose own power would be reduced) would enlist doubters amongst the politicians and try to influence government against any moves towards creation of a CDF, saying that because the three services were having the mother of all turf wars about jointery, there would be no point in going further with the proposal, which is exactly what has been taking place in India; that saga is depressing. This way lies disaster for the armed forces. I have been present at a creation, and saw officers disagreeing so violently about allocation of particular appointments to this or that Service that friendships of years were sundered.[27] It can be a messy business, but it is the only way to go.

Notes

1. And to move closer to India, with which in 2007 wide-ranging defence co-operation was agreed. See 'Australia and India sign defence information sharing agreement', Department of Defence, 12 July 2007, http://www.minister.defence.gov.au/NelsonMintpl.cfm? CurrentId=6851. Australia also intended, under the former Liberal government (defeated in elections in November 2007), to sell uranium to India in support of the Bush administration's nuclear co-operation policy. The new Labour government changed this policy in 2008.
2. The BBC noted on 26 August 2000 that 'A Commonwealth summit in November 1999 endorsed the suspension [of Pakistan] and asked a Commonwealth Ministerial Action Group (CMAG) to "keep the situation in Pakistan under review and be prepared to recommend further measures to be taken by the Commonwealth if progress to democracy

is not made speedily".' (http://news.bbc.co.uk/1/hi/world/south_asia/896833.stm) But on 22 May 2004 the BBC reported that the Commonwealth had decided that Pakistan had become more democratic: 'Pakistan has been re-admitted to full membership of the Commonwealth. It was suspended in 1999, after General Pervez Musharraf seized power in a military coup. Since then Pakistan has been a front-line state in US President George W. Bush's declared war on terror, but the Commonwealth Secretary-General Don McKinnon said that the decision to re-admit Pakistan had been taken because of its progress towards democracy.' http://news.bbc.co.uk/2/hi/south_asia/3739421.stm

3. IMET, the International Military Education and Training programme.

4. *Pakistan-U.S. Anti-Terrorism Cooperation; Updated March 28, 2003*, CRS Report RL31624.

5. See, for example, the *Daily Telegraph* (UK) of 10 March 2007: 'Bin Laden has evaded capture and assassination ever since President Bill Clinton signed a secret order authorising the CIA to kill him. While President George W. Bush said after the September 11 attacks that bin Laden was wanted "dead or alive", US military and intelligence might have failed to carry out the order more than five years after the terrorist leader fled for his life after the invasion of Afghanistan and the collapse of his Taliban allies. Now the Bush administration is redoubling its efforts. "Reports that the trail has gone stone cold are not correct," an American official said.' On the other hand there was the statement by President Bush on 13 March 2002 that said 'So I don't know where he [bin Laden] is. You know, I just don't spend that much time on him, Kelly, to be honest with you.'

6. Information from a senior officer. General Franks' reaction is not known.

7. *New York Times*, 28 Jan 2003, http://mea.gov.in/bestoftheweb/2003/01/28bow01.htm

8. To the writer in May 2007.

9. BBC, 6 February 2007 (http://news.bbc.co.uk/2/hi/south_asia/6335229.stm), one of many such reports.

10. *Daily Times*, Pakistan, 27 September 2007. http://www.dailytimes.com.pk/default.asp?page=2007%5C09%5C27%5Cstory_27-9-2007_pg7_4

11. See, for this and other interesting facts and reflections, Khalid Aziz, 'Causes of the Rebellion in Waziristan', *Criterion Quarterly*, April-June 2007. Mr Aziz, a former Chief Secretary of North West Frontier Province, has a deep knowledge of the region and its problems.

12. A conversation reported to me by his interlocutor, another general.

13. By Ansar Abbasi, http://www.thenews.com.pk/arc_default.asp. The list of senior officers in the article was taken from *Wikipedia* http://en.wikipedia.org/wiki/Pakistan_Army.

14. International Institute for Strategic Studies, *Military Balance 1979–1980*.

15. Siddiqa, Dr Ayesha, 'Soldiers of Fortune', *Newsline*, December 2006. http://www.newsline.com.pk/NewsDec2006/cover1dec2006.htm

16. I had discussions with the AG, the Chairman of the Joint Chiefs of Staff Committee, the Chief of the General Staff and other senior serving officers in July–August 2007.

17. Cost estimate for protective suits is based in part on a report by the Deputy Inspector General of the US Department of Defence of 21 June 2000 to the effect that 'The Distribution Standard System records indicated that the Depot had 2,178,583 [protective] suits of the six types in our sample at 1,043 warehouse locations ... At 728 other locations that were not identified as containing protective suits, we found an additional 696,380 protective suits, worth $51 million.' The cost of masks is based on widely available commercial information.

18. There is no point in having NBC suits if soldiers are not trained to put them on and fight in them. The most horrible exercises in the British Army of the Rhine in the 1960s were when we had to don 'Noddy Suits' and try to persuade ourselves that they might extend our lives in the event of nuclear attack or distribution of fallout from our own short-range missiles. They would have not had the slightest effect, of course, and they weren't even

good for morale because we knew the whole thing was pointless as well as being excessively uncomfortable. The suits were collected after these exercises, but few could be reused, for obvious reasons. The bills must have been enormous.

19. 'India and Pakistan: Can They Arrange a Cold War?' *The Economist*, 3 October 1998.

20. Riedel, Bruce, 'American Diplomacy and the 1999 Kargil Summit at Blair House,' Policy Paper Series 2002 (Philadelphia: Center for the Advanced Study of India, University of Pennsylvania, May 2002), Internet: http://www.sas.upenn.edu/casi.

21. French, Howard W. and Dugger, Celia W., 'US India-Pakistan Mission Fails to Ease the Standoff,' *New York Times*, 16 May 2002: http://www.nytimes.com/2002/05/16/international/asia/16STAN.html. George Perkovitch is a Senior Associate at the Carnegie Endowment for International Peace and author of, inter alia, the magisterial *India's Nuclear Bomb*, University of California Press, California, 1999).

22. *Inside Pakistan's Drive to Guard its A-Bombs*, Peter Wonacott, Wall Street Journal 29 November 2007. http://online.wsj.com/public/article/SB119629674095207239.html

23. Photograph at http://www.daylife.com/search/photos/all/1?q=national+command+authority.

24. This section is an abridged version of an analysis completed for Jane's *Chemical, Biological, Radiological and Nuclear Assessments* in November 2007.

25. See http://www.pakistanconstitution-law.com/appendix21.asp of 20 April 2004.

26. http://www.infopak.gov.pk/writeups/NSC_maiden_session.htm

27. An Australian Major General berated a Brigadier, who was involved in planning the structure of the future joint service HQ, for failing to recommend that a particular appointment should be reserved for the army, with the words 'don't forget your loyalty'. It was the General who was being disloyal, of course – but the Brigadier was not promoted, in spite of being an outstanding officer.

Chapter 8

Terrorism and Tribes

President Musharraf has often been accused of failing to do enough to rid his country of terrorism,[1] and even of complicity in harbouring some of democracy's most violent enemies. Although hundreds of al Qaeda and other terrorist suspects were arrested and handed over to the United States and Britain in 2002–7, and scores of home-grown religio-political savages imprisoned, some commentators and analysts, even in the US government, seemed to be convinced that Musharraf was reluctant to take on the terrorists.

It would be strange if a man who has survived at least nine assassination plans or attempts were not anxious to counter those who seek to kill him, but the purpose of domestic and foreign terrorists in Pakistan is not focused solely on murdering its President, and there are other reasons for the government to want to counter them. The fanatics loathe the West, which they consider the root of all evil, and equate moderate governance in Pakistan with secularism and unconditional support of non-Muslims. In one of Osama bin Laden's diatribes in September 2007 he called on Pakistanis to 'rebel against the apostate' Musharraf,[2] but the wider purpose is a call to arms – quite literally – against all infidels, and senior army officers are concerned that the aim of bin Laden and his acolytes in Pakistan is to encourage unrest to the point that soldiers and even officers might regard co-operation with the US in the 'war against terror' as essentially un-Islamic (in 2007 there was evidence of this). They seek political power in order to subject Pakistan to a quasi-religious regime of autocracy in which there would be neither compassion nor tolerance, and the armed forces are a main target, along with the universities. Within Pakistan, Musharraf and his like represent all that they are determined to destroy. His Western critics may claim he did not act fast or hard enough to combat terrorism, but the terrorists don't agree, and nor do the religious extremists who support them.

In July 2005 Musharraf ordered deportation of foreigners attending religious colleges because these can be 'misused for extremism'. But he was promptly criticized internationally for doing too little, too late, to counter the spread of militant Islam, which is almost undeniable, and within Pakistan he was attacked for appearing to follow Western dictates and betraying his country's religion. He was in one corner of a boxing ring. Leaping out of the others were the terrorists, their bigoted theocratic supporters, and foreign and domestic critics, all trying to land a killer punch.

In September 2005, Musharraf, as President and head of the army, was trying to achieve a balance between his personal preference for non-confrontational, democratic Islam (which the theocrats consider a non-sequitur), and pragmatic sufferance of religious extremists who promote their highly selective interpretation of Islam as the sole arbiter of all aspects of social and political life. Pakistan's Islamic zealots use their faith as both tool and justification for their assaults on laws and customs based on Western jurisprudence and common sense. Forceful movement against them is presented as anti-Islamic while their own violence is portrayed as the inevitable consequence of persecution by kafirs, or non-believers. In spite of limitations on Musharraf's choices for action, hard-line Islam was being contained through a combination of reluctance on the part of the educated classes, especially the business community, to embrace seventh-century religiosity, and the government's measured, if sometimes hesitant responses to extremists' provocation. In 2000–5 the army appeared largely content with Musharraf's espousal of 'enlightened moderation', but later there were incidents that indicated a disturbing trend away from enlightenment.

One leader of Pakistan's group of politico-religious parties (the Muttahida Majlis-e-Amal (MMA), or United Action Front) is Qazi Hussain Ahmed, a preacher-cum-politician and head of the Jamaat-e-Islami party, who has courted arrest by increasing the intensity of his rhetoric. He endorses the Taliban's militant resurgence in Afghanistan and attacks Western and especially US influence (although two of his sons are US-educated, one of them an American citizen), and is implacably opposed to Musharraf's agenda of anti-terrorism and enlightened Islam. Hypocrite or not, he is a dangerous demagogue. The government ordered the arrest of some 800 suspected Islamic militants in July 2005 but the subsequent call by Qazi Hussain for civil disobedience to protest a 'global conspiracy' against Islam was unsuccessful, which was an encouraging sign, as were the August 2005 local elections because, although they were in theory non-political, many of the more rabid of the MMA's supporters failed to win votes. It still held sixty-seven of the National Assembly's 342 seats, from the 2002 national elections, but it seemed that Qazi and his ilk might be losing popular appeal.

The test for any government in Pakistan would be the arrest of 'Qazi Sahib' or other prominent religious leaders who openly support terrorism.

The MMA has sought confrontation, and although it appeared Musharraf might be in a position to accept the challenge he had to weigh up the possible consequences of action against the wild men.

Unfortunately Musharraf, as Byron had it, 'nursed the pinion that impelled the steel', in that in 2002 he endorsed the election efforts of the religious crackpots in the interests of sidelining the two mainstream political parties. The results were not wholly catastrophic for the country, but they gave Qazi and his supporters confidence that they could flex the religious muscle that was first given them by Zulfiqar Ali Bhutto who cultivated them to the extent of forbidding alcohol (an act of ridiculous humbug by a Scotch-bibbing Westernised sophisticate), and Zia ul Haq who cultivated them because he was himself of similar persuasion. But Musharraf engineered himself into a peculiar position of semi-alliance with the sort of people who were and remain entirely opposed to his agenda for the country.

Musharraf had a pressing personal interest forced upon him: he had to destroy terrorists lest they get him first. But his domestic considerations, not least his own political survival, made it inadvisable for him to move as fast as his Western detractors demanded in his campaign against Islamic militancy. Widely publicized foreign criticism of his efforts assisted his ultra-Islamic adversaries while not contributing to their neutralization. A poll in September 2007 indicated that only 38 per cent of Pakistanis supported Musharraf (a dramatic slump within a year), while Osama bin Laden's approval rating was 46 per cent – and the poll did not include the tribal regions of North West Frontier Province.[3] (As discussed below, later polls indicated further slippage in Musharraf's acceptability.)

The most sensitive factor is the army itself. Just how far has it gone in endorsing extremist Islam?

The army of Pakistan, like all institutions of state, is religiously based. Undoubtedly there are some religious extremists among its officers and soldiers, but the promotion and selection process from colonel up to major general was closely overseen by Musharraf, who rarely vetoed an appointment and preferred his subordinates to agree that officers whose priorities centre on religious devotion rather than professional competence should not be posted to positions in which they might influence others. Promotions of major generals to lieutenant general are not subject to a selection board as such: the army chief speaks with such of his principal staff officers as he may care to consult, then contacts corps commanders for their views. A retired senior officer told me in September 2007 that 'He [Musharraf] had a grid made out with Corps Commanders listed on one side vertically, and horizontally several columns indicating input (this I saw as a result of several one-on-one discussions).' This informal process appears to have worked well enough, as there appears to have been no three- star officer appointed whose religious practices and beliefs could be described as immoderate and unenlightened. They are perfectly good Muslims, but do not seek to run the army on purely religious lines.

One component of Pakistan's society that is decidedly immoderate, as well as being startlingly and sometimes terrifyingly unenlightened, exists in the Federally Administered Tribal Areas and, in fact, throughout much of North West Frontier Province. The tribes are ungovernable, as they have always been, but a disquieting development has been the increase in the power of clerical tyrants (as distinct from tribal leaders whose posts are held at the will of the majority), which has had an adverse effect on the morale and efficiency of army and Frontier Corps units engaged in operations in the Province. There is evidence that some soldiers have been so influenced by religiosity as to have doubts about their being regarded as Shaheed in the event of being killed in conflict with fellow Muslims who are held (by extremist clerics) to be engaged in fighting against infidels.[4] This has resulted in incidents of refusal to take part in operations in the tribal areas, which indicate a serious malaise. The complexity of the tribal system, combined with growth in intensity of religious fervour and the anarchic situation across the western border, is presenting a challenge to the Pakistan Army that it is finding difficult to meet.

One revelation is that:

> Statements [by terrorists captured during an army operation] and [other sources] leads to one inevitable conclusion, that deep in their hearts ... [some of the] troops have sympathies for AQ/Taliban who, in their perception are fighting a holy war against non-Muslims now occupying Afghanistan. This feeling has got further impetus and strength because of the US invasion and occupation of Iraq and a partisan approach towards the Palestinian issue. Print and electronic media, anti-US sentiments among the general public, bitter criticism by opposition leaders of our government's policy regarding Afghanistan [and] support to the Coalition (US) forces in combating terrorism ... and the anti-Islam propaganda by the west, have further reinforced the perception of the common man that Muslims all over the world are being victimised. These feelings have obviously ... penetrated the rank and file of the Army despite our best efforts that whatever we are doing is in the overall best interests of the country. Having identified this weakness, we now need to apply all our command and leadership skills to educate our troops on the logic and necessity of what we are doing.[5]

This is disturbing for the army and the country, but at least it is realized by those in positions of command that a problem exists, and it is apparent that action has been and continues to be taken. The fact remains that the influence of malevolent religious fanatics has held sway to some extent, as they have been able to play on the sentiments and beliefs of soldiers who are not in an intellectual position to confound or contradict the specious persuasiveness of semi-educated, essentially barbaric, but ostensibly devout con men.

Afghanistan, the Frontier and the Taliban

No Man who has ever read a page of Indian history will prophesy about Frontier.

Lord Curzon, 20 July 1904.

As indicated in Chapter 5, since independence in 1947 Pakistan's governance of the Federally Administered Tribal Areas (FATA)[6] in North West Frontier Province has never been complete, and was conducted relying on: the time-tested British tactics of bribery ('subsidies'); personal contact between government representatives (the Political Agents) and tribal representatives (maliks); tribal custom and precedent in resolving disputes; acceptance and understanding of Islam as an ethical force; and the underlying threat of severe punishment for transgressions of the ancient (1901) and still extant Frontier Crimes Regulation. There were four large areas along the border with Afghanistan in which no military presence had ever been effected until 2001–2, and neither the military nor ordinary citizens from the rest of Pakistan were welcome anywhere in the tribal lands. They are even less welcome now.

Being Pashtuns, as are their counterparts over the border, the tribes are as ruthless when fighting among themselves as they are at combating strangers, and their partiality for mayhem and murder makes them untrustworthy allies and barbarically dangerous enemies.[7] Attempts have been made for decades to bring the tribes into mainstream Pakistan, but in many regions their attitude has been unco-operative. On some occasions they have appeared to agree to road construction, for example, only to obstruct projects on various pretexts once they began. This has by no means been universal, and in several Agencies, notably Mohmand and Orakzai, the army managed to build roads, schools and clinics in 2002–4 – but many of the schemes have since been destroyed because of the growing insurrection in FATA and even in the so-called 'settled areas' of the province.

Encouragement of tribesmen to join the army was welcome in much of FATA as it was an opportunity for unemployed young men to make a living with the opportunity of practising violence, a well-nurtured inherent skill. Care had to be taken in apportioning recruits to units for reasons of tribal rivalries (the Mahsuds and Wazirs of South Waziristan Agency are forever at feud, for example), and few problems were experienced. Although precise figures are not officially provided, it seems that

Pashtuns amount to perhaps a fifth of regular army soldiery, about 100,000 men, as a result of recruiting drives since the 1970s. (The Frontier Corps of 65,000 in NWFP is almost entirely Pashtun.) But when major offensive operations began in the tribal areas in 2004 there were some incidents of refusal to fight by Pashtun soldiers on tribal grounds. Some later developments were disquieting, and in 2007 there were more instances of indiscipline. It appears that reluctance to engage militants is not based only on disinclination to kill fellow tribesmen, which would create blood feuds, but stems to some extent from antipathy against fighting fellow-Muslims, an attitude played on by extremists. Another factor is the widely held belief that the counter-insurgency war in FATA (for it is an all-out war, not simply an increase in the tempo of operations by militants and the army) is not being conducted on behalf of Pakistan but is waged at the behest of the United States. This perception is encouraged by religious leaders and also, if unintentionally, by Washington whose officials have on countless occasions publicly rebuked Pakistan's government for failing, in their perception, to enter wholeheartedly into the US 'war on terror'. Recent unrest in the tribal areas dates from the time of the US invasion of Afghanistan, which was the beginning of Washington's open-ended, worldwide drive to eradicate Muslim extremists.

US military action against the Taliban in Afghanistan began in late 2001. The operation at Tora Bora, close to the border with Pakistan, that was mounted in the first week of December, was not co-ordinated with Pakistan, no matter what might be claimed to the contrary, and was a military nonsense. The tiny US force of about forty special forces and CIA heavies relied on bribing Afghan militia leaders and rag-bag tribal groups to achieve the objective, which was to kill or capture Osama bin Laden. In early 2007 a senior member of Britain's Secret Intelligence Service told me he was close to Tora Bora, where some twenty of the UK's Special Air Service troops were involved, and indicated that there were command and control problems during the operation.[8] Other independent reports, including one from a member of the SAS now in civilian employment but still unable to speak openly, are scathing concerning overall direction of the battle in which failure, in the words of a former CIA operative, Gary Bernsten, was due to 'Lack of flexibility, lack of creativeness, a reliance on bureaucracy and doctrine. That's what it was.'[9]

General Tommy Franks wrote on 19 October 2004 in the *New York Times* (described as 'a member of Veterans for Bush'[10]) that 'Pakistani troops also provided significant help [during the Tora Bora operation] – as many as 100,000 sealed the border and rounded up hundreds of Qaeda and Taliban fighters.' But on 27 December 2001 Mr Donald Rumsfeld had said that 'They [Pakistan] must have seven or eight, nine battalions along the

Pakistan-Afghan border, which is clearly a deterrent to people trying to come across – trying to escape from Afghanistan,' and 'we took custody of about 20 people turned over to us by Pakistani authorities. These detainees are now being held in facilities at Kandahar. And that brings us to 45 total right now Taliban and Al Qaeda personnel in custody.'[11] The border was not 'sealed' and there were no 'hundreds' of fighters rounded up.

The facts are that on 8 December 2001 the Director General Military Operations, Major General Ashfaq Kiyani[12] contacted senior commanders on the western border and, according to one of them, 'discussed the implications of coalition forces operation in Tora Bora and the possibility of deploying our troops in the areas opposite the Tora Bora Mountains. Interestingly, our coalition friends had not informed us about their operation in Tora Bora and we came to know about it through the press.'

In spite of having no prior knowledge of the operation, within three days the Pakistan Army's XI Corps deployed 5,000 soldiers along the border about which Mr Rumsfeld said at the time is 'a long border. It's a very complicated area to try to seal, and there's just simply no way you can put a perfect cork in the bottle.'[13] The problem was lack of co-ordination between US and Pakistani forces, and this set the tone for the years to come. The effect on the Pakistan Army was complicated. Senior staff officers and commanders had a certain understanding for the imperatives of their US counterparts, in that they realized the need for security and thus concealment of operational details, and appreciated that in some cases the requirements of secrecy could override the need to provide fore-warning of movements and mission intentions. But on the ground this can lead to confusion and so-called 'friendly fire' fiascos in addition to the killing of civilians, which is a major cause of bitter outrage in Pakistan as a whole, but especially in the Frontier – and in the Pakistan Army and Frontier Corps.

On 13 January 2006, for example:

A missile attack on a residential compound in northwest Pakistan near the Afghan border [in Bajaur] killed up to 18 people, reportedly including numerous women and children. Some reports said the death toll was higher and included up to one dozen Islamic militants. Pakistani officials and local witnesses blamed the attack on US air forces, possibly Predator drones that were targeting top Al Qaeda leader Ayman al-Zawahri, who was not at the scene. US officials would not confirm US involvement.[14]

Next day the *Daily Times* carried a pithy editorial that summed things up:

On January 7 [2006], some troops of the US-led coalition forces in Afghanistan crossed over into North Waziristan and conducted a search operation on Pakistani territory. They arrested two tribesmen and took them away. [On 13 January] a US helicopter also fired on the house of a religious leader in the area, killing eight tribesmen, including two women and a child. Nine other people were wounded in the firing. We are now informed that Pakistan has lodged a protest with the US government over the incident, though we have no information about how the US government has responded to the protest or what internal action, if any, it plans to take with regard to its local commanders to ensure that this sort of thing doesn't happen again ...

Such incidents of American intervention pose problems for two reasons. First, General Pervez Musharraf is already precariously balanced on the issue of military operations in the Tribal Areas. The policy is deeply unpopular in Pakistan, not just among the tribesmen of the NWFP but also among retired military officials. Second, his main reason for deploying troops to the area was to ensure that US and US-led forces did not enter Pakistani territory in pursuit of Taliban and Al Qaeda elements who were better left to be handled by the Pakistani military. Such incidents therefore serve to weaken General Musharraf's position even within his own military constituency and make it that much more difficult for him to do the job he is supposed to do.[15]

A week later Prime Minister Shaukat Aziz told an American reporter that the US attack in the Bajaur Agency was not co-ordinated with the Pakistani government and 'not one shred of evidence' had been found indicating that any Islamic militants had been at the site of the attack. He condemned the incident and called for greater US-Pakistan co-ordination. This was the furthest he could go, but the damage had been done; and for very many people the Bajaur catastrophe epitomized all that they disliked in the actions and attitude of US forces in Afghanistan and, indeed, worldwide. During my visits to Pakistan in 2006 several army officers told me that what they most objected to was being blamed for lack of action against 'miscreants' on the Frontier when it was obvious the army was doing all it could to contain violence, to the extent of having had by mid-2006 over 400 soldiers and some 300 Frontier Corps troops killed. One senior officer was particularly acid about the State Department's co-ordinator for counter terrorism, Henry Crumpton, who at a press conference in Kabul in May had said, 'Has Pakistan done enough? I think the answer is no. I have conveyed that to them, other US officials have conveyed that to them.' 'He's talking rubbish,' the Pakistani officer said. 'And why is he saying this sort of thing in Kabul?' Ironically, on the day that Mr Crumpton delivered his criticism, 'militants in North Waziristan distributed leaflets containing an alleged message from Osama bin Laden urging Muslims everywhere to aid in the fight against Pakistani forces in the tribal areas.' His exhortations may have borne fruit – they were certainly given impetus by the next missile strike in Bajaur, which took place in the early hours of October 2006 when three Hellfires destroyed a madrassa at Chingai village, near the main town, Khar, and killed eighty-three people, all but three of them aged between fifteen and their early twenties.[16] Apparently it had been thought that Ayman al-Zawahiri, said to be the highest-ranking member of al-Qaeda, was present, which he was not, although a notable religious figure of the area, a Taliban-supporting rabble-rousing cleric called Maulana Liaquat, was killed, along with his sons. One apparent target, Maulana Faqir Muhammad, was not killed in the strike, but the following day he appeared at a local rally and urged 'mass suicide attacks on Pakistani forces', one of which took a week later place at the Punjab Regiment's training centre at Dargai in neighbouring Malakand district, killing forty-two soldiers and wounding some twenty.[17] Since then there have been many incidents of suicide bombing, the most horrific of which were those that killed 180 people during a procession held by Benazir Bhutto in Karachi to celebrate her return to Pakistan in October, and the assassination of Bhutto in Rawalpindi on 27 December 2007, when another thirty died.[18]

Pakistan has a short history of suicide bombings, the first recorded being in 1995 when an Egyptian citizen tried to drive a bomb-laden truck into the Egyptian Embassy compound in Islamabad. There were two suicide bombing attacks in 2005, both of which were caused by the dispute between Sunni and Shia extremists (most Sunnis and Shias get along perfectly well in Pakistan, but the wild men are always on the lookout for an opportunity to encourage hatred by bombing or otherwise murdering those of the differing persuasion). In 2006 there were six: two Shia-Sunni, the others aimed at US and security forces' targets. In 2007 there were over fifty, most of which directly targeted military forces, especially compara-tively soft objectives such as bus transport linking residential areas to military bases. In Rawalpindi, in November, there were attacks on check posts and buses that killed sixteen people, and on 10 December an air force school bus at Kamra, close to Islamabad, was hit by a suicide car-bomber, injuring five children. It seems likely that the Bajaur strikes had at least some influence on the extremists, and that the army's action at the Lal Masjid, the Red Mosque, in Islamabad in July 2007, when seventy-three armed fanatics were killed in an assault by the Special Services Group, probably encouraged other bombers. One para-military soldier and two members of the SSG were killed in the course of the siege and ten SSG during the storming of the mosque, which operation, contrary to wide-spread belief, was conducted with admirable competence. (In the eighty-room complex the soldiers fought through a warren of booby traps covered by the fire of dedicated Islamic revolutionaries for over thirty hours, and received scant praise in their own or any other media, although in the aftermath the al Qaeda figure Ayman al-Zawahiri, who called the operation 'a dirty despicable crime', received much local and international publicity for his tirade against it.)

The Lal Masjid was the fiefdom of two brothers, Abdul Aziz and Abdul Rashid Ghazi, both fanatics whose equally crazy father, the founder, was killed by unknown gunmen at the mosque in 1998. (In many international media reports it was declared with appropriate intakes of breath that the mosque is close to the headquarters of the Directorate of Inter Services Intelligence, the ISI, with which organization almost everything vaguely suspicious in the subcontinent is linked by perfervid reportage.[19] I suppose ISI HQ is indeed fairly near the mosque, just as is every other building in central Islamabad, but I found it a long and sweaty walk when I tried to verify the claim.) Abdul Aziz tested the waters by announcing in 2004 that Pakistan Army soldiers killed in Balochistan (his family is Baloch) and Waziristan should not be buried according to Islamic custom, and his challenge went unmet. His uncompromising confrontation continued, but in the interests of not rocking the boat the government declined to arrest him. On 31 March 2007 he gave an ultimatum concerning Sharia law – as the *Daily Times* reported: 'Maulana Abdul Aziz, the prayer leader at Lal Masjid and principal of Jamia Hafsa, on Friday gave the government a week's deadline to "enforce Sharia" in the country, otherwise "clerics will Islamise society themselves". "If the government does not impose Sharia within a week, we will do it," Aziz told a gathering after Friday prayers. Similarly, he gave the Islamabad administration a week to shut down 'brothels', otherwise 'seminary students will take action themselves'. 'If we find a woman with loose morals, we will prosecute her in Lal Masjid,' he said.[20] Obviously the government (and the opposition parties, for Islamabad brothels have never had political or even religious barriers)[21] could not permit a parallel system of quasi-legal prosecution, but the situation festered until on 18 May Maulana Abdul Aziz threatened suicide attacks throughout the country and then attempted to extend his influence by encouraging defections from the police, para-military forces and the army. The crisis began to come to a head on 3 July when 'students' in the complex fired on police and the para-military Pakistan Rangers who were attempting to maintain order outside the mosque, and took prisoner four policemen whom they tortured. When it appeared that government reaction would almost certainly involve force, Abdul Aziz decided to leave the premises, which he did dressed in a burqa. After being unveiled, as it were, by a policewoman, he was shown to be a coward and a joke, and most of the young male and female student activists remaining in the mosque – some 1,100 in all – decided they would also leave, which they did without incident. His brother, Abdul Ghazi, remained in the complex and tried to negotiate his freedom, but his demands were both minatory and excessive, involving pensions for family members, pardon for all involved in the siege and his own safe passage to an unspecified country. He was killed in the SSG attack on 10/11 July.

Thus yet another rift was created between military (and patriotic, Constitutional) duty as exemplified by what the SSG did at the Lal Masjid, and the normal loyalty any Muslim owes to his or her religion. On the one hand there was a group of fanatics determined to subvert and destroy the laws of the land, and on the other the majority of the people of Pakistan who wish only to be able to get on with their lives unhindered by self-righteous thugs whose highly personal and supremely selective interpretations of the word of God can be accepted in neither intellectually analytical terms nor in practical, common-sense, day-to-day living. The people of Pakistan were (and are) confused about their religious leaders, who they have been reared to respect; but some of them take advantage of ignorance – the weapon of religious bigots throughout the millennia – to purvey their own self-serving explanations of the Quran and the Hadith.[22] The army is in the middle, being assailed by wild-eyed pulpit-bashers while attempting to abide by 'enlightened moderation' as espoused by their chief (General Kiyani's views are similar to those of President Musharraf). And a major consequence appears to have been the steep rise in suicide attacks specifically directed against army targets.

A central figure in the tribal areas is the Governor of North West Frontier Province, Lieutenant General (Retired) Ali Jan Mohammad Aurakzai, who was Corps Commander in Peshawar from 2000 to 2004. After retirement (and a period as Director Defence Production) he was appointed Governor in 2006. During his tenure as chief military officer in the Province he used his influence to bring to the tribes to negotiations, using the classic *jirga*, the semi-formal gathering of tribal elders, to assess general feelings and take all nuances into account when reaching decisions, or – as is more usual – gently indicating to the tribes that nothing can be done without their combined agreement concerning future action. A skilful negotiator such as Ali Aurakzai will even persuade his interlocutors that the entire idea for improvements actually came from them, and the government was waiting only on their esteemed approval to be allowed to continue.

Certainly, Ali Aurakzai stood on some sensitive toes when he was military commander. The then Governor could not expect to accept lightly what was, after all, a degree of interference in his prerogatives. But it must also be said that Aurakzai, himself a tribal, born and brought up in the Orakzai Agency in a hamlet miles from civilization, was the right man at the right time for the job, and that by means of deft persuasion he succeeded in calming the fervour of the wild men who resist on principle any intrusion from the settled areas. His expertise in tribal affairs and his rapport with even the most recalcitrant of tribal mavericks has been invaluable, but it seems that every time he made a gain there would be an incident that would set back his advance to some degree.[23]

In 2005 and 2006 there were at least three incidents of kidnapping of Frontier Corps soldiers by tribesmen, which were essentially parochial affairs – although serious enough for the victims who suffered privation and even death. But at the end of August 2007 came a much graver episode, in which over 200 soldiers and para-military troops, including a lieutenant colonel and nine other officers, were taken captive by militants near Wana township in South Waziristan Agency. They were released on 4 November following a reciprocal freeing of some twenty-five convicted tribal terrorists. The affair was disturbing for the army and the country, especially as the rebels had murdered three soldiers, but Musharraf reacted in an unexpectedly laid-back fashion and permitted the drama to run its course which ended in the usual tribal way, with concessions on both sides. In almost all Western eyes this compromise was seen as craven submission to the dictates of criminals, and in tenets of Western-style law there is indeed no admission of such an advanced style of plea-bargaining. It cannot be expected that the practise of negotiation will be endorsed by Pakistan's critics, or even by those many Pakistanis who consider the tribal regions to be as foreign as any South Sea island. But it is the way of the region, and although it may stoke up trouble for the future, it is well to consider what could have happened in this and other instances of tribal lawlessness. Again, however, it was the army in the middle, and it is the army's shoulders that will bear the weight of criticism from friend and foe alike. Fortunately, the shoulders are broad.

A 2007 poll in November (19–28), released on 13 December,[24] found that:

> The Pakistan Army has long been the most respected institution in the country; in IRI's first few polls [five in 2006–7] its favourability rating was consistently at the 80 percent level. In the last poll, however, the Army's rating dropped 10 points to 70 percent and slipped to third behind the media and the courts. In this poll, the Army dropped 15 percentage points to a rating of 55 percent. The media remained on top with 78 percent. The drop in the Army's prestige is likely due to the unpopularity of Musharraf. When Pakistanis were asked if the performance of Musharraf affected their opinion of the Army, 31 percent said that they now had a higher opinion due to his actions and 20 percent said that their opinion had not changed, while a plurality of

41 percent said that Musharraf's performance caused them to now have a lower opinion of the Army.

and that:

> Voters also expressed concern regarding rising Islamic fundamentalism; 66 percent agreed that religious extremism was a serious problem in Pakistan. Further, 63 percent said that the Taliban and Al Qaida operating in the country was also a serious concern. However, only 40 percent of Pakistanis supported the Army operations in NWFP and Tribal Areas and just 15 percent felt that Pakistan should cooperate with the United States in its War on Terror. Finally, respondents expressed a desire for the separation of military and state; 56 percent agreed that the Army should not play a role in civilian government and 74 percent said that Musharraf should resign as Army Chief of Staff. [Which he had done by the time the poll ended.]

The army is in a difficult situation, and the most confusing indicator is the fact that although so many people are worried about the Taliban and al-Qaeda, so few support the army's counter-terrorism operations in the tribal areas. All that the army can do is maintain its loyal obedience to civilian government, no matter if it is led by those proven to have been corrupt and inept in former years. (The murder of Benazir Bhutto in December 2007 served not only to create even further chaos in the country but confused the political scene, there being no other figure of national standing in her party, save for the barrister Aitzaz Ahsan who, unfortunately, was sidelined by the slightly undemocratic passage of party leadership by inheritance.)

A civilian government is essential for Pakistan, even if its likely incompetence will result in disruption in the (comparatively) short term; but there should be no conditionality in the manner in which the army carries out its duties as required by elected civilian leaders. The army must also strive to eradicate religious extremism, however limited that may be, from its ranks.

I do not advocate a secular army, any more than I would be so presumptuous as to propose a secular Pakistan. I do, however, suggest that the Army of Pakistan should have no religious influence on society, and that it should have no casting vote in governance of the country. It has half a million voters in its ranks. Let them be its contribution to democracy.

Notes

1. See, for example, Beehner, Lionel, 'Musharraf's Taliban Problem', Council on Foreign Relations, 11 September 2006. http://www.cfr.org/publication/11401/
2. *Guardian* (UK), 20 September 2007. http://www.guardian.co.uk/alqaida/story/0,,2173071,00.html

3. A further poll, in November, found that 67 per cent of the population wanted Musharraf to resign (Most Want Musharraf to Quit), http://www.washingtonpost.com/wp-dyn/content/article/2007/12/13/AR2007121300702.html. The *New York Times* had the same headline and coverage, but as the BBC pointed out (http://news.bbc.co.uk/2/hi/south_asia/7141911.stm), 'The BBC's Jill McGivering in Islamabad says that this snapshot of opinion is already slightly out of date. The opinions were sampled in November – after the imposition of the state of emergency – but before President Musharraf took other important steps such as standing down as head of the army and confirming that elections would go ahead in January. It was also completed before he said that would end the state of emergency on 15 December.' In spite of all the criticism of the BBC's Overseas Service, one can usually rely on it to cover all sides of a story.

4. Private information from a number of senior officers in the period 2004–7. A Shaheed (otherwise Shahid) is, literally, a martyr who has died fighting for the faith. His place in Paradise is guaranteed and he is, when practicable, buried in the clothes in which he was killed, the bloodstains indicating his status.

5. Private information, for obvious reasons.

6. The North West Frontier Province government has an excellent description of the region at http://www.fata.gov.pk/index.php

7. The Victorian notion of the noble savage is entirely suspect, although the sense of 'honour' is certainly apparent. In the 1990s I travelled extensively in the tribal areas without interference, having no more than verbal assurances that my safety would be guaranteed. Since 2002, however, I have not cared to take the risk, as feeling is such that any foreigner is suspected of being an American and thus fair game. When planning a visit in 2006 I told an old friend that if anyone had a shot at me they would perforce be involved in a blood feud with the tribe of the person I intended to visit. 'And a fat lot of good that would do *you*,' he said. I took his advice.

8. He told me more, but I signed the Official Secrets Act a long time ago. Given the climate of jobsworth bureaucratic vengeance that applies in Britain it would be unwise to elaborate. I was refused permission by the UK MOD to describe the SAS involvement which resulted, among other things, in a major being awarded a Military Cross. Absurdly, the citation is classified. The officer later commanded 22 SAS Regiment and his name is well known. The obsession with secrecy is all-pervasive, unhealthy and often ridiculous.

9. Interview with the US Public Broadcasting Service 20 January 2006. (The British source put it a little more pungently.) http://www.pbs.org/wgbh/pages/frontline/darkside/interviews/berntsen.html

10. *New York Times*, 19 October 2004, http://www.nytimes.com/2004/10/19/opinion/19franks.html.

11. CNN, 27 December 2001, 'Donald Rumsfeld holds Defence Briefing' [General Myers, Chairman of the Joint Chiefs of Staff also answered questions]. http://edition.cnn.com/TRANSCRIPTS/0112/27/se.02.html

12. Later Director General Inter Services Intelligence, then, in October 2007, Vice Chief of Army Staff, and, on 28 November 2007, Chief of Army Staff.

13. Germain, David, 'Guerrilla Warfare and the American Military' http://www.mathnews.uwaterloo.ca/Issues/mn8808/newsclips.php

14. *Pakistan Chronology*, Congressional Research Service, Washington.

15. http://www.dailytimes.com.pk/default.asp?page=2006\01\14\story_14-1-2006_pg3_1

16. See *The Economist* for a balanced report: http://www.economist.com/displaystory.cfm?story_id=8112163; also a valuable summation in *STRATFOR* at http://www.stratfor.com/products/premium/read_article.php?id=279397. There is an interesting exchange of views by tribals and others at the blog http://www.khyberwatch.com/forums/archive/

index.php?t-445.html, and good cover by *The News* (Pakistan) at the time, http://www.thenews.com.pk/top_story_detail.asp?Id=3945.

17. *Guardian*, 9 November http://www.guardian.co.uk/pakistan/Story/0,,1942914,00.html. Its regional reporter, Declan Walsh, is admirably accurate and reliable, as is the *Daily Telegraph*'s representative, Isambard Wilkinson. The *Telegraph*, however, is somewhat selective about publishing material concerning Iraq, Afghanistan and Pakistan.

18. In Karachi the government provided security precautions on the same lines as given to any VIP cavalcade, a fact not reported by the media. There were jamming devices at vulnerable points, and an armoured passenger vehicle was supplied from the Karachi pool. There are conflicting versions of events in Rawalpindi, and it is not known if precautions were similar to those in Karachi. Her vehicle was blast-proof, but she chose to stand up through the roof. No matter what anyone might think or say about Benazir Bhutto – and I am among the many who did not admire her – the fact is that she knew the risks in appearing in public, and was prepared to take them. She showed courage. And that isn't a bad epitaph.

19. 'The mosque is located near the headquarters of Pakistan's shadowy ISI intelligence service, which helped train and fund the holy warriors, and a number of ISI staff are said to go there for prayers.' BBC, 27 July 2007. There were indeed ISI and agents of other intelligence services having a look at the mosque and its adherents, but one wonders just who it was who said they went there for prayers.

20. *Daily Times*, 31 March 2007. http://www.dailytimes.com.pk/default.asp?page=2007\03\31\story_31-3-2007_pg1_2

21. Only a very few years ago I attended a post-retirement party given by an Islamabad Madam, who in her large and elegant apartment facing the Margalla Hills had brought together a remarkably eclectic group of people (some with impressive beards), whose initial embarrassment at being so gathered was rapidly diffused by their realization that in spirit they had a great deal in common.

22. There are two types of Hadith, or descriptions of the deeds and sayings of the Prophet: the *Sacred Hadith*, in which God speaks through the Prophet; and the *Noble Hadith*, the sayings of the Prophet as recounted by his followers. Arguments concerning relevance and degrees of validity can go on forever, but the opportunities for revisionist interpretation and plain manipulation are, unfortunately, limitless.

23. Aurakzai resigned on 5 January 2008.

24. By the International Republican Institute in Washington – http://www.iri.org/mena/pakistan/pdfs/2007-12-12-pakistan-poll-index.pdf. The poll was conducted before Musharraf announced his standing down as Army Chief and the ending of the state of emergency, but it is probable that even these major declarations would have had little effect on perceptions.

Chapter 9
Pakistan In Danger

In a strategy that runs the risk of sending contradictory signals to Islamabad and the world about the nature of Indian policy, the government has followed the handing over of a dossier linking "elements in Pakistan" to the November 26-28 Mumbai attacks with a full-throated accusation that the terrorists who killed more than 160 people "must have had the support of some official agencies in Pakistan."

Siddharth Varadarajan,
The Hindu, New Delhi,
January 8, 2009[1]

On the evening of November 26, 2008, a number of well-trained militants came ashore from the Arabian Sea on small boats and attacked numerous high-profile targets in Mumbai, India, with automatic weapons and explosives. By the time the episode ended some 62 hours later, about 165 people, along with nine terrorists, had been killed and hundreds more injured. Among the multiple sites attacked in the peninsular city known as India's business and entertainment capital were two luxury hotels—the Taj Mahal Palace and the Oberoi-Trident—along with the main railway terminal, a Jewish cultural center, a café frequented by foreigners, a cinema house, and two hospitals. Six American citizens were among the 26 foreigners reported dead. Indian officials have concluded that the attackers numbered only ten, one of whom was captured.

K Alan Kronstadt, ongressional Research Service, Washington, DC,
December 19, 2008[2]

The terrorist attack in Mumbai came as a severe blow to what was at best a limping approach to dialogue by both India and Pakistan. It destroyed the low but improving level of mutual confidence that had been achieved by years of back channel diplomacy and open meetings between officials and political

197

figures.[3] Stage by stage in the following weeks the countries became more aggressive. Understandable resentment and tension in India were heightened by the media, whose headlines and general reportage, electronically and in print, were chauvinistic to the point of bellicosity.[4] This was reciprocated in Pakistan, which, officially and in its independent media, professed with at least some degree of justification to be at a loss to understand why so much adverse comment was forthcoming from India before completion of the investigation or even issue of an interim report that provided evidence to support any findings.

This may have been disingenuous, but it fed the feeling in Pakistan that much more attention was being paid to the Mumbai atrocities than had been the case in the suicide bombing of the Marriott Hotel in Islamabad on September 20, 2008, when 54 people were killed and over 250 injured. The fact that the Mumbai attacks were much more dramatic and protracted (it took security forces almost three days to kill nine of the terrorists and capture the tenth) was the obvious reason for greater international cover, but the major difference was that the attack in Islamabad was a home-grown affair while that in Mumbai was caused by terrorists who, compelling evidence suggests, came from Pakistan. The point, however, is whether or not they were supported in some fashion by other "elements"[5] in Pakistan.

This is as firmly believed in India as it is denied in Pakistan, and India's newly-appointed Home Minister, Palaniappan Chidambaram (formerly finance minister, and a highly intelligent, level-headed person), gave his opinion that the attack could only have involved "state or state-assisted actors" in Pakistan. He was quoted as saying on January 4, 2009, in an interview with "Walk the Talk" on India's NDTV, that "somebody who is familiar with intelligence and who is familiar with commando operations has directed this operation. And that cannot be a non-state actor."[6]

The implications of this open declaration of Pakistan's presumed national guilt by the Indian government minister most closely associated with the investigation are intriguing.[7] It is unlikely he would have delivered the accusations without being convinced of their validity, yet there is a certain ambivalence detectable, if only because the obvious path for any country believing that an act of war has been carried out by or at the behest of a detectably enemy nation is to itself declare war, or at least place the matter before the UN Security Council. It seems that the war option was not "off the table" (in the words of the Minister for External Affairs, Mr Mukherjee), so far as India was concerned, and Pakistan took military precautions accordingly, further justifying its actions when the Indian Chief of Army Staff, General

Deepak Kapoor, said on January 14 that "we in India are keeping all our options open and that must be clearly understood."[8]

The observation by the outgoing US Secretary of State Condoleezza Rice that the aim of the Mumbai operation was "probably to stir up trouble between Pakistan and India,"[9] appeared close to the mark. In this vein the *Indian Express*, with whose editor the Chidambaram interview was conducted, recorded that "Mincing no words, the Home Minister said it would now be upon Pakistan to ensure that such acts are never repeated by its citizens against India. 'The price they will pay if this is repeated will be enormous,' he warned," which was a disquieting threat.

No government can give a guarantee that any of its citizens will or will not take a course of action in relation to a foreign country. If there is another externally-rooted terrorist attack in India, which is more than probable, there will be much pressure on the government to take military action, which would be disastrous for the sub-continent. The problem for Pakistan is to maintain a balanced force along the border with India, to be prepared for what has been publicly threatened, while countering a sizeable insurgency in the west.

In 2006–2008 the Pakistan army reinforced its presence in North West Frontier Province (NWFP) by redeploying units and formations[10] from the east, most notably 14 Infantry Division, normally based at Okara, 60 miles south west of Lahore, and subordinate to 2 Corps, one of Pakistan's "Strike Corps." The division was given responsibility for South Waziristan, and other brigades and units from the east were placed under command of divisions of 11 Corps, with its HQ in Peshawar. Some 60,000 extra troops were moved into NWFP to assist those of 11 Corps, which had a strength of about 40,000, and results were at first disappointing. (The strength of the para-military Frontier Corps, commanded by regular army officers, was also about 40,000 in NWFP, but its standard of training was inadequate to cope with the tactics of the Taliban and their tribal supporters.)

Most incoming units and their superior headquarters were prepared for open warfare in the Indian border area and were very good at armor-infantry cooperation, but had not had much practice in, for example, convoy movement through territory subject to low-level insurgency. There is a great deal of difference between advancing through a minefield and moving by roads and tracks that in all probability have improvised explosive devices (or mines) placed along the way.

Units in the east had concentrated, quite properly, on the tactics required to defeat an Indian armored advance into Pakistan and were trained to take the war across the border by rapid movement to seize territory. Fighting tribesmen and "guest militants" (as foreign elements might be called) were quite a different matter, and some initial operations were most unsatisfactory. The GOC[1] 14 Division, Major General Tariq Khan[11] and other commanders established temporary schools to retrain officers and soldiers in counter insurgency skills, which required a major effort, not only in selecting instructors and training areas, but in logistics and, above all, in operational commitment. Like the Sri Lankan army, which since 1982 has suffered from the twin and usually conflicting demands of conducting training while concurrently countering the Tamil Tigers, 14 Division and other formation headquarters had to balance the requirement to impart important skills with the urgency of patrolling, getting to know the terrain and people, and mounting operations to dominate the area. This took several months, but was effective, although the main target, Baitullah Mehsud,[12] could not be found. In May 2008 the *Dawn* newspaper reported on an operation in South Waziristan, where a group of journalists had been flown in by the army:

> A senior army commander pointed towards a huge compound which, according to him, was the real cause of all the trouble. We were told that the abandoned compound, with several small rooms, and a small mosque, was in fact "a nursery for preparing suicide bombers." According to Major General Tariq Khan, who commands the 14 Division, "it was like a factory that had been recruiting 9-12-year-old boys, and turning them into suicide bombers."

> The suicide nursery was being run by one Qari Hussain who is regarded as the man leading the campaign of suicide bombings in Pakistan. He was given protection by Baitullah [Mehsud] and has become the biggest ideologue of the militants and someone who specializes in indoctrinating teenagers in violence in the name of Islam. He is still at large and it is not clear where he has established his new nursery of young bombers.

> Army officers stationed there admit that until the operation started they only had some idea about such activities, and it was only in January [2008] that they discovered how organized these militants were in their mission to recruit, indoctrinate and launch suicide bombers. The computers, other equipment

---

1   General Officer Commanding

and literature seized from the place, some of which were shown to us, give graphic details of the training process in this so-called "nursery." There are videos of young boys carrying out executions, a classroom where 10-12-year olds are sitting in formation, with white band of Quranic verses wrapped around their forehead, and there are training videos to show how improvised explosive devices are made and detonated.

The scale of militant presence and activity in the tribal areas and in other parts of North West Frontier Province, notably the Swat District, was not only surprising but operationally taxing for the army and especially the Frontier Corps. (It should be noted that in October 2008 only 38 percent of people thought that the army should be "fighting extremists in NWFP and FATA" and 50% disagreed; see footnote 24). The influence and depth of "Talibanisation" has had a considerably detrimental effect on social life, not least in education and health, and there seemed to be little that the security forces could do about it.

In January 2009 a self-styled Taliban "commander" in Swat, Shah Dauran ordered citizens to stop sending their daughters to school. His warning was given over a banned FM radio station the authorities appeared powerless to close down, adding to the general perception that the government writ did not extend to Taliban-controlled areas, no matter the operations of four well-commanded army brigades in the Valley. In Mingora, the principal town in Swat, a sign on the wall of a large bazaar, formerly known as the Women's Market, announced that "Women are not allowed in this market." Barbers have been forbidden to shave beards, and shops selling videos and CDs, and even tailors' shops, have been burned down, the latter being punished for making western-style clothes. Of even more consequence, as of mid-January 2009, 181 schools had been blown up or burned down.

The region is controlled by religious fanatics and the problem appears to be spreading, although when voters are able to indicate their ballot-box preferences, religious parties are thoroughly trounced, as happened in the February 2008 elections.[13] Irrespective of what the people may desire, however, the overwhelming reality is that of dominance by extremist clerics and their adherent fanatics at the expense of traditional tribal and elected leaders, and even further marginalization of police, who dare not take action against Taliban or tribesmen, no matter the nature of the offense. As one newspaper's editorial had it in January 2009, "The situation in Swat is grotesque. It is shameful that we have allowed this to happen in our midst; that in Islamabad the government keeps up pretence of normalcy and claims it is succeeding against militancy. The situation in Swat receives sporadic media attention; occasionally human rights activists speak out against it. Far more urgent action is needed."[14]

So far as the army is concerned the priority has been to destroy the militants and their bases while ensuring security for civil authorities involved in administration and development. This has proved to be extremely difficult, and in the period July–December 2008 security forces suffered 142 killed. It will take many years before the tribal areas, and even such "settled" areas as Swat District, will be properly governed, with access by all to education—because it is education of which the mullahs are fearful (as are feudal landowners elsewhere in Pakistan). Widespread literacy would erode their power.[15]

In 2008–2009 the army continued to stay out of politics and governance,[16] and concentrated on operations in the west. As discussed above, however, the tenor of statements and comments from official and other sources in India was such that there seemed a possibility that India would conduct a strike on what New Delhi might consider to be a terrorist facility within Pakistan. Even were the area struck to be so proved, Pakistan could not ignore such action (although apparently powerless against US Predator attacks in the west that have killed several alleged terrorists and many undoubted civilians), and would have to react, if only for reasons of national confidence and integrity. In consequence of the apparent threat, several formations, including 14 Division, were ordered to return to the eastern border region, leaving considerable gaps in the tribal areas which would probably suffer from reintroduction of militants, although very many had been killed – probably some 600–700. It was postulated at the time by some observers that Pakistan had moved troops away from NWFP in order to impress upon the US authorities the seriousness of the Indian threat and to excuse the lack of success in the western border region. While this is a possible explanation, it perhaps reads too much subtlety into what was explained to the author as "precautionary [redeployment]; what else could anyone expect us to do?"[17] As some army units gradually withdrew from five of the seven Tribal Agencies (Malakand, Bajaur, Mohmand, Orakzai, Khyber and Kurram), so the Frontier Corps, revitalized and better equipped than ever before in its history, moved in to take over responsibility for operations against militants and dissident tribesmen, and, along with semi-integrated police units,[18] for general security.

(In June 2008 a Frontier Corps patrol in Mohmand Agency was mistaken for militants by US troops. The twelve 500-pound bombs that were then

202

dropped by US aircraft killed an officer and 10 soldiers. Government reaction was to protest that the attack was "a gross violation of the international border" that "tends to undermine the very basis of our cooperation."[19] According to sources in Pakistan the attack caused considerable anti-US feeling in the army and FC, especially as the dead army officer left a widow and two baby daughters.)

By mid-January 2009 it seemed that both "ordinary" crime (the usual inter-tribal squabbles, kidnapping, murder and other violent antisocial activity) as well as militant operations had decreased markedly in much of FATA, although the FC suffered a setback on January 10 and 11 when "hundreds of Taliban militants poured into northwestern Pakistan in a large frontal attack on a paramilitary base [the small fort of Mama Gat] . . . that left at least 40 militants and 6 Pakistani soldiers dead, according to Pakistani security officials. The attack, on an outpost of the Frontier Corps paramilitary force in the Mohmand district, appeared to be the heaviest assault on Pakistani troops in months. And in a reversal of usual patterns, it involved a large number of Taliban forces from Afghanistan attacking into Pakistan, signaling coordination among militants on both sides of the border."[20] This confrontational raid from across the border was unusual, but highlights the difficulties of policing the region – on both sides. Pakistan's security forces have received much criticism for being unable to stop incursions into Afghanistan, but as a senior Pakistani official pointed out to the author,[21] the one good thing about the raid was that it "might shut [the coalition forces in Afghanistan] up" about Pakistan's supposed deficiencies in policing cross-border movement.

Strikes inside Pakistan by US Predator aircraft continued into 2009, and by mid-January the total was estimated at about thirty,[22] concerning which Maleeha Lodhi, a distinguished and most effective former ambassador in Washington and high commissioner in London[23], wrote that "the dramatic rise in attacks by unmanned Predator aircraft in the country's border regions inflamed public opinion, threatened to undercut Pakistan's own counter insurgency efforts and risked destabilizing the country. Islamabad's feeble protests gave grist to the mill of its critics who accused it of a covert deal with Washington on this count."

Militants and tribesmen became more apprehensive about such raids, as they appeared to have been successful, according to anonymous US sources, in killing "high value" individuals. Although such claims cannot be confirmed[24], it was obvious that the tempo of attacks was increasing, and, in turn, that militants and tribesmen had increased their efforts to discover and kill those they suspected of passing information concerning the identity and location of desirable targets. There is little doubt that human sources were intended to complement technical means for this purpose (see Chapter 7), especially as electronic communications by Taliban, other militants (including the highly sophisticated drug-smuggling networks), and supposed al Qaeda cadres have been minimized. In the period January 5–7 in North Waziristan, two Afghans were shot and hanged from a tree on the Bannu-Miramshah Road at Naurak village, with a note in Pashto stating that they were spying for the US; the bodies of another four alleged but unidentified spies were thrown on to roads; and the bodies of two Afghans, Habibullah and Khan Muhammad Babar, were left with notes to say that anyone found spying would be similarly dealt with. There was little or nothing that the army, even with considerable presence in North Waziristan, could do about such killings, some of which are probably the result of inter-tribal rivalry, drug-gang fighting for territory and influence, or simply personal hatred, of which in FATA there is abundance.

In 2008 Pakistan had a year of living dangerously. It was subjected to many terrorist attacks, notably the suicide bombing of the Marriott hotel in Islamabad in September, and, according to the *Daily Times* newspaper "Some 725 Pakistanis – 149 Law Enforcing Agencies' officials and 576 civilians – were killed in 63 terrorist attacks, averaging 61 killings per month." (India suffered 424 civilians and security forces' personnel killed by Maoist extremists in eight states, in addition to 444 deaths in the restive north east.) The insurrection in the west was barely contained, and Islamabad was blamed for the suicide attack on the Indian embassy in Kabul in July, and the terrorist outrage in Mumbai in September. As 2009 began the population had a low level of confidence in national leadership, although there was no sign that the return of Pervez Musharraf would be welcomed. Unintentionally, he had lowered trust in the army, largely because his political machinations were considered to be linked with his position as army chief.

No matter the fact that the country was under severe threat from terrorism, the main concern of its citizens was inflation, which gravely affected day-to-day living, rather than apprehension that there could be further attacks, but there were indications that the army's image was improving. A poll in October by the International Republican Institute[25] showed that 68 percent of the population approved of the army, as compared with a low of 55% in November 2007 and 60% in June 2008. (Only the medical profession was more highly regarded, at 72%, and approval of the government and political parties stood at 31 and 39% respectively. 20% approved of Asif Zardari and 18% of Osama bin Laden, but only 3% thought that Musharraf would do a good job in running the country.) Another question was, "Some people say the military has the right to take over from civilian leaders when they have become too corrupt or fail to govern. Under what circumstances should the military be able to do this?" 11% did not offer an opinion; 18% said in no circumstances and 56% said they would approve but only in an emergency; while 15% had the opinion the army should take over whenever it wants. In June 62% considered that the army should have no role in civilian government, but in October this had fallen to 49%.

The thread of this book has been the failure and thus undesirability of military involvement in the governance and civilian administration of Pakistan. There is little doubt that some civilian governments were so morally polluted and inefficient that the army's takeover was regarded as a merciful release from corrupt incompetence, but military rulers also lost sight of the basic premise of good government: that above all the voice of the people should be heard. There is no indication that another era of military control is likely, and the army, under General Kayani, is tenaciously adhering to the maxim that it should be seen (but not too much) and not heard at all. It has enormous responsibilities, and it is to be hoped that, as it and the Frontier Corps gradually restore order in North West Frontier Province, there will be energetic action by Islamabad to create representative government in the tribal areas and bring the region into civilized modernity, if that is not a contradiction in terms. Pakistan is in danger, and a loyal army will continue to be its mainstay in countering threats to its existence as a state.

Notes

1 http://www.hinduonnet.com/2009/01/08/stories/2009010859721000.htm

2 Congressional Research Service papers are not publicly available, which is unfortunate because they are of the highest quality in description and analysis of US and world affairs.

3 The Indian foreign minister was particularly downbeat in an interview with the *Times of India* on January 17, 2009: "I believe Pakistan's position since Mumbai attack has put a very large question mark over the achievements of the composite dialogue process over the past 4½ years. The absence of a sincere and transparent position on terrorism has eroded the value of the dialogue process. If one takes a broader view, this is not a good development because it places a long-term question mark on the utility of dialogue as a mean to resolve bilateral issues with Pakistan."

4 See, among many examples : December 1, 2008: "Investigators said on Monday the militants who attacked Mumbai had months of commando training in Pakistan, adding to rising tensions between the neighbors as recriminations mounted at home." (http://www.indianexpress.com/news/we-took-mumbai-attack-orders-from-pakistan/392860/); December 21, 2008: "Defense Meet Keeps Option of Pak Strike Open" (http://timesofindia.indiatimes.com/Defence_meet_keeps_option_of_Pak_strike_open/articleshow/3867650.cms); January 5, 2009: "FBI to Confront Pak with 26/11 Evidence"(htttp://www.indianexpress.com/news/fbi-to-confront-pak-with-26-11-evidence-us/406883/).

5 "New Delhi's foreign affairs ministry said the terrorists who attacked Mumbai were linked to "elements" in Pakistan, a charge Islamabad has said is without proof." *Guardian* (UK), 5 January 2009 (http://www.guardian.co.uk/world/2009/jan/05/mumbai-terror-attacks-india-pakistan).

6 As above; and "State actors involved in 26/11 Attacks: Chidambaram", *Hindustan Times*, January 4, 2009.

7 The "dossier" of factual account supposedly linking Pakistan, qua Pakistan, with the terrorist atrocity in Mumbai can be accessed courtesy of *The Hindu* newspaper, at http://www.hindu.com/nic/dossier. htm. It is an interesting compilation – and there is no doubt that citizens of Pakistan committed the atrocities – but in no terms can it be assessed from the facts provided that any government agency in Pakistan was responsible for, or aware of, the Mumbai attack.

8 *AFP* January 15. The general continued that "It is not to raise any kind of hysteria for war... but I am referring to the keeping of all our options open – whether diplomatic, economic or, as the last resort, a fighting option."

9 State Department : http://www.state.gov/secretary/rm/2008/12/112999.htm..

10 Combat units are regiments (armor) or battalions (infantry), varying in strength from 600-900; formations are brigades, usually 5000 strong, and divisions, with about 17,000 all ranks.

11 He had been GOC 6 Armored Division and in early 2007 was selected to command 14 Division, specifically to take it into South Waziristan. After a successful tour of duty he was appointed Inspector General Frontier Corps in Peshawar in mid-2008. An outstandingly competent officer.

12 Mehsud has been named in connection with many atrocities, most notably the assassination of Benazir Bhutto, but there is no clear evidence of his involvement, although his rhetoric is extreme and there is no doubt he has committed or ordered acts of the utmost barbarity.

13 See the Centre for Strategic & International Studies (Washington) excellent report on the elections at http://www.csis.org/media/csis/pubs/sam116.pdf. The religious grouping, the MMA, obtained only 6 seats in the February 2008 elections, as against holding 59 in the previous National Assembly, from 2002-2008. Another notable CSIS report 'FATA - A Most Dangerous Place' was published in January 2009; its principal author, the distinguished scholar Shuja Nawaz, has been appointed the first Director of the South Asia Center of the Atlantic Council of the United States.

14 'Horror amid the hills,' *News International*, January 14 , 2009.

15 Before the régime of President (and general) Zia ul Haq in the 1980s mullahs were rarely politically powerful. Naturally they had some influence over the population, which was not averse to their assumed extension of power that became possible after the US-supported Directorate of Inter Services Intelligence enlisted their help to mount a cross-border 'jihad' against the Soviet Union's occupation of Afghanistan. This was energetically supported by Zia, who was ultra-religious. The power of the tribal leaders, the maliks, was eroded because the historic instrument of influence and persuasion since British times –

money – was channeled in increasingly greater amounts through religious leaders, or those purporting to be so. Concurrently the power of the government-appointed District Officers was reduced, and thus the authority of the central government. It all went downhill from there.

16 See, for example, "Quiet General Tries to Keep Army Out of Politics," *Wall Street Journal*, August 22, 2008..

17 Senior Pakistan army officer to author, January 2009.

18 The army now trains NWFP police at the Punjab Regiment's Center in Mardan.

19 "Air Strike Damages Trust in Pakistan-US Alliance," *Reuters*, June 12, 2008.

20 *International Herald Tribune* January 12, 2009.

21 By email on January 15, 2009.

22 "Al-Qaeda chief killed in Pakistan, US claims," *The Guardian* (UK) January 10, 2009, by Saeed Shah, an excellent and enterprising reporter.

23 Countries belonging to the Commonwealth of Nations (formerly the British Commonwealth) use the term 'high commissioner' instead of 'ambassador' in each other's countries. Likewise the phrase 'defense adviser' is employed instead of 'defense attaché,' lest there be connotations of information gathering, which between fellow commonwealth nations would be unthinkable. (Perhaps.) A few years ago, in speaking of her DA, a newly-appointed high commissioner (not Maleeha Lodhi) asked me "but who does he advise?" "*You*, of course," I told her.

24 See, for example, a UK *Daily Telegraph* report, datelined Delhi, January 9, 2009, that "The leader of al-Qaeda in Pakistan, Usama al-Kini, and one of his senior henchmen have been killed in an American air-strike, according to intelligence sources."

25 See *The News*, December 20,2008 (http://www.thenews.com.pk/print1.asp?id=152892), and the IRI website. The poll, of course, could not include the 7 Tribal Agencies.

Index

214